Core Technology Competencies for Librarians and Library Staff

A LITA Guide

Edited by Susan M. Thompson

For the
LIBRARY AND INFORMATION TECHNOLOGY ASSOCIATION

Neal-Schuman Publishers, Inc.
New York   London

Published by Neal-Schuman Publishers, Inc.
100 William St., Suite 2004
New York, NY 10038

Printed and bound in the United States of America.

The paper used in this publication meets the minimum requirements of American National Standard for Information Sciences—Permanence of Paper for Printed Library Materials, ANSI Z39.48-1992.∞

Library of Congress Cataloging-in-Publication Data

Core technology competencies for librarians and library staff: a LITA guide / Susan M. Thompson, editor.
    p. cm. — (Guide ; #15)
    Includes bibliographical references and index.
    ISBN 978-1-55570-660-9 (alk. paper)
    1. Librarians—Effect of technological innovations on. 2. Library employees—Effect of technological innovations on. 3. Technological literacy. 4. Librarians—In-service training. 5. Library employees—In-service training. 6. Library education. 7. Information technology—Study and teaching. 8. Core competencies. I. Thompson, Susan M., 1952–

Z682.35.T43C67 2009
020.71'55—dc22

                                                        2008046174

Table of Contents

iii

**PART III: SUCCESSFUL COMPETENCY
IMPLEMENTATION PROGRAMS**

v

List of Figures and Appendices

FIGURES

APPENDICES

Preface

Core Technology Competencies for Librarians and Library Staff provides a practical look at the skills, technological know-how, and personal attributes that enable librarians and staff to take full advantage of technology to deliver dynamic library collections and services. The rapid pace of change in technology and library services has made it difficult for libraries to determine just what technology skills various types of library personnel *should* know, much less actually ensure that they *do* know them. By identifying core competencies we are trying to separate out from all the possible and desirable abilities those key skills that are considered essential to working effectively, in this case working effectively in the technological environment of the modern library.

This book discusses both the core technology competencies needed by all library staff and the specialized technical skills needed in the library's technology support department, commonly referred to as the "systems department." Defining technology competencies helps both librarians and non-MLS staff understand what is expected of them in terms of technological skills and knowledge. Having adequate technical competencies empowers library staff to control and make the best use of the various forms of technology their jobs require. The higher the skill levels are of the librarian and staff, the more they can take advantage of technology to improve library collections and services. High levels of technical expertise developed by staff in traditional library function areas also creates opportunities to distribute expert help throughout the staff and may allow some technical work to shift out of the systems department to other areas of the library.

Library systems departments have come into existence relatively recently, in the past 20 years or so, but there have already been significant changes in what these departments do and in the technology their staff need to understand in order to develop the next generation of library applications. In addition to changes in traditional library technologies, the expansion in the variety of technologies available in libraries today has also impacted the type and level of skills needed in systems departments, particularly because many of the new technologies come with little or no vendor-provided support.

Core competencies for the library systems personnel depend on and build out from the level of technical competency of the library staff as a whole. General librarian and staff competency levels significantly impact the work in library systems. A knowledgeable library staff can lessen the amount of basic support provided by systems personnel. However, as staff become more sophisticated technology users, support needs change, requiring that systems staff skills keep pace with more complex technology levels.

The information in *Core Technology Competencies for Librarians and Library Staff* should be of interest to any librarian, staff member, and new professional entering the library field who would like to know what technology skills are expected in libraries today. Library administrators, technology managers, and systems librarians will find the definition of core competencies particularly useful in three areas:

1. Updating job descriptions and hiring specifications
2. Establishing employee orientation and assessment criteria
3. Developing training and professional development programs

The book is divided into three parts. Part I, "Overview of Technology Competencies for Today's Librarians and Library Staff," provides an overview of technology competencies expected of librarians and non-MLS library staff today. To give some context, Chapter 1, "History and Overview of Technology Competencies in Libraries," looks at changes over time in library technology and the kinds of technology competency expectations that currently exist for both traditional library positions and new jobs that have appeared over the past few years. Chapter 2, "The Library School's Role in Preparing New Librarians for Working with Technology," examines how library education programs are meeting some of the general technical competency standards and includes a sample syllabus and an assignment to design a library automation system. Both chapters include extensive literature reviews and data based on surveys of practitioners in the field.

Part II, "Core Competencies for Library Technology Specialists," discusses the kinds of skills needed by the library's technical specialists, particularly those who head library technology departments. Chapter 3, "Management and Technology Competencies for the Systems Librarian," and Chapter 4, "Core Competencies for Non-Librarian Systems Managers," look at core competencies for systems librarians and non-librarian technology managers, respectively, and include job descriptions for the two types of positions. Chapter 5, "Social Survival Skills for the Lone Information Technology Librarian," presents the unique competency issues faced by solo systems librarians, in particular focusing on the social communication skills needed.

Part III, "Successful Competency Implementation Programs," presents three case studies describing the best practices of academic and public libraries and how they use the concept of core technology competencies to determine job classifications, develop training and professional development programs, establish employee assessment criteria, and improve technology support, among other things.

The extensive appendices for these chapters include core competency lists, personnel assessment checklists, job descriptions, and training curricula.

Core Technology Competencies for Librarians and Library Staff is intended as a starting point for individual libraries to define their own core technology competencies. There is no single best inventory of technical skills that suits all types of libraries. Size, staff resources, the parent organization's technical support structure, the specific technologies available in the library, and the library's technology goals are some of the factors that can significantly impact which competencies are appropriate for a particular library. It's also worth noting that technology competencies are often considered to be more than just a set of technical skills. Other personal and management attributes, such as the ability to communicate well, work with teams, manage projects, and learn quickly and independently, may also be considered core competencies for technology.

Finally, technology keeps changing, making any definition of appropriate skill sets a moving target that needs regular evaluation and updating. In fact, expecting mastery of a specific set of technology skills may not be the best (or most realistic) goal of a core competency program. Developing the transferable skills that allow us to control and shape technology to our needs, combined with flexibility and comfort with learning, may serve us better in the long run.

Acknowledgments

I would like to acknowledge the contribution of the Heads of Library Technology LITA interest group, whose lively discussions introduced many of the ideas in this book. Their 2006 ALA conference program, "Core Competencies in Library Technology: What IT Is and Where IT's Going," proved there was an interest in this topic, and all of the presenters have contributed to this book. Last, but not least, I would like to thank my husband, Bruce Thompson, for his constant willingness to wordsmith and provide editorial insight.

Part I

OVERVIEW OF TECHNOLOGY COMPETENCIES FOR TODAY'S LIBRARIANS AND LIBRARY STAFF

Chapter 1

History and Overview of Technology Competencies in Libraries

Susan M. Thompson

Overview

Technology competency is the fundamental knowledge and ability that enables effective use of digital technology to accomplish tasks and to support and develop computerized systems. The history of technology in libraries shows a steadily increasing demand for technology competency, resulting in the development of new positions and "librarian 2.0" expectations that take advantage of the advanced capabilities of current technology. Although it appears that technology competency expectations in general are higher for librarians than for library staff, a number of basic competencies have been identified as important for all who work in libraries. Today's rapid pace of change, combined with the increased breadth and depth of technical knowledge needed, makes technology mastery an unrealistic goal; but, an understanding of a technology's underlying principles helps develop transferable skills that, combined with flexibility and comfort with constant learning, result in competencies that adapt well into the future.

Introduction

The term *core competencies* may imply that this book has all the answers—that there is one perfect set of credentials for working with library technology. This is not the case. The idea of core competencies for technology is not something that can be perfectly defined and then fixed in place. There is not one list of competencies that is appropriate for every institution. Different sizes and types of libraries have different technology skill needs. What's more, as libraries change, so do their technology needs. The success stories in later chapters of this book represent several types of libraries and library environments. The authors describe why they decided to define core technology competencies for their libraries and how these competencies have improved their staff's use of technology.

This chapter looks at technology competencies from the viewpoint of general, nontechnology specialist librarians and staff. Librarians are distinguished from other types of library staff as having completed a Master's of Library Science (MLS) degree and as working in a professional, librarian-classified position in the library. Much of the literature I reference is written by librarians for other librarians, often in academic libraries. However, most of the information applies just as well to non-MLS staff positions in all types of libraries. I start by looking at what is meant by competency in the context of technology. Next, I summarize developments in the past 40+ years of library technology. Finally, I discuss how the history of technology influences current library work and the competencies we need today.

Competencies

What Is Meant by Core Competency?

> Being competent means the ability to control and operate the things in the environment and the environment itself.
>
> —L. Ron Hubbard (accessed 2008)

Core competency is the fundamental knowledge or ability related to a specific subject area or skill set. The *core* part of the term refers to the underlying understanding from which an individual can build specific abilities related to a task or job. *Competency* implies that this understanding goes beyond a basic ability to being well qualified or proficient at the task, although some experts assert that competencies should simply define the abilities to adequately perform the role (McNamara, 2008).

Terms like *skills* and *ability* are often used as synonyms for *competency*. These words can be useful in understanding what competencies are and often appear in competency descriptions. However, it can be dangerous to think of competencies as the same as either of these terms. Defining technical *skills* can be too specific and lead to just compiling a list of technologies, such as knowing how to use a word processor, Microsoft Excel, and the local integrated library system (ILS), without understanding their roles—how they will be used. A technology skill, in and of itself, is just a tool to accomplish some other primary task. On the other hand, *abilities* tend to be too vague. Ability implies potential, which may or may not be actualized in a particular area of work. Examples of abilities might include "able to use a computer" or "able to learn new technology quickly."

Competency relates abilities and skills to the context in which they will be used. Usually core competencies are an agreed upon set of standards for work-based activities. In "Competencies for Information Professionals," Webber (1999: 28) defines competency as "the set of knowledge and skills that enable an employee to orient easily in a working field and to solve problems that are linked with their professional role." In other words, to be competent goes beyond just knowing how to do something to understanding how to adapt that skill or ability to your work.

Why Define Competencies?

Organizations usually use core competencies to serve one or more of the following purposes:

1. Define job descriptions, classifications, and hiring criteria
2. Establish employee orientation and performance evaluation standards
3. Develop training and professional development programs
4. Improve or change library services
5. Improve or change the technology support structure

Typically, competencies are general descriptions of the abilities needed to perform a role in the organization. Competencies can be thought of as just a different way of looking at information you already have about the work performed in the library. Job descriptions, job hiring criteria, job evaluations, professional development goals, and training curricula all have elements of competencies built into them. The circulation clerk's job description might specify that he or she is responsible for circulating library materials; the job evaluation might talk about how well he or she circulates library materials; a professional development goal might be to learn how to modify automated circulation policies; and the circulation clerk might take a training class on editing the automation system's loan rules. All these ways of describing, evaluating, and improving the circulation job in this example depend on the employee having the technical competency to use a computerized circulation system.

Competencies most often are integrated into job descriptions and professional development goals. It's useful to compare competency descriptions with job descriptions. Job descriptions typically list the tasks and responsibilities for a role, whereas competencies list the abilities needed to conduct those tasks or fulfill those responsibilities. Job descriptions describe what you do, whereas competencies describe what you're capable of doing. A competency description may also be broader than a job description, being applicable to a job class rather than to an individual position.

Discussion of competencies can be even more tightly bound with professional development. Competencies are often used as a basis for training by converting competencies to learning objectives. Especially in the case of technology competencies, the assumption is that current employees may not have all the desired skills and need training. The employee evaluation process may be used to show which competencies are missing and to specify what training is needed. Changes in library services can also be driving forces in defining new technology competency needs. Historically, as the library's use of technology has expanded, our services have moved in new directions that many of us weren't trained for. Training plays a large role in several of the competency implementations described in later chapters. Houghton-Jan (2007) provides extensive information on creating a technology training program based on competencies in her article in *Library Technology Reports*.

The increased use of technology in libraries has significantly increased demands on the technology support structure. The library systems department, the most common information technology (IT) support provider, has greatly expanded beyond its original role of supporting the ILS. The quantity of technologies combined with the rapid pace of change has outstripped the ability of many systems departments to completely support all of the library's technologies. As a result, staff in all areas of the library are increasingly being expected to provide the initial troubleshooting and simple problem resolution for the technology in their areas. What's more, they are often expected to learn many aspects of new technology on their own without formal training programs. This trend toward self-sufficiency improves communication and takes some of the support burden off the library IT department. It also bolsters employees' confidence in their technical skills. On the other hand, it increases the demand for staff training programs and makes the need for an understanding of core technology competencies for the various positions throughout the library especially acute.

Defining Technology Competencies

Technology competency refers to those abilities that either require the use of digital technology to accomplish a task (e.g., a library clerk's ability to use a computer, bar code scanner, and circulation software to check out books to patrons) or require an in-depth understanding of the technology itself in order to support existing systems (e.g., the help desk staff's ability to understand computer hardware, operating systems, and software to fix a computer). People with the first level of ability are often called *users* and people with the second level are called *information technology (IT) support.* A third type of competency could also be distinguished—*creators*, who develop new or customize existing technology. Some examples of creator competency might include the abilities to create a Web site, develop an interactive tutorial, or establish an RSS feed to the catalog. Creators often need as much or more expertise in technology as IT support, at least in the area of their creation. They may also need an understanding of library goals and expertise in the specific library field pertinent to the application.

No hard line exists among these types of technical competency, but rather they can be considered a continuum with users at one end and full-time IT support at the other. Creators may fall in the middle or exist far beyond IT support in this competency continuum depending on the level of technical knowledge needed. Traditionally, most librarians and staff in the library had technical skills closer to the user end of the spectrum where they used technology created and maintained by someone else to do their job. The support and creation of new technology was primarily the realm of IT specialists and systems librarians. However, one of the interesting developments in the past decade or so (and perhaps one of the reasons for the increased interest in competencies right now) is the growth of the "power user." Power users blur the boundary between user and IT support. They may provide their own technical support and are often responsible for creating new uses of the technology. Power users are often motivated by personal interest and their expertise may go deep into the technology in their particular area of interest, but they may not know as much about the broad range of technology as IT support does.

Power users have been around as long as libraries have been automated. They were often the first ones to move into the formal library systems/IT role. However, what is interesting now is the acceleration both in the number of power users and in the depth of their expertise. While individuals are still motivated by personal interest to take on this deeper level of technical knowledge, the library organization itself is increasingly recognizing and formalizing these power user competencies in three areas. First, various staff in the library may be expected to develop deeper levels of technical expertise to accomplish their traditional work. For instance, instruction librarians may be expected to create their own Web pages or use online course management software to disseminate instruction materials. Second, technical work formerly done in the library's systems or IT support department may be moved out to other departments. For example, reference or public service may take on responsibility for basic troubleshooting and repair of computers in public areas. Circulation staff may directly edit the loan rule table in the library automation system. Finally, new technology-dominated areas of the library are being created and staffed outside of the library systems department. Digital repositories are an example of a new library service that requires significant technical ability but is not necessarily located in the systems department.

In part, this increased expectation in technical competency is due to the spread of technical knowledge in all areas of the library. Recent library school graduates tend to have a higher level of technical savvy that they bring to whatever area of the library in which they work. Other departments in the library may also deliberately hire technology experts to support their particular initiatives. Digital projects often grow in separate areas outside the systems office and so they may hire their own personnel with systems-type qualifications.

Another factor influencing the spread of deeper technical expertise throughout the library is change in the ILS, which make them easier to use and maintain. ILS systems no longer need a lot of complex customization using an arcane command language and so may not need specialists or dedicated programmers located in the systems department. Instead, technically competent librarians working outside the systems office are often able to handle the requirements for their portion of the ILS.

One competency role we haven't talked about is that of "planner." The ability to plan, anticipate, and envision the future is a competency in and of itself. The planner is the person who understands the big picture, ideally of both the library and the technology itself, and can make decisions regarding appropriate technology to be acquired, changes that should be made in the library's use of technology, and future directions to pursue. A planner requires competency in a specific, hands-on technology, including a deep grasp of the theory, trends, and capabilities of that technology and an understanding of the needs of the library and its users in order to spot trends and anticipate future possibilities.

While this book focuses specifically on technical competencies, technological proficiency also requires other competencies. For example, to be truly competent with the library's automated circulation system, we would also expect a circulation clerk to be competent with the library's circulation policies and procedures in order to make judgments on when to override the computer system to waive a fine or extend a loan period. Diane Neal explores this idea of "soft skills" in more detail in Chapter 2.

It is worth exploring briefly how an understanding of laws, policies, and ethics impact the library's use of technology. Knowledge of various laws, controversies, and local policies combined with a good understanding of library ethics and mission is important in making many seemingly technological decisions. Many of the laws do not have hard and fast rules but allow interpretation. It's important for library staff to look at and really understand these in the context of their own library and users rather than just accept industry interpretation or blanket policies handed down by the parent organization.

Some examples include the impact of the Children's Internet Protection Act and Internet filtering policies on public and school librarians' ability to provide Internet access. It is also important for these librarians to understand how the filtering technology itself works in order to assist users in their searches. School and academic librarians need to understand technology as it impacts copyright, fair use, plagiarism, and other intellectual property concerns. The Digital Millennium Copyright Act's limits on the ability to manipulate media data can impact the use of media resources. Software licensing and vendor contracts can impact deployment of technology and access to electronic collections. Anyone who edits Web pages should understand the impact of the Americans with Disabilities Act (ADA) with regard to creating accessible Web pages. Privacy, one of American Library Association's primary ethics, may be unwittingly compromised by newer, nonlibrary-specific technologies. For instance, user logins may be captured and saved on network logs for months or even years after use of library computers.

Even so, all of these competency roles come home to the technology itself. At the most basic level, the technology available in the library defines what technical competencies are needed. You need the ability to develop Web pages only if the library has a Web site. And, of course, trends in technology have a huge impact on the technology competencies needed in libraries.

History of Library Technology and Technology Competencies

The current state of technology determines to a large extent the type of technology competencies library staff need. However, writing a book about technology competencies immediately anchors those competencies to a specific time and state of technology. Unfortunately, as everyone knows, technology is a moving target. In fact, I shall argue that technology, like the universe, is not just moving but accelerating and expanding with the passage of time. So, how do we capture a concept like "technology competency" in a way that will be useful for some time to come?

It is helpful to discuss technology competencies in the context of how technology in libraries has developed over time, especially because our expectation of appropriate technological knowledge of our staff does not always match the current reality. For instance, competency standards that emphasize only knowledge of the library automation system may overlook the value of using office productivity software and the Web to carry out daily responsibilities and to interact with the traditional library automation systems. By anchoring our discussion in the history of technology in libraries, we can better see what outdated competency expectations we may still be holding onto, what technical competencies are appropriate at this place and time, and what competencies have adapted well over time and so may continue to be relevant in the future.

We can't look at technology competencies without looking at the state of technology itself. Ten or twenty years ago it wouldn't have occurred to me to include the creator role in the list of competency levels. Before personal computers (PCs), it wasn't even possible for ordinary librarians and library staff to significantly change existing applications, much less create new ones. Even after the introduction of PCs, library technology was dominated by applications oriented to the major library operations, such as the ILS and journal index databases, which were built and supported by external vendors. It was only when PCs were joined by Windows and the Web that an environment was created that actively encouraged, even demanded, change, customization, and creation by individual library staff members. Technology developed in the past decade or so has given us the ability to create and customize at an unprecedented level. Now defining competencies has to take into consideration the ability to choose among options. Rather than just editing Web pages, do you want your instruction librarian's Web competencies to incorporate wikis, blogs, and other social networking components? Should she be able to test the page's usability, ensure that it meets the ADA accessibility guidelines, or incorporate multimedia elements?

Library Technology by Decade

It is useful to look at the history of library technology as a series of periods or stages. A decade-by-decade description of changes in technology in fact tracks fairly closely with the periods or stages identified by other authors, so such a description will serve our purpose.

1950s

The first experiments with computers for library applications occurred in the 1950s. The earliest use of computers focused on their number crunching ability, but after World War II the computer's equally useful abilities to store, organize, and retrieve information efficiently were recognized as particularly appropriate for libraries. One of the landmarks from that period includes IBM's early work with library circulation systems. The use of computers in libraries was recognized early and satirized in the movie *Desk Set* (Lang, 1957), starring Katherine Hepburn and Spencer Tracy. This 1957 movie envisions an early form of Google—a computer able to answer any reference question—but not always accurately. While these search capabilities were more fiction than fact at that point, the 1960s started to move it into reality. The 1950s period of library automation, although interesting, had little direct impact on the lives or competencies of most librarians and staff.

1960s

The 1960s saw the beginning of more sustainable library automation efforts. Some of the most significant developments, initiatives, and standards from this period still with us today include the major government databases Agricola, ERIC (Education Resources Information Center), and Medline; the establishment of OCLC (Ohio College Library Center); and, perhaps most significant, the creation of the MARC (Machine Readable Cataloging) record format by the Library of Congress. The computers used in these early automation efforts were offline, batch-processing systems, typically using punch cards for data entry.

During this period automation became a reality for many libraries, albeit the largest and best supported institutions, as specific areas of library operations incorporated discrete automation elements. Also during this period, the library profession's major associations developed technology-specific chapters. The International Federation of Library Associations and Institutions (IFLA) formed its Committee on Mechanization in 1965. The American Library Association's (ALA) Library and Information Technology Association (LITA) was established in 1966 and began publishing the *Journal of Library Automation* (which later became *Information Technology and Libraries*) in 1968.

Although work on automating the library was occurring on several fronts, for the most part users saw technology only at the circulation desk. Library staff in specific areas of library operations, such as circulation or acquisitions, incorporated discrete automation elements into their normal analog workflow. Library staff fortunate enough to have technology were restricted to a limited user role and expected to follow step-by-step procedures to use the computerized devices. A typical library staff competency needed during this time would have been transferring typewriting skills to keyboarding and operating punch card machines.

1970s

By the 1970s, computer technology had advanced to online "time-sharing" systems that could be directly accessed via terminals, although batch-processed punch cards were still used. The 1970s' technology was still dominated by mainframe computers requiring special air-conditioned clean rooms serviced by white-coated techies, but minicomputers would become the dominate force by the end of the decade. Typically, only larger libraries and utilities had access to this technology.

The 1970s saw significant strides in the automation of the major library functions: acquisitions, cataloging, circulation, and bibliographic database searching. Automation software continued to be function specific, automating discrete functions within specific library areas with the emphasis on back-end technical tasks. Although many of these systems were developed by individual institutions, initial development efforts begun in laboratory and university environments began to transition into commercial business ventures, and automation vendors began to appear, including Innovative Interfaces, Data Research Associates (DRA), and Dialog search services.

One of the driving forces in the 1970s was the conversion of bibliographic data into electronic form. By 1977, OCLC had become available to libraries nationwide. Applying the MARC standard and inputting records into OCLC fell into the cataloging area, and soon other elements of the cataloging process began to be automated too. Acquisitions and circulation also underwent significant development during this era. The one exception to technology in these "back office" functions was the new database search service offered by some reference departments. Mediated searching provided access to major government, and, increasingly, commercial databases and introduced sophisticated search techniques using Boolean logic and KWIC (keyword in context) indexes.

In general, staff were still relegated to a limited user role with little direct control over development or support of the technology. Typical library staff competencies still focused on the ability to follow step-by-step procedures to use computerized devices plus the ability to navigate choices on a terminal screen. Examples of additional skills for catalogers might include knowledge of the MARC format and the ability to input records into OCLC using terminal and modem technologies. For reference librarians, new skills were focused on searching bibliographic databases using specialized commands, modem protocols, and Boolean logic.

1980s

The earlier innovations had set the stage, and by 1980 technology was ready to explode in the library world, particularly from the library staff and user viewpoints. In the 1980s, libraries consolidated their previous gains in library automation, added significant new functions, and then spread the word. Although not all libraries were automated in the 1980s, by the end of the decade, libraries that weren't automated felt guilty about it and wished they were. More than any other decade during library automation's short history, the state of technology at the beginning was very different from that at the end. Libraries went into the decade with passive, big iron technology dealing independently with each major library system and went out with ILSs covering almost every library function on minicomputers that the library could actively control. Staff could input data directly into the computer via terminals. Even more significant, small, customizable PCs were changing life at staff workstations and the definition of service in public reference areas.

The 1980s were a pivotal decade. Arguably the first 20 years of library automation could be seen as concerned with discrete, independent functions in the back end of the library. During the 1980s, a major change was seen as second-generation ILSs were introduced. Now information created in one part of the library, for instance acquisitions, could be used in another area, for example, cataloging, resulting in more efficient processes, better communication, and better service. However, it also meant the walls dividing processes between one department and another began to come down, and, more and more, work in one area could directly affect another.

These new ILSs were designed as turnkey systems, which is to say that they did not require extensive technical assistance to operate. The original library automation systems were typically built by an in-house IT department, but by the 1980s a growing field of library vendors had taken over the market. For example, Northwestern University's system became NOTIS in the 1980s and Virginia Tech's in-house automation system became VTLS (Breeding, 2007). Both to facilitate dissemination and to meet library demands for control, these new ILSs were designed to exist outside of the separate, privileged computer room environment constantly fed and pampered by IT experts, who were often external to the library organization.

For the first time it was possible for the library to take control of its technology and use locally trained experts. While vendors were still responsible for major support of the technology, the computer systems no longer required the cadre of white-coated lab techies. Now these turnkey systems could be controlled locally by a "power user"—a library specialist (librarian or library staff) who had the interest and ability to learn the technology involved. Because many of these early technology innovations and adoptions took place in departments such as cataloging and acquisitions, the library's first technology experts tended to come from the technical services area. In particular, the early emphasis on the bibliographic database tended to build technology skills in the cataloging department.

This local librarian or staff person was trained by the ILS vendor to handle the simpler maintenance, troubleshooting, and configuration tasks. As these local experts found "systems" dominating more and more of their duties, their responsibilities changed, and many eventually became systems librarians. By the end of the decade, these lone systems experts were beginning to form departments with multiple experts—including techies without any library background. These new technology staff members reported to the library rather than to a computer center and were often supervised by a librarian, usually the systems librarian.

The introduction of desktop computers brought about further changes. Librarians and staff began to experience computers at a personal level. For the first time staff could have a computer at home. Although the penetration was low and the computers had limited capability, these early adopters could write letters to grandma, play computer games, experiment with programming, and just get comfortable with computer technology in general. More significant was the fact that staff with computers on their own desktops could began to experiment with word processing, spreadsheets, and even creating databases to accomplish all those little chores not handled by the big automation system. Computers were now out of the laboratory and in the home, introducing the concept of individual ownership and individual responsibility for understanding computers (Childers, 2003).

As significant as the changes were in the back end of the library, even more important changes were happening out front. Earlier technology efforts were successful in their goal of increasing the effectiveness of back-end operations, and, as a result, more staff time and technology resources were increasingly available for the "front of the house." In the 1980s, library users finally gained direct access to the library's technology. Truly effective automated, public access catalogs for library users became widely available. *American Libraries* celebrated the increasing ubiquity of automated catalogs in their 1982 contest "101 uses for a dead catalog" (*American Libraries*, 1982). By the end of the decade compact disc (CD) databases on PCs (and Macs) began to replace paper periodical indexes.

Users could now search the library collection much more efficiently, but first they had to learn how to use both the equipment and the software. User training programs began to expand beyond library-specific, bibliographic knowledge to include technology and search system instruction. The reference librarian was the one who had to step in and learn how to teach these new technologies to the library users. Bibliographic instruction began to give way to information literacy.

Staff and librarian competencies during this period focused on becoming expert in the function-specific technology and dedicated hardware in the individual's particular department. Reference librarians needed to understand how to search new computer database interfaces and how to teach these skills to users. The first big surge of interest in technology competencies appears in the library literature of the early 1980s. According to Childers (2003), these early articles considered how to support technology in the library and the impact of technology in changing roles of specific areas, such as cataloging. Childers (2003) also noted that by the late 1980s an increasing number of articles were about systems librarians, indicating that this new specialization had become established. While the library was now directly responsible for maintaining computer technology, in-depth technical know-how was still limited to select experts, namely, the systems librarians. Library staff in other areas of library operations were not expected to directly control or support technology in their areas beyond the basic user level.

1990s

Two important changes in library automation that started in the late 1980s came to fruition in the 1990s and continue to have a significant impact on technology in libraries. These two developments were networking at multiple levels and the introduction of client–server systems. Also a dominant force was the increasing ubiquity and ease of use of personal computer technology—first at work and then at home.

Networks had been a part of library technology for over a decade by the 1990s, from terminals with hard-wired connections to the library automation server to modems providing data-sharing access to bibliographic utilities. However, these were limited technologies dedicated to specific functions. The greatly increased role of evolving network standards, which enabled shared communication across devices and systems and even across locations, drove much of the development during the 1990s.

Local area networks (LANs), which allowed institution-wide communication and shared technology, were introduced in the late 1980s and were a key player in the expansion of technology experienced by libraries in the 1990s. What was communicating on the local networks were PCs, in the generic sense. Whether Apple or IBM, personal computers were rapidly replacing dumb terminals, which had a significant impact on the way people worked. Rather than walking to a shared location to use a terminal dedicated to a specific library function—such as cataloging, circulation, or mediated reference database searches—library staff more and more could expect to have a computer on their desk that was capable of performing any or all of these functions.

By the time the Windows operating system was introduced in the mid-1990s, the third generation of ILSs was enabling access to automated functions from library staff's desktop computers. This "client–server" environment took advantage of the LAN to off-load some of the server's tasks to the intelligent desktop computers. Library staff no longer had to share a few dedicated terminals but could work at their own desktop computer, combining their traditional work with other tasks involving word processing, spreadsheets, and, increasingly, e-mail. Finally, the "personal" in personal computers came into its own as people began to get ideas and try new things, leveraging the highly controllable and customizable PC environment.

As significant as the evolution in PC technology was in libraries, the next development was revolutionary—the advent of the Internet and the World Wide Web as a widespread service in libraries. While libraries had access to certain functions of early forms of the Internet, it wasn't until after a combination of developments in the early 1990s that it became popularly available. In 1991, Tim Berners-Lee's hypertext protocol was introduced as the World Wide Web. Around the same time, the National Science Foundation (NSF) eliminated restrictions on commercial use of the Internet, allowing much more content to become available to the public. Finally, the advent in 1993 of the first graphical browser, Mosaic, pulled these earlier developments together, as its graphical interface made it much easier to search for this new content using the hypertext protocol (Wikipedia, 2007).

14

With all these pieces in place, the stage was set for library technology to explode out of its isolated, library-specific role. Until this networking era, library technology was largely independent from technology in other parts of the library's parent organization and inaccessible by the outside world (with OCLC and LC the long-term exception). For instance, while academic library automation systems were designed to work with multiple functions across the library, the system functioned in isolation from other technology efforts on and off campus. LANs and the Internet along with new national and international communication standards made it possible to communicate among systems from different vendors. As a result, the automation environment became more supportive of collaboration, and it became possible to integrate different systems. With the combination of the Web and Windows PC technology, libraries started to greatly expand their services and to realize that the priorities of the end user had taken control. In particular, users could access more and more library content and services without actually coming to the library.

During the 1990s, staff continued to develop their competence in the components of the ILS pertaining to their specific work area, including adding new features and learning how to operate the automation system in the Windows environment. All librarians and staff learned to use PC technology, including the basics of the Windows operating system, word processing, and other office applications. E-mail became an important method of communication—inside the library as well as outside. Everyone became familiar with using the Web, and a few began to develop skills in creating Web pages as the library began to create an online presence providing a user interface to the library's electronic content and some services. In addition to the ILS, more function-specific applications were appearing, such as interlibrary loan systems and cataloging authority systems. The number of bibliographic databases expanded and began to move online, requiring new skills for reference librarians and acquisitions staff. Library systems staff were under increasing pressure not just to support all types of new technology but also to spot trends and specify acquisition of new technology.

2000s

We live in a much different world than even just 10 years ago. The 2000s have seen an explosive growth in digital resources, integration of systems, and development in client–server technology that allows a whole new level of customization. Central to these developments is the Web online environment. Networks are no longer just for connecting technologies to accomplish work but also for social connections and recreational use. Users and (most) library staff are increasingly confident in their technology abilities and often have the same or even more advanced systems at home. The Internet, Web search engines, and e-mail are a regular part of our lives—both at work and at home. In fact, network technology is blurring the distinction between home and work. However, with all this seamless networking, security has become much more of an issue.

One of the distinguishing aspects of technology since 2000 is integration. After adding more and more new technologies during the previous 30 years, we now want to make these technologies work together. The complex back end of multiple applications, equipment, and institutional relationships are now being connected to talk to each other. In particular, libraries have become interested in creating a seamless search environment for users. Today the ILS represents only one aspect of the overall automation environment. A number of new products have been introduced to manage and deliver digital content combined with better ways to navigate this sea of electronic information. Some of these products, including link revolvers, metasearch engines, and tagging, are focused on improving users' success in finding relevant information. Integration of independent systems, along with improved authentication and authorization services, are creating a friendlier, easier-to-use information environment. The goal is to make a simple environment for users that focuses on their goals and tasks rather than on requiring them to learn a variety of individual technologies. Increasingly this environment also provides the user with ways to personalize and customize the library interface.

Library technology is also starting to break away from the constraints of vendor-defined systems. Open-source technology allows technically proficient librarians to control and enhance the user experience. Open-source initiatives include ILS applications, institutional repositories, and infrastructure components (e.g., Apache Web server, Linux operating system). The emergence of national and international standards beyond MARC—RDF (Resource Description Framework), XML (Extensible Markup Language), Dublin Core Metadata, OpenURL—have played an important role in enabling these common linkages.

The distributed environment has become the wireless environment with even less control or rigid expectations of what users do in the library. Not only have print materials become digitized but also libraries are buying more and more information that is born digital. In addition, although libraries still primarily purchase information from publishers, now libraries are creating their own digital content. A quiet revolution is taking place as libraries look at copyright and intellectual property with new eyes and begin to create alternate digital repository systems.

The advent of the Web with its pervasive network of information also brought new concerns regarding information overload, in which users felt overwhelmed by the amount of information available and tended to make poorer choices of information sources. While we are still concerned about information overload, librarians by 2000 had largely given up the idea that we could control access to the Web via catalog-type access. Instead we're teaching skills on how to search effectively and evaluate sources in the open search environment.

Many librarians are finding that their systems departments are no longer able to handle all the demands from the many different types of technology now available in the library. Library staff are increasingly expected to provide some level of technology support for themselves. Fortunately, the simplicity promised

16

by the Windows operating system along with increased hardware reliability makes it easier to maintain PCs. On the other hand, the increased capabilities of new systems offer a number of choices and opportunities to customize systems that add new complexity. Concern is less with how to use technology and more about how to use it well. We're not just interested in the skills to create a Web page but in how to make a Web page that incorporates multimedia, that can interact with users, and that is usable by all types of users. In addition to the "hard" technical skills, the past decade has seen an increase in technology-related "soft" skills. Usability, accessibility, marketing, desktop publishing, graphic design, security, and online instructional pedagogy are just some of the skills that librarians and staff are developing.

The year 2000 was a significant milestone in library technology. Although new technology continues to develop at a breathtaking rate, the current level is finally powerful enough to enable the library to focus more on its core mission. In some ways, technology is beginning to return to us the original purpose of libraries to find knowledge rather than to learn how specific technologies work. Technology today is less concerned with *how* we operate than with *what* we actually do. Computers have solved the mechanics of access, transmission, and reproduction of information. Librarians can now focus on the information itself.

History of Computer Literacy

Since early in the history of computers, including library automation, the concept of computer literacy has existed. It is an interesting notion to be as competent at computers as we are at reading. Looking back at computer literacy expectations in the past, we can see that they closely mirror the technical competencies expected in libraries of the time. One of the earliest mentions of computer literacy was by President Nixon when he urged adding the study of computers to the science curriculum in 1968. However, the interest in computer literacy really took off in the 1980s. Childers (2003) found that the number of articles on computer education in the *Reader's Guide* went from nothing in the 1970s to a significant number by the mid-1980s and then fell to a reduced level that nevertheless indicated an ongoing interest in the late 1980s through the 1990s.

What is meant by *computer literacy* is hard to pin down. While we now tend to think of computer literacy as the most basic level of understanding about technology, it has been defined at a variety of levels in the past. Computer literacy standards ranged from simple ones aimed at everyone to those designed to explain a course of study for computer science majors. For instance, Donald Norman (1984: 222) defined the lowest computer literacy level as including "basics" like algorithms, and from there his standards went on to programming knowledge and, at the highest level, "an understanding of the science of computing," His idea of computer literacy is aimed at a level more appropriate to computer science majors rather than to the needs of everyday users. Even today, the technically sophisticated may fall short of

Norman's expectations (and probably don't even miss it just as even the most experienced drivers have little reason to know how to rebuild a carburetor).

The problem with using computer literacy as a measure of core competency is that it plays into the idea that one standard of computer ability applies to everyone. In fact, today, technological competency is a continuum with various levels of appropriate ability. My favorite definition of computer literacy is Eric Lease Morgan's: "You are computer literate when you feel you are telling the computer what to do and not the other way around" (Morgan, 1998: 39). To me, this means we must move beyond the idea of memorizing a rote set of commands. Instead we should combine a basic knowledge of what the computer is capable of doing with our understanding of library processes to determine what technology's role will be in delivering library services.

Why Now?

I've presented the history of technology in a linear fashion, assigning certain technologies to certain decades. In reality, each individual library experienced its own historical time line of events. Early adopters might have gone through each of these developments in sequence, but libraries coming in later may have leapfrogged over one or more generations of technology. The same can be said for the individuals working in libraries. Recent graduates might leapfrog over existing staff's comfort and ability with technology, creating a disparity in abilities. Should the newcomers "dumb down" their skills, or should the old-timers "catch up"? Bringing everyone up to the same level of competence is often the motive for competency training programs.

This leapfrog effect of new graduates with a high technology competency level is not just impacting regular librarians and staff. IT support and systems librarians are also feeling the pressure. In a 2005 LITA Heads of Library Technology interest group meeting, a recent masters of library science graduate stated that she felt her programming skills were better than many in her campus IT department—in fact, they often asked her for help (Thompson, 2005). On the other side, a library systems department head expressed the view that one of the new IT support challenges was new librarians and power users who used technology at a level well beyond the average level established in the library. This caused problems for the systems department because of both the effort needed to support nonstandard technology and the fact that the technology might exceed the knowledge of the IT support staff.

The need for technology skills in libraries has steadily increased over time. Beile and Adams' (2000) study of academic library jobs shows growth in required computer skills for public services and technical services positions from 40 percent in 1988 to 67 percent in 1996 (up to 80 percent if we include preferred skills). A survey of research libraries found that by 2000 over half of the library positions in which librarians wanted to work involved a significant degree of technology in one capacity or other (Simmons-Welburn, 2000).

Defining Today's Technology Competencies

Increases in Pace, Breadth, and Depth of Change

What the preceding history shows is that, although libraries have the reputation of being traditionalists wedded to books, they were actually very early adopters of computer technology. The introduction of technology into libraries revolutionized library operations. The amount of technology to learn was intimidating, but, looking back, the pace of change of the earlier technologies in the 1970s and 1980s seems quite steady. As new technologies were put in place, staff had time to learn and adapt to them. What's more, staff usually had to deal with only one or two new technologies at a time—typically the automated application in their function area and its supporting equipment, such as terminals and printers. When PCs were first introduced, the number of applications to learn was still limited—word processing, spreadsheets, and, perhaps, databases, were about all. The depth of knowledge needed for these applications also tended to be at a simpler level. For example, with the word processor, one needed to know how to open and save documents, type something such as a letter or a list, and possibly use basic formatting such as bold and italic.

Acceleration in number and variety of technologies in libraries over the past decade or so has greatly increased technical competency demands on librarians and staff. Today, library staff are dealing with technology in an environment of constant change. This change has three characteristics. First is the rapid speed or pace at which the change takes place. Second is the number of different technology types in use, in other words, the breadth of technology. Third is the depth at which we need to understand individual technologies.

The *pace* of change is concerned with the rapid updating of existing technology and constant introduction of new technologies. It's not that earlier generations of technology in libraries didn't require change. Rather, it is that the rate of change today is more rapid—on the order of months rather than years—and it is accelerating. This rapid pace of change started to come to general attention in the 1990s. A 1996 *Library Journal* survey found that 75 percent of library staff said their jobs had changed in the past three years (St. Lifer, 1996). By the end of the 1990s the popular literature had begun to refer to technology change in "Web years," implying that the pace of change was too fast for normal years to measure.

Illustrating this rapid and accelerating pace of change is a time line from my own library. I come from a very young university. California State University San Marcos (CSUSM) was established in 1989. When we moved into our library facility in 1992, we leapfrogged over several generations of library technology. Not only did we start with an ILS in place but we also had fully networked computers on every staff desktop as well as function-specific terminals and computers. Nevertheless, we have experienced significant technology changes in our short existence, including the proliferation of new technologies and the accelerated pace of changes in technology. Figure 1-1 illustrates the pace of major changes in some of our Web-based applications. We start off relatively quietly in the early 1990s, but by the early 2000s major changes are occurring more than once a year.

Breadth refers to the wide variety of technologies involved in library jobs today. Originally, library staff were responsible for technology just specific to their particular area of library operations. As automated systems became more integrated, the number of functions increased, providing staff with more capability but also with more things to learn. Even so, the changes at that time all focused on well-understood library processes. An example would be the addition of CD-ROM databases, which were a fairly direct manifestation of the paper journal indexes that reference librarians had used for years.

In the 1990s, libraries began to add more and more technology-based services that they had not traditionally offered. The biggest addition was the library Web site. For the first time, libraries could create a virtual library presence capable of offering many of their traditional resources and services to users in their homes. Web technology also offered new ways to organize and access library collections. Now, patrons are increasingly able to customize and control their electronic library experience. For patrons who do visit the physical library, technologies are available that may not be directly related to accessing library resources. For example, office productivity and media editing software allow patrons to complete their entire research process from the initial search for sources to creating the final product. This capability extends the library's role from just providing information access to supporting all aspects of the research process.

Not only do library staff have to plan, develop, and support all this new user-centered technology but they are also using many more types of technology in their jobs. For instance, when our library changed to Innovative's Millennium system, reference librarians found they could easily access information about the collections that had previously been the purview of the acquisitions department.

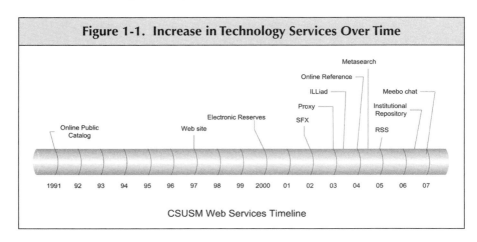

Figure 1-1. Increase in Technology Services Over Time

CSUSM Web Services Timeline

The technology made it easy to get information about the collection, such as how frequently materials circulated by call number, but it also led to new responsibilities as bibliographers were now expected to track their own spending.

The last category of change is the *depth* of technical knowledge expected of library staff today. Librarians and staff are expected to use technology with a higher level of sophistication and think creatively about how to apply technical solutions to their work. Integrated library systems provide more and more ability to make choices and customize the application. In fact, we have more options and control in all our software, whether it's changing our screen background or using macros to automate common ILS tasks. Take a rather narrow function such as reserves. In addition to all the technological aspects of putting print reserve material on the shelf (creating an ILS entry, establishing a circulation loan rule, and printing labels), library staff need to understand the electronic reserve system. Electronic reserves not only involves the specialized software but also requires an understanding of technologies to input the documents (scanner, electronic file transfer), special protocols to manage such things as copyright or disability issues, and, possibly, external access systems, such as course management systems.

Increasingly staff are also expected to support their own technology to a much larger extent. In this context, support means both troubleshooting problems and taking the initiative to learn new technology on their own. We can no longer wait for an IT specialist to take care of a technology problem or to provide thorough training on how to use each new technology. In addition to understanding the technology itself, staff are also expected, at least tacitly, to understand the impact of recent laws and interpret old concepts, such as copyright, for a new electronic environment.

The current state of technology creates a very stressful but exciting environment with lots of opportunities to enhance and change library services. So how does this increased pace, breadth, and depth of technical abilities impact competency? Let's take a look at the reference librarian's responsibilities before and after the Windows/Web explosion. Before the Web, technical competencies for a reference librarian included the ability to use the PAC terminal to help patrons search the catalog and use the CD-ROM PC to help patrons search one or two journal databases. In addition, she might have performed custom searches on something like DIALOG or used a PC word processor and printer to create handouts. If a technical problem was encountered, she called in IT support or the vendor.

After the advent of the Web, the reference librarian still supports the patron searching the catalog and journal indexes, but the number and complexity of these indexes have greatly increased, especially considering that each has a different search interface. In addition, the reference librarian also supports searching the open Internet. She may also be more involved in technical support, often providing the first level of troubleshooting of equipment and software in public areas. If the patron encounters a problem, the reference librarian has to diagnose whether the

21

problem is with the patron's understanding of how to use the information source, in which case she educates the patron, or with the technology itself, in which case she may solve the problem herself or call in IT support. In addition to supporting library-specific applications, she may also support patron use of office productivity software or media applications. Support of off-site patrons has greatly increased with technology such as 24/7 chat services, blogs, wikis, and, of course, the ubiquitous e-mail. In addition to direct support of patrons, reference librarians still create paper support documents, but increasingly they are also creating Web pages. Reference librarians who teach are also involved in a multitude of instructional technologies, which is another discussion in and of itself.

Give Up the Concept of Mastery

One of the most important competencies in this new age of technology is the ability to handle constant change. Given the rapid pace, breadth, and depth of change, one of the most useful strategies for gaining competency is to give up the concept of mastery. It may seem radical in a book about competency, but I recommend that expecting *not* to know everything about a technology can be more beneficial than attempting to master it.

Historically, librarians and staff have been justly proud of their thorough knowledge of all aspects of their fields of expertise. When library automation systems were introduced, they were essentially just a direct replacement of specific manual processes in well-understood areas of library operations. Thanks to in-depth training from automation vendors, and documentation that often detailed tasks down to the specific keystrokes to press, staff learned these new systems thoroughly. Contrast that with today, when software often doesn't even come with a manual and the pace of change is on the order of months rather than years. Few of us have the time to master even one technology before it changes, much less all the different types of technologies we deal with every day.

As a result, I have come to feel that this expectation of mastery can, ironically, be detrimental to building and maintaining technical competency. If we think we do know all about a technology we use, it may actually be a symptom that our focus has become too narrow and that we may be missing what else is out there. I see three reasons in particular for giving up the concept of mastery. First, you can't easily master the moving target that is today's technology. Much has been written about the rapid changes in technology, so I will just say that we should bear in mind that technology is secondary to the primary purposes of most of our jobs. We need to know only enough about it to get the job done. Second, mastery tends to set skills in concrete. In my experience, the biggest difficulty in moving from an existing technology to a new technology can be librarians' and staff's comfort in their knowledge of rote procedures specific to the old technology. For example, when the PC operating system changed from DOS to Windows, the experts who knew all the DOS keystrokes to perform their tasks had a harder time translating these skills into the Windows environment and resisted the "inefficient" mouse and menu system more than less expert staff. Third, there is a tendency to wait to use new technology until you feel you really understand it or until it has proven its benefits (usually by seeing how someone else has used it). While it certainly makes sense to avoid the "bleeding edge" of untried technologies, waiting until one is comfortable with the technology may mean that an opportunity has been missed or, even, that the technology may be reaching the end of its life cycle.

In place of mastering the specifics of a technology, the more important competency is to understand the theory—the underlying metaphor behind the technology—and develop transferable skills. Staff are commonly frustrated when they learn a new technology and then see it change or go away in the next iteration/generation. However, while the specific applications may have gone, often the skills learned are still useful. What is important is to understand the principles by which the program works. Once you learn the underlying functionality, you know what the new program can do, and so your learning task is reduced to just figuring out how to find the equivalent commands in the new application. An example is the word processing programs WordPerfect and Microsoft Word. While the commands and menu structure are different, the underlying ability to open documents, select fonts, format, print, and so forth, are almost all the same. In addition, certain sets of features, such as fonts and character formatting, tend to travel together in both programs, making it easier to find related functions. People familiar with one program can use this knowledge to inform their learning of the unfamiliar program, greatly shortening their learning curve. They may be a little slower with the new application at first, but they can have confidence that they will be able to use the features they need. (However, it can be difficult to give up an emotional attachment: some of us do still mourn the loss of WordPerfect's "reveal codes" command, which seems to have no equivalent in Word.)

The bottom line is to be fluid and comfortable with constant learning. This type of competence may be difficult to define and measure objectively, but it is a critical skill. Job advertisements trying to describe this ability often use terms like *flexibility*, *willingness to learn*, and *ability to handle change*. An environment supportive of a willingness to try new things expects employees to "play" and experiment and doesn't penalize the occasional failure. While it may be difficult to teach this skill directly, I've found that it helps to discuss the concept and to point out to staff the extent of knowledge they already possess to give them confidence that they will be able to transfer these skills to new areas. I've seen the success of this strategy in my own library. In our recent change to Microsoft Office 2007, staff shrugged off the inconvenience of having to learn a new system with comments like "it's a pain to use now, but I can see how its features are going to be more useful than the old way." The library staff didn't need hand-holding or convincing; they were confident in their own judgment of the new technology's worth and their own ability to figure it out.

In his blog on the more adaptive, "2.0 jobs" now needed in libraries, Michael Stephens (2006) concluded, "In the 21st century, library professionals will encounter a world where playing around with a new tool (toy?), experiencing new things without fear of failure (or success!), and spending time trendspotting, dreaming, and keeping an eye on emergent technologies will be built into our jobs. We'll be expected to play."

Technology Expectations for Library Jobs Today

Technology is changing the work we do in libraries as well as the services we offer. Technology competency is not an option, it is critical for all librarians and staff. Non-MLS staff may be particularly impacted as they move into a more "parapro-fessional" role, taking on many of the duties once associated with librarians as well as gaining new responsibilities, often related to the technology itself. Various organiza-tions have tried to define the basic technology competencies needed by library staff in general and by specific function areas. Diane Neal in Chapter 2 includes a selection of the efforts of statewide and national organizations to define technology competencies for librarians and library staff.

Competencies can be described at various levels. One method is to start with the most basic skills. The California Library Association (2005) uses this approach in its *Technology Core Competencies for California Library Workers*. For instance, the section "Parts of Your Computer" describes the steps involved in starting up the workstation, shutting down the workstation, and using the mouse and keyboard. However, I would recommend instead that libraries focus their competency efforts at a higher level. For instance, Latham (2000: 39), in her discussion of IT skills for library professionals, not only states that "every professional should be familiar with all components of an office suite" but goes on to specify that they "should be able to choose the appropriate application for the anticipated result" and "make use of extended capabilities of an application—to create charts, import graphics, attach files, etc." Another way to think about it is to compare technology competencies with reading literacy: do you want to be sure everyone knows their alphabet, or do you want them to be able to read library policies and write coherent reports?

There should no longer be any question that all library staff should know PC operating systems and applications such as word processing and e-mail. Instead, libraries should focus their examination of competencies on skills that build on this base. According to Woodsworth (1997: 46), "Basic competencies for every librarian include knowing what the Internet is and is not; evaluating and using hardware, software, and networks; and understanding basic computer and infor-mation science concepts." One of the most interesting competency lists in the past few years does not even come from the library community. Nevertheless, Turner's (2006) "20 Technology Skills Every Educator Should Have" includes all the skills I consider important for librarians and staff today:

1. Word processing skills
2. Spreadsheet skills
3. Database skills
4. Electronic presentation skills
5. Web navigation skills
6. Web site design skills
7. E-mail management skills
8. Digital camera skills
9. Computer network knowledge applicable to your school system [or library]
10. File management and Windows Explorer skills
11. Downloading software from the Web (knowledge including eBooks)
12. Installing computer software onto a computer system
13. WebCT or Blackboard teaching skills [most applicable to instruction librarians]
14. Videoconferencing skills
15. Computer-related storage devices (knowledge: disks, CDs, USB drives, zip disks, DVDs, etc.)
16. Scanner knowledge
17. Knowledge of PDAs [although PDAs are fading in importance, small devices from cell phones to iPods are increasingly important as information devices]
18. Deep Web knowledge
19. Educational copyright knowledge
20. Computer security knowledge

25

Active discussions in the library blogosphere following the initial appearance of Turner's list corroborate the relevance of her competency list for librarians. Blogger StevenB (2006) looked at how well academic librarians currently meet the 20 skills. The *Shifted Librarian*, in addition to endorsing the list, added five more items: blogs, instant messaging, RSS, wikis, and audio e-books (*Shifted Librarian*, 2005).

The trend is clear, at least for librarians, that a higher level of technical competency is expected. By having higher competency expectations, we can get on to the "good stuff." I would even advocate pushing the limits and expect staff and librarians to know technologies not often included on the baseline competency lists, in particular, Web editing, Web 2.0, and even media skills. The Web is pervasive and has come to serve as the library's primary communication channel. Everyone should know how to move around in and contribute to this environment. While it certainly makes sense to control the ability to edit pages on the library's public Web presence in order to protect site usability and stability, most libraries have some sort of intranet or development Web space that everyone should be able to participate in. Think back to when only secretaries could type up documents and the bosses were stuck with handwriting or dictating (well, maybe they enjoyed being "stuck"). The Web is the new word processor, and everyone should be able to use it.

Enough has been said in many other venues on the importance and value of Web 2.0 technologies, especially for communicating with our public. Communication technologies such as blogs, wikis, and instant messaging (IM) are just as valuable for internal library communication. To improve library services, everyone should be encouraged to explore technologies like RSS feeds, tagging, and podcasting. While the library systems department can help set up Web 2.0 applications, these technologies are designed at a low enough threshold that everyone should be able to hop on and try them for themselves. A library that encourages exploration will benefit with a more capable staff and improved library processes.

Media is everywhere and especially relevant to our younger patrons (as in under age 40). A rich variety of multimedia information sources exists today, and students frequently incorporate multimedia elements into their research products. We in the library world need to know more than just how to check out a video. Librarians and staff should be able to find a video online and play it, help a user to transfer an MP3 audio file, or edit a photo. In this area particularly, library employees can feel constrained by the fun factor. Learning how to use many of these technologies can be a lot of fun, as evidenced by the fact that many of us choose to pursue media-related hobbies in our spare time. However, just because learning it is enjoyable doesn't mean these aren't valuable technology skills to learn for the workplace as well.

Meredith Farkas (2006) took a different approach to competencies in her blog article entitled "Skills for the 21st Century Librarian" in which she focuses on personal attributes rather than on the specific skills needed for technology success. In particular, she was concerned with the role of library schools and the tendency to treat technology skills as not particularly relevant to traditional library specialties. However, rather than expecting library schools to teach specific technical skills, she advocated that they need to teach students "big picture topics" that would enable them to keep up with and use technology well (Farkas, 2006). Her basic competencies included the following:

1. Ability to embrace change
2. Comfort in the online medium
3. Ability to troubleshoot new technologies
4. Ability to easily learn new technologies
5. Ability to keep up with new ideas in technology and librarianship (enthusiasm for learning)

Farkas's technology-friendly attributes resemble the types of competencies mentioned in the previous section in which flexibility and comfort with constant learning replace a dependency on mastering specific technologies. Interestingly, she also goes on to advocate for higher level competencies that start to cross into management territory and look beyond the immediate unit to the needs of the library as a whole. Her higher level competencies include the following:

1. Project management skills
2. Ability to question and evaluate library services
3. Ability to evaluate the needs of all stakeholders
4. Vision to translate traditional library services into the online medium
5. Critical of technologies and ability to compare technologies
6. Ability to sell ideas/library services

Specific technical competency needs can vary among different positions in the library. I have been interested in two questions with regard to this variation in competency expectations. First, is there a difference in technology expectations for non-MLS staff versus librarian classifications? Second, if so, is this difference due to actual differences in job responsibilities or simply to how employees are classified? Unfortunately, much of the studies of library competencies is focused on librarians with little mention of staff. I decided to conduct my own small survey to investigate the perceived importance of various technology competencies for three types of positions: librarians, library staff, and systems librarians (discussed in Chapter 3). I performed two quick surveys using the instrument developed by Diane Neal (Chapter 2)—one involving my own California State University San Marcos (CSUSM) librarians and library staff and the second using the other authors in this book, who are all library systems professionals.

My results show that there is indeed a difference, a significant difference, in expectations between the staff and librarian classifications. Figure 1-2 shows that both groups of survey respondents ranked technology skills for staff as less important than for librarians. The surveys rated the majority (67 percent) of the technology competencies as somewhat or very important for librarians versus 44 percent

27

Figure 1-2. Technology Competencies Ranked as Somewhat or Very Important by at Least 60 Percent of Respondents for Each Position Classification

	AUTHOR SURVEY		CSUSM SURVEY	
COMPETENCIES	STAFF	LIBRARIAN	STAFF	LIBRARIAN
General technology	33%	40%	27%	47%
Internet-related	47%	80%	13%	67%
Hardware peripherals	53%	73%	53%	87%
Library technology	25%	75%	33%	67%
Percent of all competencies	**44%**	**67%**	**28%**	**67%**

(authors) and 28 percent (CSUSM) for staff. For three of the four technology categories, significantly more technology skills are expected for librarians than for staff. In the Internet-related competencies the difference is particularly striking. The CSUSM survey respondents rated only two skills as important for staff—evaluating Web pages and searching electronic databases. This represents only 13 percent of the listed skills versus 67 percent expected for librarians. The author survey largely concurred with these expectations, with the exception of Web 2.0 technologies, which more than half of the authors rated as important for both librarians and staff. Appendix 1-1 lists all of the competencies surveyed.

The skills in the first category of general technology competencies were considered less important overall for staff and librarians. However, the type of technologies thought important was similar for both librarians and staff, although expectations for staff were lower. A few competencies were rated as more important for staff to know than for librarians, in particular, knowledge of the ILS and scanner peripherals. This makes sense, because staff positions in areas such as interlibrary loan and circulation desks frequently use scanner equipment. However, I was surprised that knowledge of the ILS is considered less important for librarians than for staff. My speculation is that respondents may have been thinking of the back-office functions with which many librarians in areas such as reference have little contact, rather than the OPAC. Figure 1-3 lists the ten technology competencies rated highest in importance for each classification. Interestingly, there is more consensus between the author and CSUSM survey respondents for the librarian competencies than for the staff ones. The competencies that are the same for both classifications are indicated in boldface.

Many of the differences between the authors and CSUSM respondents in the results may be attributable to local practices. For instance, the author respondents rated tablet computers as low in importance, whereas the CSUSM respondents rated them higher, particularly for librarians. This seems to correspond with the fact that we have been experimenting with the use of tablets in the CSUSM library, particularly for instruction. Two more instances are virtual reference services and online information literacy technologies—60 percent of the authors rated them as important for librarians versus 100 percent of respondents from CSUSM, where librarians regularly use both of these technologies. The results may also reflect a difference in organizational culture. Both respondent groups rated the importance of librarians in library technology planning at 100 percent, but the CSUSM respondents also rated it highly for staff—71 percent versus 20 percent.

Although the surveys didn't really explore my second question of whether these different technology expectations are based on job responsibilities, it should be noted that in fact staff frequently use technology as often as librarians and in ways that require comparable, if not greater, proficiency. I suggest that some of the differences in expectations may be due more to preconceptions related to position classification schemes than to the actual needs of the job and that these are

Figure 1-3. Top Ten Most Important Competencies for Staff and Librarians

	STAFF			LIBRARIANS	
TOP TEN STAFF COMPETENCIES	AUTHORS	CSUSM	TOP TEN LIBRARIAN COMPETENCIES	AUTHORS	CSUSM
Office productivity software	100%	100%	**Office productivity software**	100%	100%
Office printers	100%	95%	Electronic database searching	100%	100%
Integrated library systems	100	94%	**Evaluating Web sites for validity**	100%	100%
Computer operating systems	100%	89%	**Federated search tools**	100%	100%
Bar-code scanners	80%	95%	Library technology planning	100%	100%
Basic PC troubleshooting	80%	94%	**Office printers, color printers**	100%	100%
Computer security	100%	72%	**USB drives**	100%	100%
Evaluating Web sites for validity	100%	67%	Link resolvers	100%	83%
Federated search tools	100%	65%	CD/DVD writable media	80%	100%
USB drives	80%	78%	Blogs	100%	75%

preconceptions managers would do well to guard against when defining core competencies. As the historical overview has shown us, the current wave of technology is now concentrated on the Web, yet this is the one area that the survey respondents thought to be significantly less important for staff. Are we being shortsighted, or is this just the reality given the type of responsibilities common to staff positions? I consider it equally important for both staff and librarians to have a robust set of technology skills, including Web technologies, for reasons ranging from the increasingly paraprofessional role of many staff to better patron service to improved office procedures. But will it be possible for staff to build their technical competencies? Staff positions are often constrained with a very rote set of assigned duties. As a classification, they may have less time to experiment and are not generally encouraged to use their own initiative to try new things. The library could be missing a major resource if staff are kept at a lower level of technological know-how because of unquestioned assumptions that have lowered expectations.

New Jobs

In addition to the changes technology has made in traditional library positions, it has also resulted in the creation of a number of new specialties that deal specifically with the technology itself and with the new services it makes possible (Braun, 2002). Arguably the oldest of these new positions is that of the systems librarian. Chapter 3 will go into this specialty in more detail, but, briefly, the systems librarian came about in the 1980s specifically to develop and support the new library automation systems, especially the integrated library systems provided by remote vendors.

Although the office and responsibilities of the systems librarian grew through the 1990s, other types of technology-specific positions didn't really begin to appear in significant numbers until the past few years. Since 2000, several trends have combined to create a fertile environment for new positions. First, the success and increased number of earlier technology initiatives, such as electronic databases and library Web sites, have stretched the capability of current staff to meet all the new demands within the constraints of existing positions. Second, new technologies have created opportunities to expand and change library services. Finally, the pressure of changing user expectations combined with advanced, customizable technology have encouraged libraries to break outside the boundaries of their traditional approach to services and create new ways to reach their audience.

With these new digital initiatives have come new library positions. Some of these have simply spun out portions of existing positions that have become too large or complex and made them into independent positions. Positions that might fall into this category include metadata cataloger, electronic resources librarian, and instructional design librarian. While it's interesting to look at the technology competencies specific to these new positions, it is also useful to note that many of these competencies often still apply to some extent to the original positions. Therefore, many cataloging positions today require some knowledge of metadata practices in addition to traditional cataloging ability whether or not the position is listed as a "metadata specialist." Certainly any instruction librarian needs to be able to deliver instruction via the Web or electronic courseware as well as in person.

To see what kinds of new jobs are out there, I did a quick review of the job announcements in *College & Research Libraries News* from the 2006 and 2007 issues. Because I only looked at the print version of *C&RL News*, the number of jobs may be underreported in that there may be a tendency to advertise technology-related jobs more frequently in electronic-only form. Figures 1-4 and 1-5 list some of the competencies included in these position announcements.

Of the more than 60 technology-related positions I identified (not counting systems librarian positions), almost half fell into the "spin-off" category of new technology jobs. These spin-off jobs tend to be high-tech versions of traditional library positions and are often located in the same department. By far the most popular new job was that of the electronic resources librarian, with 13 job announcements. The title was highly variable but usually included "electronic resources" or "electronic collections." The title was also combined with "serials" in several listings, and most of these positions included serials responsibilities. It's also worth noting that many of the traditional serials librarian jobs also required knowledge of many of the skills listed for the electronic resources librarian. Figure 1-4 lists some of the most notable competencies for this position.

Instructional design librarians were charged with developing innovative learning technologies. While there were six positions specifically advertised with instructional technology as a primary duty, many of the traditional instruction positions also shared similar competency expectations. Responsibilities typically included collaborating with faculty and information technology staff to develop both curricula for online delivery and electronic resources to support the information literacy program and reference. At least two positions were also responsible for the library's Web site. These positions were often tasked with advocating for emerging technologies.

At least ten metadata-specific cataloging positions were advertised, although it was somewhat hard to distinguish these positions because many of the more traditional cataloging positions also required at least some facility with metadata. In general, the metadata catalogers were expected to be familiar with metadata standards and to participate in digital projects. Some of the positions also included

Figure 1-4. Technology Positions Spun Off from Traditional Library Specialties

POSITION	TYPICAL COMPETENCIES
Electronic resources librarian	Support networked electronic resources ILS serials module OCLC, MARC formats, AACR2 e-Resource license and publishing industry issues Electronic resource management system infrastructure Web-based technologies: XML, XSL, HTML Metadata applications Support linking technologies such as SFX
Instructional design librarian	Online instructional design and pedagogy Course management tools Web authoring Web 2.0: blogs, podcasting, RSS, wikis, online chat Graphic design and multimedia tools Web site management and scripting languages
Metadata cataloger	Metadata standards: METS, MODS, Dublin Core, TEL Other standards and formats: MARC, OCLC, AACR2, VRA, DC, OAI Excellent computer skills (spreadsheets, MS Office) Web authoring Current and emerging library trends and standards

Figure 1-5. New Technology Specialist Positions

POSITION	TYPICAL COMPETENCIES REQUESTED
Digital collections librarian	Institutional repositories and digital collections Digital asset management system Digital imaging technologies Web technologies: page design, portals Social networking technologies: podcasting, RSS, virtual worlds Project management Grant writing Developing partnerships and working in teams
GIS librarian	GIS software Digital geospatial data Current and emerging technology High degree of computer literacy
Web librarian	Web design, architecture, and usability Web authoring: Dreamweaver, HTML, Web 2.0 tools Content management systems Web search and tagging Web scripting: PHP/MySQL, JavaScript, etc. Graphic and multimedia Instruction design and courseware Social networking: blogs, wikis Improved browser experience, "hack OPAC" Continuous learning
Data research scientist	Research experience, experimental preferred Software and tools for data management Standards and applications: Dublin Core, METS, OAI Proficient with XML and metadata
Literary studies and digital scholarship for humanities	High computer literacy Understand changing scholarly communications issues Use technology in humanities Know metadata, XML, and information architecture
Project management Social science data librarian	Experience with electronic government or social science data Statistical packages: SPSS, SAS Metadata standards: DOI GIS software

responsibilities for markup of digital text in XML, linking URLs to full-text and federating monographs. All the metadata positions also required traditional cataloging duties.

Several entirely new specializations have also come about in response to new technology-enabled services. Most notable of these is the digital collections librarian, with 12 job ads—more than any other specialty other than electronic resources. Actually this position has multiple names, but they all deal in some form with the creation and dissemination of digitized content. These digital collections may come about to preserve archival collections, to provide access to unpublished materials such as theses, or to provide another avenue for scholarly publication. In addition to technical competencies, these positions often also required skills in project management, grant writing, and partnership creation.

Probably one of the oldest of the non-IT support technical specialties is the geographic information system (GIS) librarian. However, this is a rather rare specialty—only two were advertised in the *C&RL News* during the time period reviewed. Another type of new position is that of Web librarian, with six positions advertised. Responsibilities for the library's Web site were originally part of other existing positions, usually in the library systems office but sometimes in other areas of the library, such as reference. Positions devoted to developing the Web site started to appear around 2000. While constant technology change is widely acknowledged in all areas of library technology, this was the only specialty that regularly listed "continuous learning" among its competencies.

The other new specializations had many fewer positions advertised, but this is perhaps not surprising given that some of these positions explore completely new areas of library service. Three of the most interesting of these originated out of the reference subject specialist position. I've collectively called these specialties "data specialists," because the responsibilities revolve around electronic data in one form or another. All of them also expect knowledge of metadata standards. One of these new positions is Data Research Scientist. This person is responsible for collaborating with and coordinating faculty and student research using digital data collections and is expected to actively participate in research projects, developing methods of data discovery and capture, creating applications to manage and access data sets, and developing innovative concepts in database technology. No less interesting is another position focused on the humanities, Librarian for Literary Studies and Digital Scholarship in the Humanities. This librarian is also expected to work with faculty and students on research projects involving digital technology. In this case, the responsibilities include maintaining an awareness of changes in scholarly communication, researching and developing new services using software and digital tools, and fostering awareness of new technologies. The third data specialist was Social Science Data Librarian, who was responsible for planning and delivering numeric data services using government and nongovernment sources. Interestingly, this last specialty requires some GIS knowledge.

A final group of technology positions advertised fall somewhere in the management and leadership area. These positions seem to focus on either library-wide responsibilities or on managing several departments, often including technical services as well as IT support areas. All of these positions seem to directly address the need for the "planner" role mentioned earlier in this chapter. Three positions advertised in *C&RL News* were responsible for determining strategic technology directions across the library. Two were upper administration—associate librarian

33

for technology applications and director of information technology. A third, the emergent technologies librarian, was empowered to explore and champion emergent technologies. As might be expected, the administrator positions supervised other areas of the library concerned with technology, including systems, digital initiatives, and, in at least one case, electronic resources. Three other positions were more directly concerned with managing multiple departments, including systems (IT support), digital projects, and traditional technical services areas such as acquisitions and cataloging. Titles for these positions included associate librarian for information management, director of access services (which covered systems infrastructure and technical services), and assistant dean for digital futures and technical services. In common across all six of these leadership positions was a responsibility for envisioning and advocating for new technologies.

Future of Technology Competencies

Finally, I can't leave this chapter without discussing one more trend in library competencies, that of the "Librarian 2.0." I first ran across a discussion about the Librarian 2.0 in a blog posting by Michael Stephens. The key concept is adaptive librarian positions that incorporate the ability to spot trends and make use of transformative technologies (Stephens, 2006). A similar idea is also represented in an article by John Shank (2006) titled "The Blended Librarian." The blended librarian combines traditional librarian skills with a deep understanding of technology and instruction principles with the goal of creating effective online instruction.

34

The Librarian 2.0 idea is usually applied to reference and instruction librarians. Although it doesn't have to be limited to this specialization, some of the most intriguing ideas center around the instructional design librarian. With job advertisement language like "Librarian 2.0," "gaming librarian," and "Mad Library Skills Wanted," these jobs are looking for competencies in the following:

- Web and other multimedia creation software
- Current and emerging instructional technology

The Librarian 2.0 posting for Next Generation Librarian at Wayne State (Stephens, 2006) was looking for an "information specialist with combined reference and technological orientation." Some of the responsibilities include the following:

- Implement transformative technology such as IM, podcasting, and streaming audio/video
- Recommend and implement new and developing technologies such as wikis, blogs, etc.
- Contribute to virtual service offerings, such as Web 2.0, federated searching, OpenURL resolvers
- Provide training and support for other librarians in new technologies

While much of the discussion has focused on instructional and, to some extent, reference librarians, the ideas associated with the Librarian 2.0 apply to any position that involves a high technology component, in other words, most positions in libraries today. The challenge in defining competencies for today's librarians may be less about pinning down specific technical skills that are needed and instead looking for the ability to "bring ideas to the table with a high 'wow, cool, nobody else is doing this!' factor" (Stephen, 2006).

To get there, we need to be constantly picking up new skills and ideas. Just-in-time learning is taking the place of comprehensive training. Individuals more and more are expected to take responsibility for figuring out what they need to learn instead of the organization trying to train everyone to one standard. The survey by Goulding et al. (2000) of employers found that employers considered the most essential personal qualities for library employees to include flexibility, ability to accept pressure, inquisitiveness (love of learning), and innovation.

The key is to accept the control modern technology offers us. The more technology offers us the ability to control things, the more it forces on us the necessity of doing so. Some may find this fact intimidating or even frightening. However, those who embrace the control that the new technology provides will see more opportunity than burden in it.

In the past we may have had to sit passively by because earlier generations of technology did not give us access to make changes and because we did not have the high level of technical knowledge needed. Today, we can still operate our ILS and other major systems by simply following menus and carrying out predefined tasks. However, we also have the ability to transform much of the underlying technology using sophisticated but relatively easy to understand languages and tools. Customization and personalization is possible along a whole spectrum, from deep in the bowels of the ILS to the surface of the desktop. One of the most important areas that libraries now control is the user interface, giving us the power to make or break our users' experience with library collections and services. The specific competencies may change depending on the function area of the library and task to be accomplished, but all librarians and staff are enriched by taking control and learning how to change the system to fit their need.

It is this ability to explore, learn new technologies, and simply maintain our excitement about new possibilities that may be the ultimate competency that will see us into the future. Future-proof competencies include the ability to get excited about technology and spot trends, play with and explore the possibilities, and the willingness to try new technology without guarantees that it's the "right" solution. The latter ability is accompanied by the willingness to give up existing technology when its usefulness is passed, which implies constant assessment. It's not enough to passively know how to use technology; we need to actively know how to control and shape it to our needs. While the specific level and type of knowledge is different depending on our individual capability and role in the library, everyone needs to be competent in identifying, learning, and transforming technology to their (and their patrons') needs.

References

American Libraries. 1982. "101-Uses-for-a-Dead-Catalog Contest." *American Libraries* 13, no. 10: 623. *Academic Search Premier*, EBSCOhost (accessed March 31, 2008).

Beile, Penny M. and Megan M. Adams. 2000. "Other Duties as Assigned: Emerging Trends in the Academic Library Job Market." *College & Research Libraries* (July): 336–347.

Braun, Linda W. 2002. "New Roles: A Librarian by Any Name." *Library Journal* (February 1): 46–49.

Breeding, Michael. 2007. "This Graphic Shows the History of Mergers and Acquisitions in the Library Automation Industry." *Library Technology Guides*. Available: www.librarytechnology.org/automationhistory.pl (accessed June 2, 2008).

California Library Association. 2005. "Technology Core Competencies for California Library Workers" (April 21). Available: www.cla-net.org/included/docs/tech_core_competencies.pdf (accessed June 10, 2008).

Childers, Scott. 2003. "Computer Literacy: Necessity or Buzzword?" *Information Technology and Libraries* 22, no. 3 (September): 100–104.

Farkas, Meredith. 2006. "Skills for the 21st Century Librarian" *Information Wants to Be Free* (July 17). Available: http://meredith.wolfwater.com/wordpress/index.php/2006/07/17/skills-for-the-21st-century-librarian/ (accessed June 10, 2008).

Goulding, Anne, Beth Bromham, Stuart Hannabuss, and Duncan Cramer. 2000. "Professional Characters: The Personality of the Future Information Workforce." *Education for Information* 18, no.1: 7–31.

Houghton-Jan, Sarah. 2007. "Technology Competencies and Training for Libraries." *Library Technology Reports* 43, no. 2 (March/April).

Hubbard, L. Ron. "Competency." Cybernation.com. Available: www.cybernation.com/quotationcenter/quoteshow.php?type=subject&id=252 (accessed February 18, 2008).

Lang, Walter. 1957. *Desk Set*. Produced by Henry Ephron. 103 min. 20th Century Fox. Videocassette or DVD.

Latham, Joyce. 2000. "The World Online: IT Skills for the Practical Professional." *American Libraries* (March): 40–42.

McNamara, Carter. 2008. "Specifying Job and Role Competencies." *Free Management Library*. Available: www.managementhelp.org/staffing/specify/cmptncys/cmptncys.htm (accessed June 20, 2008).

Morgan, Eric Lease. 1998. "Computer Literacy for Librarians." *Computers in Libraries* 18, no. 1 (January): 39–40.

Norman, Donald A. 1984. "Worsening the Knowledge Gap: The Mystique of Computation Builds Unnecessary Barriers." *Computer Culture: The Scientific, Intellectual, and Social Impact of the Computer* (November): 220–223.

Shank, John. 2006. "The Blended Librarian: A Job Announcement Analysis of the Newly Emerging Position of Instructional Design Librarian." *College & Research Libraries* 67, no. 6 (November): 515–524.

Shifted Librarian. 2005. "20 Technology Skills Every Librarian Should Have." *Shifted Librarian* (July 21). Available: www.theshiftedlibrarian.com/archives/2005/07/21/ 20_technology_skills_every_librarian_should_have.html (accessed June 10, 2008).

Simmons-Welburn, Janice, Comp. 2000. *Changing Roles of Library Professionals. SPEC Kit 256.* Washington, DC: Association of Research Libraries.

Stephens, Michael. 2006. "Desperately Seeking the Adaptive Librarian: On the 2.0 Job Description (Part 3)." *ALA TechSource* (December 29). Available: www.techsource .ala.org/blog/2006/12/desperately-seeking-the-adaptive-librarian-on-the-20-job-description-part-3.html (accessed June 2, 2008).

StevenB. 2006. "Technology Skills for Academic Librarians." *ACRLog* (February 13). Available: http://acrlog.org/2006/02/13/technology-skills-for-academic-librarians/ (accessed June 10, 2008).

St. Lifer, Evan 1996. "Net Work: New Roles, Same Mission. *Library Journal* 121, no. 19 (November 15): 26–30.

Thompson, Susan. 2005. "LITA Heads of Library Technology Interest Group." *Technical Services Quarterly* 23: 71–75.

Turner, Laura. 2005. "20 Technology Skills Every Educator Should Have." *T.H.E. Journal* (June). Available: http://thejournal.com/articles/17325/ (accessed June 10, 2008).

Webber, Sheila Anne Elizabeth. 1999. "Competencies for Information Professionals." *Bulletin of the American Society for Information Science & Technology* 26, no. 1 (October/November): 28.

Wikipedia. 2007. "History of the World Wide Web." Wikipedia (November). Available: http://en.wikipedia.org/wiki/History_of_the_World_Wide_Web#1992-1995:_ Growth_of_the_WWW (accessed May 7, 2008).

Woodsworth, Anne. 1997. "New Library Competencies." *Library Journal* 122, no. 9 (May 15): 46,

Appendix 1-1. Survey of the Importance of Technology Competencies for Staff and Librarians

	AUTHORS		CSUSM	
	STAFF	LIBRARIAN	STAFF	LIBRARIAN
GENERAL TECHNOLOGY COMPETENCIES				
Parts of a computer and their function (CPU, hard drive, RAM)	**60%**	**60%**	58%	**75%**
Computer operating systems (Microsoft Windows, Mac OS)	100%	80%	89%	83%
Office productivity software (Word, Excel, PowerPoint)	100%	100%	100%	100%
Computer security (antivirus, anti-spyware software)	100%	100%	72%	75%
Basic PC troubleshooting (determining why the printer won't print, why a computer locked up, etc.)	80%	60%	94%	100%
Advanced PC troubleshooting and maintenance (fixing or replacing hardware, installing software)	20%	20%	17%	42%
Wired and/or wireless networking configuration and troubleshooting	0%	40%	12%	50%
Digitizing/scanning of printed resources	20%	20%	56%	**83%**
Special needs/adaptive technologies for ADA patrons (JAWS, ZoomText)	20%	**60%**	56%	**67%**
Gaming software (Second Life, instructional games)	0%	20%	56%	33%
Photo editing/digital imaging software (Photoshop)	20%	20%	33%	33%
Database construction and maintenance (Access, MySQL)	20%	20%	28%	50%
Scripting languages (Perl, PHP, JavaScript)	0%	0%	56%	33%
Object-oriented programming languages (Visual Basic, Java)	0%	0%	56%	25%
Server administration (Web servers, ILS servers, network drives)	0%	0%	17%	33%
Total rated important by at least 60% of respondents	**5**	**6**	**4**	**7**
	AUTHORS		SCUSM	
	STAFF	LIBRARIAN	STAFF	LIBRARIAN
INTERNET-RELATED COMPETENCIES				
Web page creation with FrontPage or Dreamweaver	40%	**60%**	35%	**83%**
Web page creation with hand-coded XHTML and CSS	0%	0%	11%	58%
Internet protocols (HTTP, FTP, SMTP)	40%	**60%**	22%	**75%**
Online metadata schemas (Dublin Core, EAD)	**60%**	**80%**	17%	42%

(Cont'd.)

Appendix 1-1. Survey of the Importance of Technology Competencies for Staff and Librarians *(Continued)*

	AUTHORS		CSUSM	
	STAFF	**LIBRARIAN**	**STAFF**	**LIBRARIAN**
INTERNET-RELATED COMPETENCIES				
XML	20%	40%	12%	33%
Virtual reference service using instant messaging or a product such as QuestionPoint	20%	**60%**	58%	**100%**
Electronic database searching (e.g., using complex Boolean searches in EBSCO databases)	**80%**	**100%**	**61%**	**100%**
Blogs	**80%**	**100%**	28%	**75%**
Wikis	**60%**	**80%**	28%	**75%**
Social networking sites (MySpace, Facebook)	**60%**	**80%**	17%	58%
Podcasting	40%	**60%**	17%	**67%**
RSS	**80%**	**100%**	22%	**75%**
Thin clients	40%	20%	6%	25%
Evaluating Web sites for validity, authority, etc.	**100%**	**100%**	**67%**	**100%**
Creating online information literacy tutorials	20%	**60%**	22%	**100%**
Total rated important by at least 60% of respondents	**7**	**12**	**2**	**10**
	AUTHORS		SCUSM	
	STAFF	**LIBRARIAN**	**STAFF**	**LIBRARIAN**
HARDWARE PERIPHERALS COMPETENCIES				
Office printers	**100%**	**100%**	**95%**	**100%**
Pay-for-print printers	**60%**	**80%**	**72%**	**75%**
Color printers	**60%**	**100%**	**95%**	**100%**
Bar-code scanners	**80%**	**80%**	**95%**	58%
Digitization scanners	40%	**60%**	**83%**	**67%**
USB drives	**80%**	**100%**	**78%**	**100%**
CD/DVD writable media	**80%**	**80%**	**72%**	**100%**
e-Book readers	40%	**60%**	55%	**100%**
Personal digital assistants (Palm, pocket PCs)	20%	20%	29%	**100%**
Tablet PCs	20%	20%	47%	**75%**
Projectors	**60%**	**80%**	**67%**	**92%**
SmartBoards	0%	20%	28%	**83%**

(Cont'd.)

39

Appendix 1-1. Survey of the Importance of Technology Competencies for Staff and Librarians *(Continued)*

	AUTHORS		CSUSM	
	STAFF	LIBRARIAN	STAFF	LIBRARIAN
HARDWARE PERIPHERALS COMPETENCIES				
Digital cameras	**60%**	**80%**	33%	**75%**
Digital camcorders	0%	40%	17%	**67%**
MP3 players (iPod, Zune)	20%	**60%**	56%	58%
Total rated important by at least 60% of respondents	**8**	**11**	**8**	**13**

	AUTHORS		CSUSM	
	STAFF	LIBRARIAN	STAFF	LIBRARIAN
LIBRARY TECHNOLOGY COMPETENCIES				
Integrated library systems (Voyager, Horizon, Innovative Millennium)	**100%**	**80%**	**94%**	**75%**
Link resolvers (SFX, ArticleLinker)	**80%**	**100%**	**94%**	**83%**
Federated search tools (WebFeat, MetaLib)	**100%**	**100%**	65%	**100%**
Electronic resource management (Verde, Innovative ERM)	20%	**60%**	53%	**83%**
Interlibrary loan management (ILLiad, Ariel)	20%	**60%**	**65%**	58%
Digital asset management (Digitool, ResourceSpace)	20%	**60%**	38%	**73%**
Institutional repository software (DSpace, EPrints)	20%	60%	18%	91%
Public access systems (PC reservation software, printing control software such as GoPrint or Pharos, filtering software)	40%	**60%**	47%	58%
Magnetic bar-coding hardware and software	40%	40%	41%	33%
RFID/self-check hardware and software	40%	**60%**	38%	20%
Library technology planning	20%	**100%**	**71%**	**100%**
Request for proposal (RFP) writing for purchasing technology products	20%	40%	24%	**75%**
Total rated important by over 60% of respondents	**3**	**9**	**4**	**8**

Note: Results represent percentages of technology competencies ranked somewhat or very important by the respondents. Respondents include 6 of the chapter authors of this book and 19 librarians and staff at the California State University San Marcos (CSUSM) library. Boldface indicates competencies ranked high in importance.

Chapter 2

The Library School's Role in Preparing New Librarians for Working with Technology

Diane Neal

Overview

This chapter explores how library and information science professors might better prepare their graduates for working with technology in the library. I examine technology-related sections of core competencies statements written by library professional organizations. Based on a literature review and on a survey of library science student practicum supervisors, technology "hard skills" and "soft skills" are suggested for inclusion into a twenty-first-century library and information science curriculum. Existing technology competency entrance and graduation requirements at schools of library and information science are examined. Finally, I supply a hands-on library automation assignment and a syllabus that I have used in a course on library technology systems.

41

Introduction

In 2004, former American Library Association (ALA) President Michael Gorman wrote of a "crisis" in library education. His concerns included his perception of a growing emphasis on information science and technology in ALA-accredited library schools. To Gorman, this implied a shift toward teaching technological solutions for meeting information needs and a shift away from teaching librarianship fundamentals. He also discussed a gender divide between "male-oriented" information science and "female-oriented" library science. This article generated a range of responses from many constituents, including library and information science (LIS) educators. Dillon and Norris (2005) presented empirical data questioning the existence of this crisis. Stoffle and Leeder (2005) as well as Pawley (2005) provide compelling analyses of Gorman's arguments.

As Malone and Coleman (2005) point out, a crisis has existed within LIS education, and the library profession, for quite some time. For example, it has manifested itself as an unclear distinction between the roles and responsibilities of professionals holding the ALA-accredited master's degree and paraprofessionals who do not. The profession has also questioned whether library professionals should be required to earn a master's degree in library science, or some other form of credential, in order to officially be called a "librarian."

Rather than Gorman's concern about the increase in information science education and the decrease in library science education, the current crisis is better described as the perceived separation of library science and information science and the dividing effect this separation has on the LIS field. Dillon and Norris (2005) posit, as do Gorman and Corbitt (2002), that technology is a foundation of LIS rather than an entity to be treated separately from other library-related matters. I agree with this view. Many of today's LIS schools offer information science degree programs that enable graduates to obtain non-library employment as an information architect or a knowledge manager. However, this is merely a new form of specialization within the field of LIS, just as a student might train to be an indexer or an archivist. Information science degree programs are not a symptom of a "crisis" on track to destroy the profession.

Regardless of whose "crisis" definition is accurate (or if there is a crisis at all), it is undeniable that the need for basic technology competencies will pervade *all* twenty-first-century LIS jobs, as this chapter demonstrates. Basic competencies needed by new librarians to work with library technology are discussed, as well as possible courses of action LIS schools could consider to ensure that their graduates possess adequate technology competencies.

42

Technology and the Twenty-First-Century Librarian

Does technology have a place in all twenty-first-century library job descriptions, or is it best left to the technical gurus on staff? Individuals in all corners of the field have written about the need for librarians to possess "twenty-first-century skills." According to Wilson (2002), a need exists for the integration of technical skills with traditional librarian functions. Woodsworth (1997: 46) described a focus group she led that was "unanimous in asserting that technologies underlie all specializations within the profession." Braque (2000: 7), then a student in the School of Library and Information Science at Louisiana State University, wrote, "Library education's reservation to adapt to meet the challenge of new and emerging technologies has failed its students and the profession by not preparing its graduates for technology-rich careers. . . . They are requirements and core competencies of the profession."

The Partnership for 21st Century Skills (2004), an organization of corporations, educators, and policy creators united to frame this century's educational needs, defines information and communications technologies (ICT) literacy as "the ability to use technology to develop 21st century content knowledge and skills, in support of 21st century teaching and learning." According to Minkel (2003), librarians can take advantage of these demands by promoting themselves as educators of these new skills. While these proficiencies may necessarily begin at the elementary level of tasks, such as operating computers and troubleshooting printers, they suggest the integration of technology into teaching, learning, and literacy at a higher level.

Meredith Farkas, distance learning librarian at Norwich University, wrote on her blog in 2004 while an LIS student, "All of the core required classes are library-related and none of them really enhance computer-related competencies. A student can go through our school having taken no technology-related classes." She laments the divide between the library professors who know little about technology and the technology professors who know little about libraries. As a student with an interest in traditional librarianship principles as well as technology, her post expressed a lack of identification with both the librarians and the technology specialists. However, as the author of a popular blog called *Information Wants to Be Free* (Farkas, 2006), a monthly column in *American Libraries*, and a published book about social software and libraries, her interest in both sides of the field has served her well. Obviously, LIS education should not discourage students like Meredith. What, then, should LIS educators be doing differently to prepare the new generation of librarians?

Core Technology Competencies for All Librarians

An examination of documents developed by professional organizations outlining core competencies for specific library specializations demonstrates the need for all librarians to possess a set of core technology competencies. Web addresses to these documents are provided in Appendix 2-1. Some organizations dedicate an entire section of their core competencies to technology, while others interweave technology into broader sections of competencies. Based on these competency statements, LIS educators can feel comfortable with requiring all students to demonstrate an acceptable level of technology competency.

43

Because leading library practitioners (hiring managers!) are commonly the authors of these professional competency statements, it behooves library educators to use these documents in curriculum planning processes. If library leaders are writing these documents, they will have the expectation that new graduates will possess a majority of the competencies they or their peers have outlined—or, at the very least, show potential for developing them.

The ALA (2005) has drafted a "Statement of Core Competencies" that outlines the needed skills for an entry-level, nonspecialized librarian. Section 5 (ALA, 2005), "Technological Knowledge," delineates the following skills:

- Demonstrates a comprehension of current information and communication technologies, and other related technologies, as they affect the resources and uses of libraries and other types of information providing entities
- Has basic knowledge of the concepts and processes related to the assessment and evaluation of the specifications, economic impact, and efficacy of technology-based products and services

- Understands and can apply the principles of techniques used to continuously track and analyze emerging technologies to recognize relevant innovations
- Demonstrates proficiency in the use of standard information and communication technology and tools consistent with prevailing service norms and professional applications

ALA Divisions

Several ALA divisions have written their own core competencies documents. The Government Documents Round Table (accessed 2007) has created a tiered set of "E-Competencies." The first tier, which encompasses technology competencies for all government depository librarians, includes basic knowledge of the major computer parts. It also requires the ability to use Windows, Web browsers, e-mail, online catalogs, and URLs.

The Reference and User Services Association (RUSA) (2003) incorporates the use of technology throughout its "Professional Competencies for Reference and User Services Librarians" document. For example, reference librarians should include new technologies in their daily practice. The document suggests the use of computer-based continuing education. A reference librarian "determines the appropriate mix of technologies and delivery channels to meet the particular user group's needs" (RUSA, 2003, section 6). Also, reference librarians need to understand information system usability in order to discuss related issues with system designers.

"Young Adults Deserve the Best: Competencies for Librarians Serving Youth," by the Young Adult Library Services Association (YALSA) (2003), mentions technological competencies within other areas of required competencies. It says youth librarians need to include emerging technologies as a format in their collection development efforts. Web page links should be provided to patrons as a method of increasing information access. Youth librarians must "develop and use effective measures to manage Internet and other electronic resources that provide young adults with equal access" (YALSA, 2003, Area VI). They also need to teach information literacy skills in the context of electronic information.

In "Competencies for Librarians Serving Children in Public Libraries" (1999), the Association for Library Service to Children (1999) outlines technology competencies throughout its document. In terms of technology, this list of competencies primarily focuses on electronic documents. This includes creating them for administrative purposes or for the benefit of the children they serve. The Association for Library Service to Children's competency document also discusses the need for librarians to make electronic documents available to children as part of the collection.

A panel discussion titled "The Top Ten Things a New Sci/Tech Librarian Should Know: Developing Core Competencies," held by the STS Issues in Sci/Tech Library Management Discussion group at the 2003 ALA Annual Meeting, provided perspectives from science and technology librarians at various levels. The summary of this program states, "New librarians looking to get hired in a science/technology library position . . . should have . . . some technology competency, such as Web publishing skills" (Mitchell, 2004, section 1).

Other Professional Organizations

The Special Libraries Association (SLA) devotes an entire section of its "Competencies for Information Professionals of the 21st Century" (Special Libraries Association, 2003) document to technology. It discusses the need for special librarians to keep up with and implement new technologies, use "expertise in databases, indexing, metadata, and information retrieval analysis and synthesis to improve information retrieval and use in the organization" (SLA, 2003, section D), and maintain users' confidentiality.

The "ARLIS/NA Core Competencies for Art Information Professionals," from the Art Libraries Society of North America (2003), also dedicates a section to technology. It suggests that "Art Information Professionals have a broad understanding of information technology and are skilled in the implementation and utilization of technological tools, regardless of specific format, medium or method of delivery" (Art Libraries Society of North America, 2003, section 13), as evidenced by understanding computer and network functions, maintaining awareness of technology trends, coping with technological changes, selecting and applying technologies, and possessing appropriate skills to handle digital images. Its second technology competency states, "Art Information Professionals help shape information technology products" (Art Libraries Society of North America, 2003, section 14) through various modes of collaboration with users and vendors.

The American Association of Law Libraries' (2001) "Competencies of Law Librarianship" does not outline technology-related core competencies for all law librarians. However, it does include information technology as one of its specialized competencies. This competency discusses the need for law librarians with information technology responsibilities to be able to work with digital information using various computer applications; plan, evaluate, and implement new technologies; teach others how to use the library's information systems; troubleshoot technology problems; and manage the library's Web site.

"Health Information Science Knowledge and Skills," from the Medical Library Association (MLA) (2007), includes a section called "Information Systems and Technology." It states that health science librarians "must be able to understand and use technology and systems to manage all forms of information" (MLA, 2007, section 5). Among other things, it lists the need to understand the basics of hardware, software, networking, databases, information system design, purchasing and evaluation of information systems, and technology planning.

The Music Library Association's "Core Competencies and Music Librarians" (Hunter, 2002) document integrates information technology throughout its other competencies. For example, music librarians should be equipped to work with digitization as part of collection development, improve integrated library systems as they relate to collection organization, and "promote the effective use of all technologies" (Hunter, 2002, section 4) in fulfillment of the music librarian's teaching role. Additionally, the document includes an "Information and Audio Technology and Systems" section, mainly in relation to audio.

The California Library Association's "Technology Core Competencies for California Library Workers" (California Library Association [CLA], 2005) recommends that library staff know basic computer terminology and be able to use and troubleshoot computer hardware. The CLA also recommends that staff should be able to use word processing software, Web browsers, e-mail, and computer operating system functions. They suggest being familiar with computer security issues as well as the library's online resources. The CLA identifies more advanced competencies in these categories for "Reference, Instructional, and Management Staff."

"Essential skills" are defined in the Colorado Department of Education's (1999) "Colorado Technology Competency Guidelines for Classroom Teachers and School Library Media Specialists." These include computer use, maintenance and troubleshooting, word processing, spreadsheets, databases, networking, telecommunications, and media use (DVDs, video output setup, scanners, etc.). The document also outlines skills teachers must employ to integrate technology into the curriculum.

The State Library of North Carolina (2007) describes three levels of competencies in "Technology Competencies for Libraries in North Carolina." Level I outlines competencies for all library staff, including basic computer terminology, computer hardware knowledge and troubleshooting, computer security, and e-mail use. Level II states that public services staff should possess skills in areas such as Internet use and online searching, office productivity software, public access software, and circulation software. Level III competencies, which were written for specialized library staff, include Web page creation, audiovisual equipment operation, virtual reference, and other advanced technology skills such as computer workstation configuration and network set up.

New Competencies for New Librarians: Hard and Soft Skills

Hard Skills

LIS educators should provide graduates with a core set of technology "hard skills" to serve as a baseline for the constantly rising level of technology competency they will be expected to demonstrate throughout their careers. The argument could be made (and it would be well taken by technology proponents) that emerging technologies change so quickly that it is almost not worth teaching them to students. On the other hand, general principles underlying the basic technology skill set do not change quickly enough to warrant ignoring. In 1997, Woodsworth defined these basic competencies for librarians: "knowing what the Internet is and is not; evaluating and using hardware, software, and networks; and understanding basic computer and information science concepts" (Woodsworth, 1997: 46). A decade later, these basic competencies have not changed, although the level of competency expected by new employers has almost certainly increased. Learning the basic skills will allow librarians to learn new and more advanced skills over time.

What are the core technology "hard skills"? To find out, I conducted an online survey in late 2006. I sent an invitation to participate in the survey to librarians who were currently serving or had recently served as practicum site supervisors for MLS students in the School of Library and Information Studies at Texas Woman's University. As part of the survey, I asked them how important they thought it was for all new LIS graduates to possess proficiencies with using certain technologies upon graduation. I presented them with lists of technologies related to computer literacy, Internet technologies, computer hardware, and library automation products. (The survey instrument and selected results are presented in Appendix 2-2.) With a total of 49 respondents, over 90 percent rated the following technologies as either "Very Important" or "Somewhat Important":

- Parts of a computer and their function (CPU, hard drive, RAM)
- Computer operating systems (Microsoft Windows, Mac OS)
- Office productivity software (Word, Excel, PowerPoint)
- Basic PC troubleshooting (determining why the printer won't print, why a computer locked up, etc.)
- Digitizing/scanning of printed resources
- Electronic database searching (e.g., using complex Boolean searches in EBSCO databases)
- Blogs
- Wikis
- Evaluating Web sites for validity, authority, etc.
- Creating online information literacy tutorials
- Digital cameras
- USB drives
- Library technology planning
- Request for proposal (RFP) writing for purchasing technology products

47

Based on this brief look at one aspect of my results, one can see that these practicum supervisors, who can be considered potential hiring managers, do not expect all new LIS graduates to possess the technical competency of a systems librarian or other technical library professional. They do, however, expect new graduates to possess basic computer competencies, familiarity with Web 2.0 technologies (blogs and wikis), and proficiency in digital content creation (online information literacy tutorials and digitizing/scanning of printed resources). Library technology planning and RFP writing could be considered library management responsibilities; this is an example of the merging of technical knowledge and traditional library roles.

Soft Skills

How will the impact of librarians' formal education live on after the "hard skills" they learned while earning their master's degrees have faded into obsolescence? LIS educators should incorporate "soft skills" into the curriculum. Many library technology advocates discuss the need for various soft skills as much as or more than they discuss specific technologies that librarians must be able to use in the twenty-first century. Among other things, these soft skills ensure that librarians will be able to cope with the technological changes they will face throughout their careers (Tennant, 1998). For example, Tennant (1998: 102) lists the following as desirable soft skills for a digital librarian position:

- The capacity to learn constantly and quickly
- Flexibility
- An innate skepticism
- A propensity to take risks
- An abiding public service perspective
- An appreciation of what others bring to the effort and an ability to work with them effectively
- Skill at enabling and fostering change
- The capacity and desire to work independently

In 2006, Meredith Farkas wrote a blog post, which became somewhat famous in the biblioblogosphere, called "Skills for the 21st Century Librarian." In this post, she outlined the following basic technical competencies for librarians:

- Ability to embrace change
- Comfort in the online medium
- Ability to troubleshoot new technologies
- Ability to easily learn new technologies
- Ability to keep up with new ideas in technology and librarianship (enthusiasm for learning)

She also defined the following higher level competencies. These important "soft skills" enable librarians to learn new technology-related "hard skills" and to use these technologies in meeting the library's needs (Farkas, 2006, section 2):

- Project management skills
- Ability to question and evaluate library services
- Ability to evaluate the needs of all stakeholders
- Vision to translate traditional library services into the online medium
- Critical of technologies and ability to compare technologies
- Ability to sell ideas/library services

Change is mentioned often in library literature. Webb (1988) wrote about the need for librarians to understand change and its impact on organizations.

Woodsworth (1997) said that librarians should lead internal and external change. Adequately preparing librarians for change in all its forms will hopefully allow them to accept *technological* change as a given in librarianship and to realize that this acceptance will prevent their obsolescence (Wetherbee and Wayne, 2007).

The Role of Library and Information Science Programs

LIS programs have available many options to ensure that the students and graduates possess current technology competencies and are prepared to update their skills as technologies change throughout their careers. Appendix 2-3 provides links to selected LIS school technology requirements and competencies.

Some LIS schools offer continuing education courses to help librarians stay current. For example, the University of North Texas' School of Library and Information Sciences offers an exemplary continuing education program through Project LE@D, or Lifelong Education @ Desktop (University of North Texas, accessed 2007). Online courses cover many aspects of librarianship; technology courses include Internet basics, Web site development, and Microsoft Office training. The School of Library and Information Studies at the University of Wisconsin–Madison (2005) offers technology-based continuing education courses at many levels, including Microsoft Office skills, PC troubleshooting, networking, databases, Photoshop, Web site development, and programming languages such as Java and Perl.

Some LIS schools require students to take a technology course as a requirement for the master's degree. For example, The College of Computing and Information at the University at Albany, State University of New York (accessed 2007), requires a course called Fundamentals of Information Technology. The course supplies students with fundamental technology skills, including introductions to operating systems, hardware, software, networking, security, and databases. Students in the School of Information and Library Science at the University of North Carolina at Chapel Hill (2004) must take a course called Information Tools, which covers topics such as software and networking.

Some schools mandate that incoming students demonstrate technology competency. The University of North Texas' School of Library and Information Sciences provides an assessment instrument to new students called the Information Technology Knowledge and Skills Diagnostic Tool. Students can self-assess their competency in technology areas such as basic computer use, Internet skills, Web site development, and Microsoft Office applications. If students score low on the test, they are expected to gain the necessary technology knowledge on their own or through a noncredit course offered by the school (University of North Texas, 2006). Similarly, the School of Library and Information Studies at the University of Oklahoma (2006) expects students to possess basic computer skills such as word processing, e-mail, spreadsheet software, and presentation software. North Carolina Central University's School of Library and Information Sciences (2007) requires incoming students to possess or gain these skills as well as utilize search engines, understand various file formats, and use database management programs. If students are required to possess these competencies upon entry into their LIS programs, they will be equipped to further advance their technology skills during their coursework, better preparing them to fill jobs involving advanced technical expertise.

LIS schools also should ensure that students have access to adequate hardware and software. For schools that expect students to attend classes on campus, it is important to keep the technology in computer labs up to date so that students can have hands-on experience with the latest technology. Online distance education programs can require students to own a relatively new computer with adequate software. The School of Library and Information Science at the University of South Carolina (2007) is one school with this requirement.

Courses incorporating hands-on experience prove useful for students. While a faculty member in the School of Library and Information Studies at Texas Woman's University, I incorporated practical experience into my technology courses as much as possible. For example, a major requirement for my Library Technology Systems course was to configure the open source integrated library system Koha. Working in groups, with each student choosing the role of systems administrator, Web OPAC designer, head of access services, head of acquisitions, or head of cataloging, they configured a system using a library scenario I provided. After providing Koha systems to my class as a pilot project, the Koha provider, LibLime, started the Koha with Class Initiative (LibLime, 2006). Available to any library school instructor, LibLime will provide up to five hosted Koha integrated library system installations per course at no charge. (Appendix 2-4 contains my assignment description.) I also required students to write an RFP for a technology product and library of their choice and then to research possible products and select a product based on the needs outlined in the RFP. I received positive feedback from hiring managers and other library practitioners when I discussed the requirements of this course with them, because they believed that the course gave the students much-needed practical experience. Appendix 2-5 provides the course information and readings list for my former Library Technology Systems course.

Field experience is also very useful for students. Some schools require a practicum or internship to complete the master's degree program. These experiences will expose students to the necessity of using technology in the library, whether the experience consists of working at a reference desk, cataloging items, or performing digitization projects. I advised practicum students as a faculty member at Texas Woman's University, and their practicum site supervisors almost invariably volunteered their opinion of my students' technology skills, whether they were impressed with the students' ability to write HTML code or felt students needed more knowledge of advanced database searching.

In addition to offering courses dedicated to information technology, LIS schools can examine whether they integrate technology skills throughout all courses in the curriculum. Because technology pervades so much of today's library operations, it is important to promote the use of technology in all courses. For example, students could learn about electronic resource management products in the collection development course. Link resolver products could be discussed in cataloging class. Virtual reference tools could be covered in reference class. Project management skills could be covered in management class, including how to manage technology projects. In any course, students could create a blog, contribute to a wiki, or "attend" class in the three-dimensional virtual world of Second Life.

Where We Are Now and Where We Should Be

How well are LIS schools currently preparing students to work with technology in professional positions? More research is needed to answer this question methodically, but we do have some anecdotal clues.

Markey found that in 2002 less than half of the LIS schools that belonged to the Association for Library and Information Science Education (ALISE) required students to take an information technology (IT) course. She defined IT courses as "required courses on library automation, technical services, database management, system design, and general surveys of information technologies" (Markey, 2004: 326). Personally, I hope that more schools have decided to require IT courses since 2002. It is the responsibility of the faculty to ensure that students take courses that will help them become successful professionals. As we have seen in this chapter, IT skills (and the ability to learn new IT skills over time) are likely the most inclusive skill for all twenty-first-century librarians to possess.

That said, the very nature of completing today's LIS curriculum already requires students to demonstrate a reasonably high amount of technology competency. If students cannot operate a computer, use word processing software, send e-mail, browse the World Wide Web, and so on, they simply will not be able to complete their coursework. Many LIS schools now offer online courses (or face-to-face courses that have an online component). Papers must be written in word processing programs and then submitted electronically to the professor. These basic technology skills are enough for positions in some library settings, as we can deduce from the qualitative responses provided in response to my survey (see Appendix 2-2).

The question remains of how much technology competency should be required beyond the basics, and the answer likely depends on the setting in which a student would like to work. Basic skills will not qualify students for most positions in some library settings, as a quick online scan of open professional librarian positions can demonstrate. For example, large academic libraries seek catalogers who can write XML, archivists who can lead the technical implementation of local digitization initiatives, and reference/instruction librarians who can create interactive online tutorials.

Returning to my argument regarding the division between library science and information science in our field, we must give equal weight to both. In my experience, tasks such as XML coding, document digitizing, and Web-based application development—some of the very tasks mentioned in librarian job postings—are sometimes viewed by library science–oriented individuals as gobbledygook to be left for the technical staff. Likewise, some information scientists may view positions such as "cataloger," "archivist," and "reference librarian" as little more than an artifact of the past, although appropriate application of traditional library science expertise would certainly be welcomed in the highly disorganized online environment.

I would like to think, however, that these traditional views are changing throughout our field. Based on some of today's job postings in selected library settings, it appears that library science and information science are in the process of converging. If this is the case, the LIS curriculum of the future will need to prepare students in the context of this convergence.

Conclusion

This chapter examined the need for LIS schools to equip students with core technology competencies in order to maximize their marketability upon graduation. As we have seen through a review of twenty-first-century technology skills, core competency statements of library professional organizations, and a brief examination of needed "soft skills" and "hard skills," technology competency is not just a *preferred* skill set for new librarians to possess; it is a *required* skill set. At the very minimum, all new librarians should possess skills in computer hardware and software operation and troubleshooting, Web site development, database searching, technology planning, and social software use. If schools do not ensure their graduates possess these core competencies, they are doing their students—and the profession—a disservice.

References

American Association of Law Libraries. 2001. "Competencies of Law Librarianship" (March). Available: www.aallnet.org/prodev/competencies.asp (accessed June 15, 2007).

American Library Association. 2005. "Draft Statement of Core Competencies" (July). Available: www.ala.org/ala/accreditationb/Draft_Core_Competencies_07_05.pdf (accessed June 10, 2007).

Art Libraries Society of North America. 2003. "ARLIS/NA Core Competencies for Art Information Professionals." Available: www.uflib.ufl.edu/afa/pdc/corecompsfinal .pdf (accessed June 17, 2007).

Association for Library Service to Children. 1999. "Competencies for Librarians Serving Children in Public Libraries," revised edition (April 27). Available: www.ala.org/ala/alsc/alscresources/forlibrarians/professionaldev/competencies.htm (accessed June 15, 2007).

Braque, Donna M. 2000. "How Library Education Must Change to Meet the Challenge of New or Emerging Technologies." *Sci-Tech News* 54, no. 3: 7–8.

California Library Association. 2005. "Technology Core Competencies for California Library workers" (April 21). Available: www.cla-net.org/included/docs/tech_core_competencies.pdf (accessed June 12, 2007).

Colorado Department of Education, Educational Telecommunications Unit. 1999. "Colorado Technology Competency Guidelines for Classroom Teachers and School

Library Media Specialists" (January). Available: www.cde.state.co.us/edtech/ download/tgui.pdf (accessed June 16, 2007).

Dillon, Andrew and April Norris. 2005. "Crying Wolf: An Examination and Reconsideration of the Perception of Crisis in LIS Education." *Journal of Education for Library and Information Science* 46, no. 4: 280–298.

Farkas, Meredith. 2004. "Tech vs. Traditional in Library School and Libraries" (November 29). Available: http://meredith.wolfwater.com/wordpress/index.php/2004/ 1/29/tech-vs-traditional-in-library-school-and-libraries/ (accessed June 12, 2007).

Farkas, Meredith. 2006. "Skills for the 21st Century Librarian" (July 17). Available: http://meredith.wolfwater.com/wordpress/index.php/2006/07/17/skills-for-the-21st-century-librarian/ (accessed June 12, 2007).

Gorman, G.E. and B.J. Corbitt. 2002. "Core Competencies in Information Management Education." *New Library World* 103, no. 1182/1183: 436–445.

Gorman, Michael. 2004. "Whither Library Education?" *New Library World* 105, no. 1204/1205: 376–380.

Government Documents Round Table. "E-Competencies." Available: www.ala.org/ala/ godort/godortcommittees/gitco/ecomps.htm (accessed June 12, 2007).

Hunter, David. 2002. "Core Competencies and Music Librarians" (April). Available: www.musiclibraryassoc.org/pdf/Core_Competencies.pdf (accessed June 10, 2007).

LibLime. 2006. "Koha with Class Initiative." Available: www.liblime.com/projects/ koha-with-class (accessed August 27, 2007).

Malone, Cheryl K. and Anita S. Coleman. 2005. "Habits of Mind in the LIS Communities." *Journal of Education for Library and Information Science* 46, no. 4: 277–279.

Markey, Karen. 2004. "Current Educational Trends in the Information and Library Science Curriculum." *Journal of Education for Library and Information Science* 45, no. 4: 317–339.

Medical Library Association. 2007. "Health Information Science Knowledge and Skills" (July 13). Available: www.mlanet.org/education/platform/skills.html (accessed December 6, 2007).

Minkel, Walter. 2003. "The Next Big Thing: Why 21st-Century Skills Are a Librarian's New Best Friend." *School Library Journal* 49, no. 5: 41.

Mitchell, Victoria S. 2004. "The Top Ten Things a New Sci/Tech Librarian Should Know: Developing Core Competencies." *Issues in Science & Technology Librarianship* 39. Available: www.istl.org/04-winter/conf1.html (accessed March 6, 2007).

North Carolina Central University, School of Library and Information Sciences. 2007. "NCCU School of Library and Information Sciences Computer Literacy Expectations" (January 25). Available: www.nccuslis.org/admissions/complit.htm (accessed June 13, 2007).

Partnership for 21st Century Skills. 2004. "The Partnership for 21st Century Skills— FAQ." Available: www.21stcenturyskills.org/index.php?option=com_content& task=view&id=254&Itemid=112 (accessed December 7, 2007).

Pawley, Christine. 2005. "Gorman's Gauntlet: Gender and Crying Wolf." *Journal of Education for Library and Information Science* 46, no. 4: 304–311.

Reference and User Services Association. 2003. "Professional Competencies for Reference and User Services Librarians" (January 26). Available: www.ala.org/ ala/rusa/ rusaprotools/referenceguide/professional.htm (accessed June 15, 2007).

Special Libraries Association, Special Committee on Competencies for Special Librarians. 2003. "Competencies for Information Professionals of the 21st Century" (June). Available: www.sla.org/PDFs/Competencies2003_revised.pdf (accessed June 10, 2007).

State Library of North Carolina. 2007. "Technology Competencies for Libraries in North Carolina" (March). Available: http://statelibrary.dcr.state.nc.us/ce/competencies .pdf (accessed August 25, 2007).

Stoffle, Carla J. and Kim Leeder. 2005. "Practitioners and Library Education: A Crisis of Understanding." *Journal of Education for Library and Information Science* 46, no. 4: 312–319.

Tennant, Roy. 1998. "The Most Important Management Decision: Hiring Staff for the New Millennium." *Library Journal* 123, no. 3: 102.

University at Albany, State University of New York, College of Computing and Information. "Course Descriptions and Syllabi." Available: www.albany.edu/dis/ courses/#523 (accessed June 10, 2007).

University of North Carolina at Chapel Hill, School of Information and Library Science. 2004. "Course Descriptions." Available: http://sils.unc.edu/programs/courses/ descriptions.html#102 (accessed June 10, 2007).

University of North Texas, School of Library and Information Sciences. "Lifelong Education @ Desktop." Available: http://web2.unt.edu/cmp_lead/index.cfm (accessed June 10, 2007).

University of North Texas, School of Library and Information Sciences. 2006. "Information Technology and Skills Diagnostic Tools" (January 31). Available: www.unt .edu/slis/apppacket/ITKS/ITKSassess.htm (accessed June 15, 2007).

University of Oklahoma, School of Library and Information Studies. 2006. "For Students—Technology Competencies" (September 5). Available: www.ou.edu/cas/ slis/NewSite/Students/Tech_Compet.html (accessed June 13, 2007).

University of South Carolina, School of Library and Information Science. 2007. "Technology Requirements" (May 24). Available: www.libsci.sc.edu/program/computerreq.htm (accessed August 26, 2007).

University of Wisconsin–Madison, School of Library and Information Studies. 2005 "Education2Go." Available: www.slis.wisc.edu/continueed/ed2go.html (accessed June 10, 2007).

Webb, Gisela M. 1988. "Educating Librarians and Support Staff for Technical Services." *Journal of Library Administration* 9, no. 1: 111–120.

Wetherbee, Lou and Richard Wayne. 2007. "Not Your Mother's Library: Information Darwinianism" (May 3). Available: www.librarytechnology.com/Amigos-conf-ID-V2_ files/frame.htm (accessed August 27, 2007).

Wilson, Paula. 2002. "Technology Competencies: What Every Librarian Needs to Know." *Public Libraries* 41, no. 5: 267–270.

Woodsworth, Anne. 1997. "New Library Competencies." *Library Journal* 122, no. 9: 46.

Young Adult Library Services Association. 2003. "Young Adults Deserve the Best: Competencies for Librarians Serving Youth" (October). Available: www.ala.org/ala/ yalsa/profdev/youngadultsdeserve.htm (accessed June 15, 2007).

Appendix 2-1. Links to Professional and State Associations' Core Technology Competencies

American Association of Law Libraries. "Competencies of Law Librarianship" (March 2001). Available: www.aallnet.org/prodev/competencies.asp (accessed June 15, 2007).

American Library Association. "Draft Statement of Core Competencies" (July 2005). Available: www.ala.org/ala/accreditationb/Draft_Core_Competencies_07_05.pdf (accessed June 10, 2007).

Art Libraries Society of North America. "ARLIS/NA Core Competencies for Art Information Professionals." Available: www.uflib.ufl.edu/afa/pdc/corecompsfinal .pdf (accessed June 17, 2007).

Association for Library Service to Children. "Competencies for Librarians Serving Children in Public Libraries," revised edition (April 27, 1999). Available: www.ala.org/ala/alsc/alscresources/forlibrarians/professionaldev/competencies.htm (accessed June 15, 2007).

California Library Association. "Technology Core Competencies for California Library workers" (April 21, 2005). Available: www.cla-net.org/included/docs/tech_core_competencies.pdf (accessed June 12, 2007).

Colorado Department of Education, Educational Telecommunications Unit. "Colorado Technology Competency Guidelines for Classroom Teachers and School Library Media Specialists" (January 1999). Available: www.cde.state.co.us/edtech/ download/tgui.pdf (accessed June 16, 2007).

Government Documents Round Table. "E-Competencies." Available: www.ala.org/ala/godort/godortcommittees/gitco/ecomps.htm (accessed June 12, 2007).

Hunter, David. "Core Competencies and Music Librarians" (April, 2002). Available: www.musiclibraryassoc.org/pdf/Core_Competencies.pdf (accessed June 10, 2007).

Medical Library Association. "Health Information Science Knowledge and Skills" (July 13, 2007). Available: www.mlanet.org/education/platform/skills.html (accessed December 6, 2007).

Mitchell, Victoria S. "The Top Ten Things a New Sci/Tech Librarian Should Know: Developing Core Competencies" (2004). *Issues in Science & Technology* Librarianship 39. Available: www.istl.org/04-winter/conf1.html (accessed March 6, 2007).

Partnership for 21st Century Skills. "The Partnership for 21st Century Skills—FAQ." Available: www.21stcenturyskills.org/index.php?option=com_content&task=view&id=254&Itemid=112 (accessed December 7, 2007).

Reference and User Services Association. "Professional Competencies for Reference and User Services Librarians" (January 26, 2003). Available: www.ala.org/ala/rusa/rusaprotools/referenceguide/professional.htm (accessed June 15, 2007).

Special Libraries Association, Special Committee on Competencies for Special Librarians. "Competencies for Information Professionals of the 21st Century" (June 2003). Available: www.sla.org/PDFs/Competencies2003_revised.pdf (accessed June 10, 2007).

State Library of North Carolina. "Technology Competencies for Libraries in North Carolina" (March 2007). Available: http://statelibrary.dcr.state.nc.us/ce/ competencies .pdf (accessed August 25, 2007).

Young Adult Library Services Association. "Young Adults Deserve the Best: Competencies for Librarians Serving Youth" (October 2003). Available: www.ala .org/ala/yalsa/profdev/youngadultsdeserve.htm (accessed June 15, 2007).

Appendix 2-2. Core Competencies in Library Technology for New Library and Information Science Graduates: Survey Instrument and Results

In this survey, you will be asked to rate how important it is for new library and information science (LIS) master's degree holders to possess specific technology competencies upon graduation in four general areas:

- General computer knowledge
- Internet-related skills
- Computer hardware peripherals
- Library operations and automation products

If you are not familiar with a technology presented in the survey, or do not think it applies to your library's setting, just choose the "don't know/not applicable" option for that specific technology. If you complete the survey, you will have a chance to win a $20 Amazon.com gift certificate! Your entry into the gift certificate drawing is optional. If you choose to enter the drawing, please enter your e-mail address into the space provided at the end of the survey.

Boldface is used in the following tables to emphasize competencies that most respondents rated high in importance.

1. **How important do you think it is for all new LIS graduates to possess knowledge of the following general computer areas upon graduation?**

	VERY IMPORTANT (%)	SOMEWHAT IMPORTANT (%)	NOT VERY IMPORTANT (%)	NOT AT ALL IMPORTANT (%)	DON'T KNOW/NOT APPLICABLE (%)
Parts of a computer and their function (CPU, hard drive, RAM)	**44.0**	**48.0**	**8.0**	**0.0**	**0.0**
Computer operating systems (Microsoft Windows, Mac OS)	**58.0**	**38.0**	**4.0**	**0.0**	**0.0**
Office productivity software (Word, Excel, PowerPoint)	**96.0**	**4.0**	**0.0**	**0.0**	**0.0**
Computer security (antivirus, anti-spyware software)	**32.0**	**54.0**	**12.0**	**2.0**	**0.0**
Basic PC troubleshooting (determining why the printer won't print, why a computer locked up, etc.)	**74.0**	**24.0**	**2.0**	**0.0**	**0.0**
Advanced PC troubleshooting and maintenance (fixing or replacing hardware, installing software)	16.0	48.0	30.0	4.0	2.0

(Cont'd.)

Appendix 2-2. Core Competencies in Library Technology for New Library and Information Science Graduates: Survey Instrument and Results *(Continued)*

	VERY IMPORTANT (%)	SOMEWHAT IMPORTANT (%)	NOT VERY IMPORTANT (%)	NOT AT ALL IMPORTANT (%)	DON'T KNOW/NOT APPLICABLE (%)
Wired and/or wireless networking configuration and troubleshooting	4.0	62.0	28.0	6.0	0.0
Digitizing/scanning of printed resources	**36.0**	**56.0**	**8.0**	**0.0**	**0.0**
Special needs/adaptive technologies for ADA patrons (JAWS, ZoomText)	14.0	56.0	28.0	0.0	2.0
Gaming software (Second Life, instructional games)	4.0	38.0	48.0	8.0	2.0
Photo editing/digital imaging software (Photoshop)	26.0	54.0	18.0	2.0	0.0
Database construction and maintenance (Access, MySQL)	18.0	48.0	28.0	2.0	4.0
Scripting languages (Perl, PHP, JavaScript)	10.0	16.0	48.0	18.0	8.0
Object-oriented programming languages (Visual Basic, Java)	8.0	20.0	44.0	20.0	8.0
Server administration (Web servers, ILS servers, network drives)	8.0	24.0	52.0	12.0	4.0

2. How important do you think it is for all new LIS graduates to have experience with the following Internet-related competencies?

	VERY IMPORTANT (%)	SOMEWHAT IMPORTANT (%)	NOT VERY IMPORTANT (%)	NOT AT ALL IMPORTANT (%)	DON'T KNOW/NOT APPLICABLE (%)
Web page creation with FrontPage or Dreamweaver	49.0	38.8	8.2	0.0	4.1
Web page creation with hand-coded XHTML and CSS	8.2	38.8	36.7	6.1	10.2

(Cont'd.)

57

Appendix 2-2. Core Competencies in Library Technology for New Library and Information Science Graduates: Survey Instrument and Results (Continued)

	VERY IMPORTANT (%)	SOMEWHAT IMPORTANT (%)	NOT VERY IMPORTANT (%)	NOT AT ALL IMPORTANT (%)	DON'T KNOW/NOT APPLICABLE (%)
Internet protocols (HTTP, FTP, SMTP)	24.5	46.9	16.3	2.0	10.2
Virtual reference service using instant messaging or a product such as QuestionPoint	38.8	38.8	16.3	2.0	4.1
Online metadata schemas (Dublin Core, EAD)	12.2	28.6	38.8	4.1	16.3
XML	12.2	26.5	36.7	4.1	20.4
Electronic database searching (e.g., using complex Boolean searches in EBSCO databases)	**91.8**	**8.2**	**0.0**	**0.0**	**0.0**
Blogs	**36.7**	**53.1**	**8.2**	**0.0**	**2.0**
Wikis	**32.7**	**59.2**	**4.1**	**0.0**	**4.1**
Social networking sites (MySpace, Facebook)	28.6	46.9	18.4	6.1	0.0
Podcasting	32.7	51.0	12.2	0.0	4.1
RSS	28.6	36.7	14.3	0.0	20.4
Thin clients	12.2	32.7	22.4	4.1	28.6
Evaluating Web sites for validity, authority, etc.	**87.8**	**12.2**	**0.0**	**0.0**	**0.0**
Creating online information literacy tutorials	**61.2**	**34.7**	**4.1**	**0.0**	**0.0**

3. How important do you think it is for all new LIS graduates to know how to use the following computer hardware peripherals?

	VERY IMPORTANT (%)	SOMEWHAT IMPORTANT (%)	NOT VERY IMPORTANT (%)	NOT AT ALL IMPORTANT (%)	DON'T KNOW/NOT APPLICABLE (%)
Digital cameras	**55.1**	**34.7**	**10.2**	**0.0**	**0.0**

(Cont'd.)

Appendix 2-2. Core Competencies in Library Technology for New Library and Information Science Graduates: Survey Instrument and Results *(Continued)*

	VERY IMPORTANT (%)	SOMEWHAT IMPORTANT (%)	NOT VERY IMPORTANT (%)	NOT AT ALL IMPORTANT (%)	DON'T KNOW/NOT APPLICABLE (%)
Digital camcorders	49.0	30.6	18.4	0.0	2.0
USB drives	**71.4**	**20.4**	**4.1**	**0.0**	**4.1**
Projectors	65.3	22.4	10.2	0.0	2.0
Personal digital assistants (Palm, pocket PCs)	38.8	34.7	24.5	0.0	2.0
Tablet PCs	34.7	36.7	22.4	0.0	6.1
SmartBoards	34.7	40.8	16.3	2.0	6.1
e-Book readers	28.6	51.0	14.3	2.0	4.1
MP3 players (iPod, Zune)	42.9	36.7	18.4	0.0	2.0

4. **How important do you think it is for all new LIS graduates to possess knowledge of the following library operations and automation products?**

	VERY IMPORTANT (%)	SOMEWHAT IMPORTANT (%)	NOT VERY IMPORTANT (%)	NOT AT ALL IMPORTANT (%)	DON'T KNOW/NOT APPLICABLE (%)
Integrated library systems (Voyager, Horizon, ALEPH 500)	65.3	26.5	2.0	0.0	6.
Link resolvers (SFX, ArticleLinker)	20.4	36.7	26.5	0.0	16.3
Electronic resource management (Verde, Innovative ERM)	16.3	36.7	24.5	0.0	22.4
Federated search tools (WebFeat, MetaLib)	36.7	40.8	12.2	0.0	10.2
Interlibrary loan management (ILLiad, Ariel)	34.7	46.9	10.2	0.0	8.2
Digital asset management (Digitool, ResourceSpace)	16.3	36.7	22.4	2.0	22.4

(Cont'd.)

Appendix 2-2. Core Competencies in Library Technology for New Library and Information Science Graduates: Survey Instrument and Results *(Continued)*

	VERY IMPORTANT (%)	SOMEWHAT IMPORTANT (%)	NOT VERY IMPORTANT (%)	NOT AT ALL IMPORTANT (%)	DON'T KNOW/NOT APPLICABLE (%)
Institutional repository software (DSpace, EPrints)	14.3	30.6	34.7	2.0	18.4
Public access systems (PC reservation software, printing control software such as GoPrint or Pharos, filtering software)	34.7	32.7	16.3	4.1	12.2
Magnetic bar-coding hardware and software	26.5	51.0	12.2	0.0	10.2
RFID/self-check hardware and software	40.8	24.5	18.4	2.0	14.3
Library technology planning	**69.4**	**28.6**	**2.0**	**0.0**	**0.0**
Request for proposal (RFP) writing for purchasing technology products	40.8	44.9	6.1	0.0	8.2

5. **Have you supervised, or are you currently supervising, Texas Woman's University School Library & Information Studies (TWU SLIS) practicum students?**

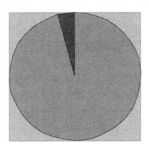

■ Yes (95.8%)
■ No (4.2%)

6. **If you answered "Yes" to the above question, do you feel the students were adequately prepared to work with library technology? Why or why not? What could TWU SLIS do differently to improve the students' preparation for working with library technologies?**

(Selected responses follow on next page)

(Cont'd.)

No. Some of the aforementioned software/hardware or technological systems require a hands-on access. I believe that individual courses taught in traditional library schools are now in need of a new technological "skeletal" framework whereby the courses can be attached. For example, the tech services folks need to be more aware of the kinds of questions that reference staff receive so that acquisitions to circulation can truly respond to the needs of electronically savvy students. Librarians have been forced into the need-to-know realm of electronic resources.

Yes, I have supervised practicum students and I felt that they were prepared in library technologies at that time; however, with ever emerging new technologies, we are playing catch up.

No. The student I supervised, although very interested and willing to learn, was pretty unfamiliar with American public libraries in general. This may be a disadvantage of the online program in that you can't actually meet such students and get a sense of what their background is.

Differences in student interests and where they planned to work. Provide opportunities to use the technology within the classes they are taking. Incorporate the tools into the curriculum. Provide access to a sandbox or development server to give students experience with the different technologies.

Yes. We have had two students and both have been very technology literate. However, we didn't need them to do Java, digitize documents and create metadata, or write specs for a new IT system. But both had the IT knowledge needed to do the tasks that were set before them.

She was adequately prepared to work with library technology (better than I was). But lacked interpersonal skills.

My student was eager to learn to work with the technologies in our library but was not comfortable using them in a lesson setting, i.e., WebQuest, hotlist, online databases, all Windows applications

Everyone should keep up to date with all technology in this day and age. Including the instructors.

They were adequately prepared with library technology in a general sense—probably even on par with many of our staff members. However, many of our staff are old timers who are not well versed with newer technology. So the more specific technological items from the survey your graduates can do, the better prepared they will be to make a difference in the organizations they go to.

They were reasonably proficient with technology. What we need are people who can learn technology quickly and help our customers with our public PCs and database terminals.

No, the student felt apprehensive or inadequate with technology.

Yes. They were very tech savvy. Very capable working with diverse staff and students.

Yes, they were quite up to date on technology and not afraid to ask about anything they had not used yet.

(Responses continue on next page)

(Cont'd.)

Appendix 2-2. Core Competencies in Library Technology for New Library and Information Science Graduates: Survey Instrument and Results *(Continued)*

The person I supervised did well with the technology I presented to her. We didn't have an opportunity to use the camera or projector, but I feel she would have done well. She was very competent. Invite vendors to demonstrate their various products in a mass session with various types of equipment, software, and applications available. Require students to visit schools and public libraries as part of their practicum to view the daily use of tech. (Not just an hour-long tour of the library.) Have students visit places where research is done using some of the reference sites and research tools mentioned. Create a handy click sheet booklet to use some of the more confusing search tools and how to access the "deep" Web search engines.

She only knew the very basics. More hands-on training would have been great.

My student seemed familiar with all aspects of technology as they related to his performance in this setting and was able to redesign a Web page for the unit he worked in.

Every library is different, but technology is something that no one can escape. Just to stress the importance of having a basic understanding of computer hardware and basic troubleshooting to enable them to resolve simple problems as they arise in the library. All staff depend on the librarian for help with basic computer problems.

7. What is your job title? (Selected responses)

Administrative Librarian
Assistant Branch Manager
Cataloguer
Coordinator for Special
  Collections
Elementary School Librarian
Head of Reference
High School Librarian
Librarian
Librarian/Teacher
Librarian/Technology Contact

Library Director
Library Media Specialist
Music/Media Librarian
Reference Department Manager
Reference Librarian
Research Support Librarian
Senior Library Supervisor
Technical Services Manager
Unit Coordinator: Government
  and Legal Information
Youth Services Librarian

8. Which best describes your library?

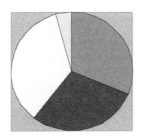

- ▨ Public Library (31.3%)
- ■ Academic Library (29.2%)
- ☐ K-12 School Library (35.4%)
- ☐ Other (4.2%)

(Cont'd.)

Appendix 2-2. Core Competencies in Library Technology for New Library and Information Science Graduates: Survey Instrument and Results *(Continued)*

9. Which best describes the number of employees at your library?

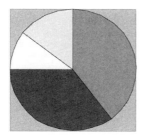

- ▤ **Less than 10 (39.6%)**
- ■ **10 to 50 (35.4%)**
- ▢ **50 to 100 (10.4%)**
- ▢ **More than 100 (14.6%)**

10. If there is anything else that you would like to share with me that might be relevant to this survey, please write it here. *(Selected responses)*

I also think that my intern needed more hands-on access to a wider set of databases. She may have only been addressing the needs of a public library system but we had a collection of over 200 databases. We spent a lot of time re-training on learning the different search interfaces of the various databases. In former years, the reference librarian had to know about the reference books and which tool was appropriate; today we need to know which database and still know which book to refer to if it is not available online. Good luck with your survey!

I recently looked at a job description on a blog for a librarian for Google. I think it is indicative of the kind of librarian that will be needed in the future. Here are the specifics: Google is seeking an information professional to serve as the domain expert and analyst for a Public Sector Content Partnerships team. The candidate must have demonstrated background and skills in conducting quantitative and qualitative analyses of government and public sector information sources in support of strategic and tactical planning. The ideal candidate will be passionate about uncovering, interpreting, and helping to improve access to public sector information.

Responsibilities:
- Conduct quantitative and qualitative analyses of the information holdings of government agencies, courts, and public sector organizations at all levels, in the U.S. and internationally
- Identify public sector information formats and subject verticals to be integrated in Google's search services
- Identify, qualify, and tier prospective partners and, in some cases, initiate communication with contacts
- Assist in developing content acquisition programs and partnership terms as well as marketing communications for prospective partners

Requirements:
- MLS, with focus in government/public sector information and 2+ years of relevant work experience; JD or legal background a plus
- Demonstrated track record in producing analytical and narrative reports
- Superior written communication skills   *(Requirements continue on next page)*

63

(Cont'd.)

Appendix 2-2. Core Competencies in Library Technology for New Library and Information Science Graduates: Survey Instrument and Results *(Continued)*

- Extreme attention to detail
- Ability to effectively operate with high energy and flexibility in a fast-paced, constantly evolving team environment
- Command of office and presentation applications
- Proficiency in a second language a plus
- Fluency in Internet and content industry economics, segmentation, and trends a plus
- Active participant in professional librarian community a plus

If this sounds like the job for you, you can apply online-

The size of the library is an important factor. An LIS graduate would have more need of tech skills in a large urban library than in a small rural library.

Many of the tasks needed an "it depends" column. If a person was specifically interested in systems, then it would be very important to know about the more complex technologies. A public services librarian needs to know how to create virtual teaching tools, but someone in tech services or ILL probably won't. But, if you tried to break it out by broad types of library positions, the survey would probably become too unwieldy!

The more hands-on technology training you can give your students, the better prepared they will be.

Students do not need to know the details about most of the technologies mentioned in this survey. They need to know that these technologies are used in the work of the library. Students should be encouraged to think creatively about how emerging technologies can be adapted for library use.

Technology changes so fast that understanding underlying principles (especially of databases) is at least as important as knowing the specific programs themselves.

A passion for helping library users is a must, and there is work for people who are personable but who have minimal technical skills. For advancement and selection into the profession, however, students must be able to learn and use technologies.

These are all very relevant questions; however, things change so rapidly in this profession they may not be useful by the time you finish your study. The camera I bought two years ago is now outdated and I hate to keep it, but it's an issue of money. That was one thing I didn't see in your survey. Librarians must be very good conservators of money and spend it wisely on technology. If they purchase the wrong thing or something that they can't use, they've wasted the taxpayers' money. I don't remember ever really having any discussions related to budgets or record keeping during my coursework. Excel, Quicken, and QuickBooks are nice, but common sense is important too. Good Luck!

It is so important that we as librarians move along with the times, and technology is the most important part of our job in most situations. If the profession is to survive, we must be more involved in the development and use of new technology. It is sad that our patrons are way ahead of us in technology.

The student cannot lose sight of the reason for knowing all these constantly changing technologies. These technologies will be outdated or drastically changed within five years of graduation. Familiarity with the current landscape is a must, but the philosophy of how information is organized is key. And the student needs to know how to investigate new technologies that arise after graduation.

Appendix 2-3. Links to LIS School Technology Requirements and Competencies

Technology-Related Continuing Education Courses

University of North Texas, School of Library and Information Sciences. "Lifelong Education @ Desktop."

Available: http://web2.unt.edu/cmp_lead/index.cfm
(accessed June 10, 2007).

University of Wisconsin-Madison, School of Library and Information Studies. "Education2Go" (2005).

Available: www.slis.wisc.edu/continueed/ed2go.html
(accessed June 10, 2007).

Required Technology Courses for Degree Requirements

University at Albany, State University of New York, College of Computing and Information. "Course Descriptions and Syllabi."

Available: www.albany.edu/dis/courses/#523
(accessed June 10, 2007).

University of North Carolina at Chapel Hill, School of Information and Library Science. "Course Descriptions" (2004).

Available: http://sils.unc.edu/programs/courses/descriptions.html#102
(accessed June 10, 2007).

Technology Entrance Guidelines and Diagnostic Tests for New Students

North Carolina Central University, School of Library and Information Sciences. "NCCU School of Library and Information Sciences Computer Literacy Expectations" (January 25, 2007).

Available: www.nccuslis.org/admissions/complit.htm
(accessed June 13, 2007).

University of North Texas, School of Library and Information Sciences. "Information Technology and Skills Diagnostic Tools" (January 31, 2006).

Available: www.unt.edu/slis/apppacket/ITKS/ITKSassess.htm
(accessed June 15, 2007).

University of Oklahoma, School of Library and Information Studies. "For Students—Technology Competencies" (September 5, 2006).

Available: www.ou.edu/cas/slis/NewSite/Students/Tech_Compet.html
(accessed June 13, 2007).

University of South Carolina, School of Library and Information Science. "Technology Requirements" (May 24, 2007).

Available: www.libsci.sc.edu/program/computerreq.htm
(accessed August 26, 2007).

Appendix 2-4. Assignment for the Koha Integrated Library System Configuration Project

I used this assignment in my Library Technology Systems course as a faculty member in the School of Library and Information Studies at Texas Woman's University. I am providing the assignment as an example of a practical, "hands-on" instructional method within a technology-related LIS course.

IINTEGRATED LIBRARY SYSTEM CONFIGURATION PROJECT
LS 5403
DR. DIANE NEAL

First of all . . . **don't panic!**

I certainly do not expect you to create a perfect integrated library system configuration by the end of the semester. What I do expect is that you will become familiar with how the "back end" of an integrated library system works. I also hope you learn how important it is to communicate effectively with team members when you do this kind of work. This project exemplifies, on a small scale, how many medium- and large-sized libraries configure and maintain their integrated systems, so this will be good practical experience for many of you.

For this project, the class has been divided into five groups of five or six students each. Each group will have a private discussion board forum in which to communicate. The group members, the URLs for the staff modules, and the OPAC for each group are posted in the discussion board.

The roles you choose for each person must be posted in your discussion group. The roles are as follows:

1. The *library systems administrator* is responsible for the overall configuration of the system. If there is someone in your group who has technical expertise or would like to become a systems librarian, that person would be the best choice. However, anybody can do it. The systems administrator will set up access for each person after each group member chooses a role. After your group has determined who will be the systems administrator, post it to your discussion board and I will e-mail the systems administrator's username and password to the designated person. The systems administrator will create accounts for each of the other team members to use.
2. The *head of access services* will configure and manage the circulation portion of your group's system.
3. The *head of cataloging* will be responsible for setting up authority records and cataloging policies. This person will also input a minimum of 10 MARC records into the system. You do not have to do original cataloging; you can get them from many places, including the MARC view in the TWU library catalog.
4. The *head of acquisitions* will configure the acquisitions portion of the system, including serials control.
5. The *Web designer* will configure the OPAC, including its appearance. Somebody who knows HTML would be best for this role. Again, however, anybody can do it.

If your group has six students, two students can share the responsibility of one of these roles. The group will decide which role to share; you can share any role except systems administrator.

Getting Help

The Koha user's guide is available at www.kohadocs.org/usersguide/. Also, there is a [?] at the top of the library staff access pages that you can click on for help, although not every page has help available in it.

(Cont'd.)

Appendix 2-4. Assignment for the Koha Integrated Library System Configuration Project *(Continued)*

Joshua Ferraro is our contact at LibLime. (LibLime is a support vendor for Koha.) Joshua has offered to help us with this project in any way possible; feel free to e-mail him with questions. Joshua has asked that you report any problems you find in the system at http://bugs.koha.org.

I will check each group's discussion board regularly to see if there are questions for me.

You can see a demonstration of a functioning Koha system at www.liblime.com/demos. There is an OPAC as well as a staff side demo there.

Other Koha OPAC examples that might be useful include the following:

West Liberty (IA) Public Library, http://opac.wlpl.org/
Nelsonville (OH) Public Library, http://search.athenscounty.lib.oh.us/
Horowhenua (NZ) Library Trust, http://opac.library.org.nz/
   cgi-bin/koha/opac-main.pl
Marseille University (FR) Mathematics Department,
   http://catalogue.cmi.univ-mrs.fr/cgi-bin/koha/opac-main.pl
Northland Baptist Bible College (Dunbar, WI), https://libcat.nbbc.edu/

OSS4LIB (www.oss4lib.org) focuses on "open source systems for libraries." Koha is an open source system, so this is a good resource for this project.

Scenario

Base your system's configuration on the following scenario.

Community Public Library is located in Community, Texas. Community has a population of approximately 350,000 citizens. Its first location opened in 1923. It now has one central location downtown and five smaller branches. It holds 250,000 titles that are distributed throughout all locations, including books, serials, media items, and electronic resources. Its 2005 operating budget was $5.5 million. The library employs 25 librarians with MLS degrees and 80 paraprofessional staff members.

The library administration has decided to migrate from its existing commercial system to Koha. Staff members have concluded that the system is not as responsive to their enhancement requests as the company should be. The library administrators believe that the money they would spend on a new commercial integrated library system could be better used in other areas, such as purchasing a federated search product (after the Koha project is complete, of course!).

When the library migrated to their current system several years ago, the system configuration decisions that were made at the time were not made carefully, and the library has suffered from these decisions for years. Therefore, they have decided to start the Koha configuration from scratch and not even take into consideration what they did with Innovative many years ago. It is a bold move, but it just might work, if it is done correctly.

The library systems administrator, the head of acquisitions, the head of cataloging, the head of circulation, and the Web designer have been charged with configuring Koha from scratch. They are about to embark on an exciting journey; none of them has ever participated in an integrated library system configuration before. The team members are about to learn that what they do in their own portion of an integrated library system configuration sometimes influences things in other parts of the system, even when they had no intention of doing so. Their library director trusts them to do high-quality work, although she wants weekly status reports from each member of the group.

Appendix 2-5. Library Technology Systems Course Description and Readings List

Course Description
LS 5403 Library Technology Systems: Planning, Selection, Migration, Implementation, and Assessment of Library-Related Software and Hardware, Including Integrated Library Systems. Overview of current library technology trends and issues.

Course Objectives
At the conclusion of this course, you should be able to:

- configure an integrated library system;
- write a Request for Proposal for a library system and make a system recommendation;
- understand the process of library system planning, migration, implementation, and evaluation;
- describe new library-oriented hardware and software; and
- evaluate usability and effectiveness of various library systems.

Lesson Topics
Lesson 1: Computer and Internet Skills; Overview of Library Technology Systems (integrated library systems, link resolvers, self-check, electronic resource management, and federated searching)

Lesson 2: The Request for Proposal (RFP) Process; Integrated Library Management Systems

Lesson 3: Circulation Systems; RFID; Open Source Software

Lesson 4: Acquisitions Systems; Serials; OpenURL; Electronic Resource Management

Lesson 5: Cataloging Systems; OPACs; Link Resolvers; MARC Records in Library Systems

Lesson 6: Computer Networks and Computer Security; Adaptive Technologies; Federated Searching

Lesson 7: Digitizing; XML; System Selection, Planning, and Implementation

Lesson 8: Digital Libraries; Library System Usability

Lesson 9: Current and Future Trends

Required Textbooks
Courtney, Nancy, ed. 2005. *Technology for the Rest of Us: A Primer on Computer Technologies for the Low-Tech Librarian*. Westport, CT: Libraries Unlimited.

Wilson, Katie. 2006. *Computers in Libraries: An Introduction for Library Technicians*. Binghamton, NY: The Haworth Press.

Optional Textbook
Cohn, John M., Ann L. Kelsey, and Keith M. Fiels. 2001. *Planning for Integrated Systems and Technologies: A How-To-Do-It Manual for Librarians*. New York: Neal-Schuman.

Useful Resources
The following resources are listed for your reference only. They are not required for this course, but they would be useful if you want to learn more about library automation and/or systems librarianship. If you have any questions about them, please let me know.

Bilal, Dana. 2002. *Automating Media Centers and Small Libraries: A Microcomputer-Based Approach*. Greenwood Village, CO: Libraries Unlimited.

Burke, John J. 2006. *Library Technology Companion: A Basic Guide for Library Staff*. New York: Neal-Schuman.Cibbarelli, Pamela R, ed. 2006. *Directory of Library Automation Software, Systems, and Services*, 2006–2007 edition. Medford, NJ: Information Today.

(Cont'd.)

Appendix 2-5. Library Technology Systems Course Description and Readings List *(Continued)*

Clyde, Laurel. 1999. *Managing Infotech in School Library Media Centers*. Englewood, CO: Libraries Unlimited.Cooper, Michael D. 1996. *Design of Library Automation Systems: File Structures, Data Structures, and Tools*. New York: Wiley.

Ingersoll, P., and Culshaw, J. 2004. *Managing Information Technology: A Handbook for Systems Librarians*. Westport, CT: Libraries Unlimited.

Jurkowski, Odin L. 2006. *Technology and the School Library*. Lanham, MD: Scarecrow Press.

Paling, Stephen. 1999. *A Hardware & Software Primer for Librarians: What Your Vendor Forgot to Tell You*. Lanham, MD: Scarecrow Press.

Singer Gordon, Rachel. 2003. *The Accidental Systems Librarian*. Medford, NJ: Information Today.

Readings List

Balas, Janet. 2002. "What Is This XML Thing and Why Do I Need to Know About It?" *Computers in Libraries* 22, no. 8: 39–41.

Balas, Janet. 2004. "Adding Substance, Not Just Frills, to a Library's Online Catalog." *Computers in Libraries* 24, no. 3: 37–39.

Breeding, Marshall. 2005. "Implementing Wireless Networks Without Compromising Security." *Computers in Libraries* 25, no. 3: 31–33.

Breeding, Marshall. 2005. "Plotting a New Course for Metasearch." *Computers in Libraries* 25, no. 2: 27–29.

Breeding, Marshall. 2005. "Re-integrating the 'Integrated' Library System." *Computers in Libraries* 25, no. 1: 28–30.

Breeding, Marshall. 2006. "Musings on the State of the ILS in 2006." *Computers in Libraries* 26, no. 3: 26–28.

Breeding, Marshall. 2006. "Reshuffling the Deck." *Library Journal* 131, no. 6: 40–54.

Brenner, Michaela, Tom Larsen, and Claudia Weston. 2006. "Digital Collection Management Through the Library Catalog." *Information Technology and Libraries* 25, no. 2: 65–77.

Cervone, Frank. 2005. "Understand the Big Picture so You Can Plan for Network Security." *Computers in Libraries* 25, no. 3: 10–15.

Coyle, Karen. 2004. "Future Consideration: The Functional Library Systems Record." *Library Hi Tech* 22, no. 2: 166–174.

Devakos, Rea. 2006. "Towards User Responsive Institutional Repositories: A Case Study." *Library Hi Tech* 24, no. 2: 173–182.

Eden, Brad. 2004. "Whither MARC? Is There a Future?" *Technicalities* 24, no. 6: 7–9.

Grogg, Jill E. 2005. "Linking Users to Open Access." *Searcher* 13, no. 4: 52–56.

"How to Evaluate and Purchase an ILS." 2003. *Library Technology Reports* 39, no. 3: 11–27.

Kaczmarek, Joanne and Chew C. Naun. 2005. "A Statewide Metasearch Service Using OAI-PMH and Z39.50." *Library Hi Tech* 23, no. 4: 576–586.

Lopatin, Laurie. 2006. "Library Digitization Projects, Issues, and Guidelines: A Review of the Literature." *Library Hi Tech* 24, no. 2: 273–289.

Maness, Jack M. 2006. "Library 2.0 Theory: Web 2.0 and Its Implications for Libraries." *Webology* 3, no. 2. Available: www.webology.ir/2006/v3n2/a25.html.

Meyer, Stephen. 2005. "Helping You Buy: Electronic Resource Management Systems." *Computers in Libraries* 25, no. 10: 19–23.

69

(Cont'd.)

Appendix 2-5. Library Technology Systems Course Description and Readings List *(Continued)*

Muir, Scott P. 2006. "An Introduction to the Open Source Software Issue." *Library Hi Tech* 23, no. 4: 465–468.

Novotny, Eric. 2004. "I Don't Think I Click: A Protocol Analysis Study of Use of a Library Catalog in the Internet Age." *College & Research Libraries* 65, no. 6: 525–537.

Pace, Andrew K. 2005. "Helping You Buy: Integrated Library Systems." *Computers in Libraries* 25, no. 8: 25–26.

"Planning Models for an ILS." 2003. *Library Technology Reports* 39, no. 3: 38–47.

Raschke, Greg and Suzanne Weiner. 2004. "Clarity in the Mist." *Library Journal netConnect* (July): 4–6, 8.

Rumph, Virginia A. 2001. "Vendor Selection Using the RFP Process-Is it for You? One Library's Experience." *Indiana Libraries* 20, no.1: 26–28.

Ryan, Terry. 2004. "Turning Patrons Into Partners When Choosing an Integrated Library System." *Computers in Libraries* 24, no. 3: 6–7, 54–56.

"Samples from Staff Requirements and RFQ." 2003. *Library Technology Reports* 39, no. 4: 55–58.

Singer Gordon, Rachel. 2006. "Helping You Buy: Link Resolver Tools." *Computers in Libraries* 26, no. 2: 15–23.

Singh, Jay, Navjit Brar, and Carmen Fong. 2006. "The State of RFID Applications in Libraries." *Information Technology and Librarie*s 25, no. 1: 24–32.

Tennant, Roy. 2002. "MARC Must Die." *Library Journal* 127, no. 17: 27–28.

Tennant, Roy. 2005. "Lipstick on a Pig." *Library Journal* 130, no. 7: 34.

Tenopir, Carol. 2006. "Thinking About Linking." *Library Journal* 131, no. 12: 29.

Turner, Steven. 2004. "Resource Integration in the Library: Link-resolvers and Federated Searching." *Mississippi Libraries* 68, no. 3: 63–66.

Vaughan, Jason. 2004. "A Library's Integrated Online Library System: Assessment and New Hardware Implementation." *Information Technology and Libraries* 23, no. 2: 50–57.

Vaughan, Jason and Jennifer Fabbi. 2005. "May: Self-Check Systems." *Computers in Libraries* 25, no. 5: 23–29.

Wayne, Richard. 2005. "T4: Top Texas Technology Trends for Libraries. *Texas Library Journal* 81, no. 1: 12–17.

Wayne, Richard. 2006. "Top Technology Trends in Texas Libraries: Wireless Networking & Anti-spyware Software." *Texas Library Journal* 82, no. 1: 48–49, 52–53.

Wayne, Richard. 2007. "Top Texas Technology Trends for Libraries." *Texas Library Journal* 83, no. 1: 22, 24–26.

Webster, Peter. 2006. "Bit by Bit." *Library Journal netConnect* (January): 16–17.

"What Is an RFP and Why Is it Worth Your Time?" 2003. *Library Technology Reports* 39, no. 4: 7–11.

Winston, Mark D. and Tara Hoffman. 2005. "Project Management in Libraries." *Journal of Library Administration* 42, no. 1: 51–61.

Wolf, Mark. 2006. "Self-Check Success." *Public Libraries* 45, no. 2: 8–10.

"Writing the RFP." 2003. *Library Technology Reports* 39, no. 4: 31–41.

Zhu, Qin. 2004. "2 Critical Stages for a Successful ILS Migration: System Profiling and Data Conversion." *Computers in Libraries* 24, no. 3: 26–30.

Part II

CORE COMPETENCIES FOR LIBRARY TECHNOLOGY SPECIALISTS

Chapter 3

Management and Technology Competencies for the Systems Librarian

Susan M. Thompson

Overview

The systems librarian evolved into a distinct library position during the 1980s as library automation systems were transformed into integrated library systems (ILSs) offered by commercial vendors. Since the 1980s, technology competencies needed by systems librarians have grown beyond the ILS to encompass a wide variety of technologies such as desktop support, servers, networks, Web-based services, and programming. Qualifications can vary widely, as there is no common set of educational or professional standards. Duties of systems librarians can also differ depending on the organization of the library's technical support structure and on the types of technologies supported. Now, systems librarians' responsibilities usually extend beyond the technology itself to encompass management and project planning duties that demand collaboration and people skills as well as an understanding of the library. As a member of the library, the systems librarian's vision and leadership is essential in library technology planning and services.

Introduction

A number of librarian positions incorporate technology in various ways. Most of these positions are newer ones that involve technology as a tool ancillary to their primary function. Historically there was just one person who dealt with technology as a regular part of his or her duties—the systems librarian. The primary interest of the systems librarian is the technology itself. Therefore, the technology competency of this position is critical. However, while the position of systems librarian is the result of the growing use of technology in libraries, it has evolved in such a way that specific technical competencies alone are not sufficient. Just as essential are vision, leadership, and the ability to work collaboratively with others.

We are fortunate in that there is a fairly rich body of literature about systems librarianship that examines topics relevant to the competencies we are discussing in this book. I summarize some of the information from these books and journal articles in this chapter, but I highly recommend that you also read the original documents. I have also drawn heavily on the discussions of the Heads of Library Technology (HoLT) interest group, which is part of the Library and Information Technology Association (LITA). Byron Mayes formed HoLT in 2001 specifically to discuss issues related to managing library systems departments. Many of HoLT's discussions over the years have touched on competency issues, and many of the chapter authors in this book are HoLT members.

The HoLT group's awkward name represents one of the dilemmas for the systems librarian position: what to call ourselves. In Foote's (1997) study of position announcements, she found that the title "systems librarian" was used only about a quarter of the time. Nevertheless, it was still the most common title used. Perhaps the term is common because it does such a good job of expressing the interrelated nature of technology. Like a human circulatory system or a highway system, technology in a library must work together as a system in order to accomplish the library's goals.

Systems librarians are not always the head of their library's technology department. Sometimes they are not even librarians. A number of HoLT members do not have an MLS, but their duties are essentially the same as others who are officially "systems librarians." In this chapter I use the term *systems librarian* in the loosest possible way to mean any position that is primarily concerned with taking care of technology in the library. She may be the sole person responsible for technology in the library, or, more commonly these days, she may be part of a team of information technology specialists—often acting as the manager of the systems department.

In 1987, Chan defined systems librarians as "the people responsible for managing computerized library systems," and this definition in its broadest sense essentially remains true today (Chan, 1987: 175). By this definition, highly technical positions, such as digital projects librarians or instructional technology librarians, do not qualify as systems librarians. The primary purpose of these positions is to provide a particular library service, such as collections or instruction; the technology responsibilities, while extensive, are secondary.

Systems librarians generally are responsible for most of the library's technologies. As a result, systems librarians are typically expected to be jacks-of-all-trades— knowing something about each technology but not necessarily being an expert in all of them. However, there are systems librarians who specialize in just one aspect of the library's technology, such as the ILS, the library's Web site, or hardware and software support. Systems librarians who specialize in a technology tend to work in larger libraries or libraries that distribute or split the function into several different positions.

There may be disconnects between what the library systems department actually does and what the rest of the library thinks the department does, which affects assumptions as to what competencies are needed to fulfill its duties. In particular, there is a tendency to consider the ILS to be the main focus of systems work. Although the ILS was the initial reason for the systems position, the reality these days is that it is just one of a constellation of technologies supported by most systems librarians.

This chapter looks at the history of the systems librarian position and its impact on the systems librarian's qualifications and role today. I then examine in depth the responsibilities typical for this position and discuss the types of competencies today's systems librarians need.

History of Systems Librarianship and Library Technology

Systems librarianship is one of the newer library specializations and perhaps one of the hardest to define. Not surprisingly, the evolution of the systems librarian position reflects the changes in technology in libraries. However, the history of systems librarianship starts a little later than the history of library technology itself. Lavagnino (1997) traced the history of systems librarians and systems departments in academic libraries using four stages, which roughly follow the decade-by-decade development of library technology that I used in Chapter 1.

1. Precomputer technology consisted of machines such as typewriters.
2. The mainframe and microcomputer technology stage saw the emergence of local technical experts in departments such as cataloging.
3. Turnkey library systems triggered the appearance of systems librarians and independent systems departments.
4. Personal computers (PCs) and client–server technologies expanded the duties of systems librarian beyond the ILS.

To this list Ross and Marmion (2000) added a fifth stage:

5. Web and widespread technology caused the systems librarian's responsibilities to expand and systems departments to grow.

1960s–1970s

Some large libraries had individuals, often called data-processing or automation experts, assigned to systems librarian-like roles in the 1960s. Even at that early date, a debate appeared in the literature as to whether these individuals should be trained in librarianship and then specialize in technology or if they should be technologists—a debate that continues to this day (Wasserman, 1965). By the 1970s, there was talk of new skills needed in the library, especially systems analysis. Systems analysis was a way for libraries to look at their processes in a logical fashion and determine how they might be automated. While the original automation systems were usually developed by programmers, systems analysis was often done by librarians. I would speculate that it is this early interest in systems analysis that gave "systems" librarians their name.

This era corresponds to Lavagnino's (1997) mainframe and minicomputer technology stage. During this time of function-specific automated library systems, certain librarians and staff began to serve as the experts for the technology in their departments. Lavagnino (1997) states that a few system librarians emerged during this time with responsibility for managing technology issues for in-house development. However, in general, the focus during this period was on hiring people with a technical background. Most of the support personnel did not have formal library training. These early systems people tended to work for bibliographic utilities, vendors, or large libraries.

1980s

The 1980s were the true beginning of systems librarianship. Corresponding to Lavagnino's (1997) stage 3, the 1980s saw library automation evolve into ILSs with public access catalogs. These new systems were designed by vendors to be "turnkey" systems capable of being managed entirely at the local site. It was at this point that many libraries hired a systems librarian or reallocated an existing librarian into this position to coordinate the selection and implementation of a commercial automation system.

The new specialization in library technology began to emerge as technology skills grew in various traditional library departments. These new experts were respected for their combination of technical systems skills and library management skills. While many of these positions originated specifically to manage the ILS, it was not long before systems librarians expanded their support to other areas of technology as libraries expanded their automation efforts. By the end of the decade, some of these lone systems librarians began to form systems departments and hire additional support staff with technology skills.

Childers' (2003) study of publication patterns concerning computer skills in libraries showed that the first big surge of interest in computer literacy occurred in the early 1980s. During this period article writers also considered how technology should be supported and discussed the changing role of librarians in specific areas, such as cataloging. By the late 1980s, articles on the new systems librarian specialization begin to appear on a regular basis.

Primary competencies for systems librarians during this era focused on the ILS—from procurement to configuration to day-to-day maintenance. Other skills included managing PC equipment and software, periodical index databases, CD-ROM technology, and some networking such as hardwired terminals and modems.

1990s

The 1990s roughly correspond to Lavagnino's (1997) stage 4 in which PCs and client–server technologies enabled the networking and distributed computing environments that have become the dominant technologies in libraries. Servers replaced mainframes, national and international standards allowed increased collaboration (and integration), and PCs became a regular fixture on library staff desktops. Until this networking era, library technology was largely independent of technology in other areas. For instance, the library automation system functioned in isolation from other technology efforts on college campuses, as did the systems librarian. However, as libraries expanded to network-based projects outside the purview of the ILS and library technology interacted more with other systems in the university, the systems librarian began collaborating more with staff in the broader organization's computing department.

The Association of Research Libraries' (ARL) 1994 survey of systems departments showed that information technology advances, particularly the Web, were starting to cause dramatic changes in the library systems function and organization (Muir, 1995). The computing environment was changing from mainframe to client–server architecture, from stand-alone to networked workstations, and from independent to integrated library systems. The library systems department was now managing more than the ILS, bibliographic utilities, CD-ROM databases, and hardwired terminal networks. The trend during the early 1990s was to add more staff to the systems office, more hardware and software, more electronic resources, and more library services delivered to remote users.

The systems librarian underwent several significant changes during this time period. She went from regarding campus computing as just a service provider to working collaboratively with users as colleagues. Collaborative activities increased both with internal library colleagues and with external partners such as vendors, consortia, and other libraries. She also became more involved in administrative tasks, in particular, supervising systems staff as it increased in number. The systems department itself was more likely to report to the library director rather than to technical services or to other areas in the library.

Publications from the mid-1990s until the early 2000s showed that much of the interest in systems librarians was in the changing roles and new skills needed. Competencies expected of the systems librarian now included knowledge of computing hardware, software, and local area networking. She also had to understand telecommunications technology in order to provide networked services that are accessible beyond the library. Lavagnino (1997) states that systems librarians' responsibilities expanded to include reviewing available technologies, strategic and budgetary planning, campus-wide standardization of technology, and, for the first time, directly serving library users.

2000s

Ross and Marmion (2000) proposed a fifth stage to extend Lavagnino's stages. Their fifth stage includes the growth of digitized resources, integration of systems, and development of client–server technology, especially as it relates to the Web.

77

The transition from stage 4 to 5 includes major components from client–server architecture and introduces patron support (providing both direct support to end users and access services such as proxy servers). The emergence of national and international standards beyond MARC, such as RDF, XML and Dublin Core Metadata, became a significant factor. The distributed environment is now becoming the wireless environment. Digitized full-text sources with authentication (e.g., electronic reserves and e-books) and integration of the library automation system, particularly the catalog, with other systems, is changing how end users access and use library resources.

Because client–server technologies cover areas outside of the library's control, such as local area networks and Internet access, the systems librarian must know who to contact about problems. Hardware has become more complex, although increased reliability makes hardware repair less important. Software is also more complex and more powerful, creating opportunities to expand the library's technical capabilities for those who know how. During the past decade or so, many more responsibilities, ranging from Web design to network security, have been assigned to the systems librarian.

Entrance into the Systems Librarian Profession

Systems librarians have seen their jobs change dramatically in the specialization's short, roughly 20-year history. It has been possible for one person during the course of his or her career to see (and to participate in) all of these changes. This has created an interesting difference between systems librarians and librarians in traditional specializations. Most librarians train for their specialty in library school. Many systems librarians have had a less formal introduction to their field. Individuals in systems librarianship come from a variety of backgrounds. Many came from other library positions, and they either deliberately chose to move into systems or accidentally evolved into that position through their involvement with technology.

Accidental Systems Librarian

Rachel Singer Gordon coined the term "accidental systems librarian" in her 2001 article describing the phenomenon of librarians who have accidentally switched careers without really planning to do so. Because of these librarians' aptitude and interest, technology-related duties simply became an increasingly large component of their jobs until it reached the point that their job title was changed to reflect their duties. As Gordon (2001: 25) stated in her article, "[systems librarians] are by personality and by training uniquely suited to adapt traditional library skills to the challenges of integrating and supporting computer technology in our libraries."

The accidental systems librarian concept is particularly important in a book about competencies. The unplanned nature of the career means that there has historically been a lack of consistency in the background and skill set from one systems librarian to the next. Although library schools have technology courses, there are still very few programs with a recognized curriculum of skills specific to the systems librarian position. (See Chapter 2 for more detail on the current state of technology education in library schools.) Unlike catalogers, who must know AACR2, or reference librarians, who must know how to conduct a reference interview, or instruction librarians, who must know the ACRL information literacy standards, there are no recognized standards or common set of knowledge for systems work.

Libraries may also need to do a reality check of what responsibilities they expect of the modern systems librarian—it is more than just the ILS or technology support in general. One of the key skills for all systems librarians in the field and away from school is the ability to identify technology trends and develop methods to keep our skills up to date. The original intent of Rachel Singer Gordon's article was specifically designed to provide a "Course in Accidental Systems Librarianship" detailing how to develop the full set of competencies that an accidental systems librarian might need—an idea she has since expanded into a book (Gordon, 2003). Richard Wayne, in Chapter 7, also provides specific information on sources to keep up with technology skills.

Qualifications

So what qualifications does a systems librarian need? As a result of the accidental nature of their entry into their positions, many systems librarians did not prepare for their career by following an organized curriculum of systems librarianship in library school. They may have had some initial formal training in a technology class in library school or with training on the ILS provided by the vendor, but learning other technology skills tended to be picked up in more informal ways. As time goes on, skills need to be updated, or the systems librarian may fall behind. Because there are no standards, the systems librarian is responsible for determining her own career path and keeping up on technology skills as needed. Just as important, the library organization itself needs to support her continuing education needs by providing sufficient time, training, and budget.

Systems librarians are usually generalists—jacks-of-all-trades rather than an expert in one area. Even so, one systems librarian can't know everything, so what should she learn? The position originated to handle the ILS, but is that still the major duty of the systems librarian? What about the basics of other major library systems, such as bibliographic utilities, interlibrary loan systems, electronic reserves, and course management systems? Should she understand the basic theories of information science? Should she know computer science basics, such as programming and data structures? Should she know relational databases and query languages? Web editing and design? Should she be able to repair and maintain microcomputer and peripherals equipment?

Clearly, the ideal qualifications for a systems librarian have changed over time. In HoLT's 2004 meeting, the participants speculated that some of the change is due to the fact that most systems departments have expanded beyond just supporting ILSs to broader technology responsibilities that require more in-depth technical knowledge than is typical of most librarians (Thompson, 2005). Another factor might be changes in the ILSs themselves, which make them easier to use and maintain. The ILS no longer needs a lot of customization and so may not need to be managed by a specialist like the systems librarian. In addition, a higher level of technical knowledge is often expected in other positions around the library these days. As a result, technically competent staff and librarians in other areas of the library are often able to handle the technical requirements for their portion of the ILS.

One question that arose was, with less emphasis on the ILS, is the Master's in Library Science (MLS) qualification as necessary today for staff working in library systems as it once was? Many felt that it was a desirable qualification that should be required for at least the systems department head, but others felt that the MLS was optional even for that position. What effect does the presence or absence of a library degree have on the systems librarian's ability to work within the library organization? The HoLT participants agreed that it was essential to be able to work effectively within the library as a colleague, manager, and change agent. Depending on the local library culture and personnel practices, this is sometimes possible only with an MLS degree. Classification as a librarian may give us credibility with other library staff. Older library staff, in particular, may relate better to technical support people from a library background. In some libraries, only librarians may manage departments. Also, in academic institutions, members of the systems staff who are part of the library faculty may be better able to participate in and contribute to the whole institution. Kevin Herrera, in Chapter 4, will discuss in more detail the relevance of the MLS degree to systems work.

What do actual systems librarians in the field think their responsibilities and skills should be? Xu and Chen, in the companion study to their 1999 position announcement analysis, surveyed both newly hired systems librarians and their library directors specifically as to the degree requirements for the systems librarian position. In their original analysis, Xu and Chen (1999) found that more than two-thirds of the systems librarian positions required an MLS degree. Supporting this finding, in the follow-up study Xu and Chen (2000) found that 75 percent of the surveyed librarians had an MLS as their primary qualification. However, less than half (44 percent) of the systems librarians themselves thought an MLS-only degree was the best qualification. About a quarter of the respondents felt that the ideal systems librarian should have a combination of degrees—an MLS with either a computer science (CS) bachelor's or master's degree. About 17 percent felt some other form of technical background—CS minor, training, or work experience—should be expected with the library degree. Finally, 11 percent of the respondents felt that a CS bachelor's or master's degree without an MLS was the appropriate educational requirement.

The fact that over half of the systems librarians (and library directors) think technical education or experience in addition to an MLS is an important qualification for a systems librarian has significant implications. Is it possible for library schools to take a leading role in training for this specialty, or should other technical disciplines be involved in certifying this specialization? In particular, what is the role of the information science master's? While often not accredited by the American Library Association (ALA), the coursework for this degree is can be very relevant for systems work. Perhaps some sort of joint MLS/MIS degree would be appropriate for systems librarianship preparation (Diane Neal, e-mail communication, June 3, 2008).

One other interesting finding in Xu and Chen's (2000) study relates to the prior experience expected of a new hire. Two-thirds of the academic and public library job postings expected one to five years of experience. However, the majority of the positions (61 percent) were filled by respondents with no library work experience.

Finally, Eric Lease Morgan offered concrete advice on qualifications for career changers interested in moving into the systems librarian role. He identified five technologies as crucial for librarians interested in moving into systems work (Morgan, 2005). First, and most important, was knowledge of XML. XML is becoming the *lingua franca* of online information resources capable of unambiguously transmitting information while also serving as data that describe that information. Other critical technical skills included relational databases, indexing, Webserver administration, and programming/scripting.

81

Systems Organization Structure

The environment in which systems librarians work is part of what defines their responsibilities and ultimately their competency needs. Many of the members of HoLT have seen their positions grow and change dramatically over the years— from a single systems librarian position to managers of growing departments (Thompson, 2005). Many of us were heads of our libraries' technology departments when that meant being the only systems librarian. As our libraries' use of technology increased, many of us started our first systems department, adding personnel and expanding the types of technology we were responsible for. Technologies managed by the library systems department may now include such things as digital imaging, Web services, and server farms as well as third-generation ILSs and networked computers throughout the library.

The biggest change over time is the greatly increased role of management and planning responsibilities of the systems librarian. Xu and Chen's (1999) review of the literature found that this trend was particularly true for positions in public libraries and in medium to large academic libraries. Systems librarians in smaller college libraries tended to be engaged in more of the day-to-day operational work.

Systems librarians in smaller libraries also did more training of both library staff and public users. Xu and Chen also found that interpersonal skills tended to be emphasized more in academic library job ads than in public library ads. I would speculate that this difference may be due to the more collegial faculty environment that tends to prevail in academic libraries.

As time went on and automation spread throughout the library, systems librarians went from being a fairly isolated single worker to being part of their own department, typically in the same area of the library organization as the department from which the systems librarian originally came—usually technical services. As the technology began to focus more on the public side, systems departments began to report higher in the organizational structure. This change expanded "ownership" of technology support from any one area of the library and made it easier to provide equal access to technology support for all areas of the library. The 2002 ARL survey found that about 60 percent of systems departments reported directly to the library director, with the remainder reporting to another upper administrator (Muir and Lim, 2002). Ross and Marmion (2000) suggest that changes in the library organizational structure reflected the need for a technology person at the upper management level. Now, systems librarians themselves can be found in upper levels of the library administration as they take charge of all aspects of library automation, supervise multiple technology-related departments, and provide overall direction for library technology efforts.

Centralized versus Decentralized Technology Support

Most libraries started with a relatively simple model for technology support— a single systems librarian position developed specifically to support the ILS. However, as technology needs increased, two divergent support models developed. Most commonly, a central systems department came about to handle support for most of the library's technology. The department consisted of the systems librarian and several staff members who were competent in a variety of technology areas. Typical technologies supported in centralized systems departments include the ILS, other library-specific applications, desktop computers and software, servers and networking, and the library's Web site.

However, in some libraries technology support has been distributed across several areas, both inside and outside of the library. The ILS function, and possibly the systems librarian, may still be part of the technical services area. The library's Web site and database technology support may be in the reference area. Server and networking technology may be the purview of an outside information technology (IT) department, and desktop support may be taken care of by a library technology department. Other distributed environments may be more "every man for himself," with each library department responsible for hiring technical support personnel to take care of the equipment and software specific to that department. The 2002 ARL survey found that over 80 percent of its member libraries had centralized systems functions, and 17 percent were decentralized (Muir and Lim, 2002). There was also discussion that other models may be evolving, often involving a central systems department with one or more significant functions, such as digitization projects, in another department.

In the past ten years, there have been significant changes in who performs the technological duties in the library organization. What I've discussed so far are conventional types of technical support positions usually located in the systems department where the focus of the position is on the technology itself. However, the responsibilities for technology have splintered as more types of technology specialties appear and as other departments in the library take on significant technical responsibilities.

New technologies, such as digitization for institutional repositories and electronic resource management (ERM) systems, are creating their own specialized positions. Even though technology is central to these positions, these new technology positions may not reside in systems departments, and the technical experts for these functions may have a background in the underlying library function area. For instance, digitization projects often concern archival or special collections material, and the digital librarian may work either in the department where the material comes from (e.g., the archives) or a new independent department that is formed. My review of 2006–2007 position announcements published in *College & Research Libraries News* (see Chapter 1) found that the two most frequently advertised positions outside of systems were digitization project librarians and ERM librarians. This brings up one of the issues HoLT identified as a concern— the need to be aware of, collaborate on, and possibly manage technology projects originating in other areas of the library outside of systems.

Relationship with the Broader Organization

Libraries rarely exist as a completely independent entity. Academic libraries are part of a college or university, public libraries are part of the municipal government, school libraries are part of the school system, and so forth. As a result, the broader organization's IT department often has responsibility over at least part of the library's technology infrastructure.

The relationship between the library's systems department and the broader organization's IT department can be very important in defining the responsibilities of the systems librarian. How are technology responsibilities divided? The network is often under the broader organization's IT department for both practical and security reasons. The larger organization's IT department may be able to provide more favorable procurement deals with vendors that may make it desirable to purchase hardware and software through them. Often the IT department will have more staff, so it may be a more efficient use of library manpower to focus on library-specific technologies and use campus-level support, for instance, for standard technology, such as PCs and office productivity software.

In my library, for example, we eventually developed a shared support structure. Library systems gave up some of its direct control over certain library technologies, and campus IT agreed to customize certain campus configurations and protocols to the library's specifications. The ability to work successfully in this shared support environment depends on an atmosphere of trust and excellent communication among the systems librarian, systems staff, and campus IT. Of course, it is also sometimes the case that the library does not have a choice concerning when it can use campus IT and instead must give up control of certain areas of library technology. Good communication becomes even more important in this the case.

So what do these organizational strategies mean for systems librarian competencies? The systems librarian must develop management and leadership skills, especially if she is the head of the systems department. Often the systems librarian acts as liaison between the systems department and other areas of the library and between the library and outside IT departments or service providers such as vendors. This liaison role calls for good communication skills and some understanding of the politics of the organization. Finally, systems work is almost always done in collaboration with others both inside and outside the library. In addition to the other skills mentioned, collaboration requires an understanding of the goals of the other units and an ability to manage projects in a way that meets everyone's goals.

Systems Librarian Responsibilities

The core competencies that a systems librarian needs are primarily determined by the needs of the library in which he or she works. More than any other library specialty, the actual duties of a systems librarian are highly variable and can be very different from library to library. Of course, any job has different requirements from one institution to another. Nevertheless, the general duties expected of traditional library specialties, such as cataloging and reference, are based on a common understanding and are usually similar no matter the type or size of institution. Job titles for these more typical library careers can be considered the "nouns" and the work associated with the job its "verb." Catalogers catalog, reference librarians refer, and instruction librarians instruct. The same is not true for systems librarians.

Several significant career decisions or turning points can impact a systems librarian's responsibilities. Most important is management versus hands-on systems work. Management duties typically include planning, coordination, and supervision. Hands-on work involves direct support of library technologies, including troubleshooting, providing user support, and integrating new technology.

During many systems librarians' careers, they have acquired more and more management duties. However, as management duties grow, these librarians often find that they have less time for hands-on technology support, and, as a result, their technology skills may erode over time. The questions for systems librarians in primarily management positions is how many and what types of technical competency standards they should meet, and how can they can maintain these skills?

The question of what technology skills, beyond directly providing technical support, that a library systems manager needs is particularly important for two reasons. First, the type of workers systems librarians manage tend to respect technical knowledge, as do the people in campus IT, with whom systems must often work. Second, the systems librarian is often responsible for recommending new technologies and acting as a change agent in the library. Both roles require that even systems librarians who are primarily managers be technologically up to date and aware of future trends.

On the other hand, systems librarians who are primarily involved in direct technology support also have two paths they can follow, albeit ones that may not be generally recognized: that of developers and that of maintainers. Again, looking back at the history of library technology, the original systems librarians were expected to just maintain the library automation system. The solving of serious problems or the development of new capabilities was strictly the purview of the automation vendor. However, over time, systems personnel have become more and more involved in customizing applications and developing new ones. This was necessary because there were no large vendors offering complete support packages for the new PC and Web technologies. Personnel in library systems had to figure out on their own how to do most of the support work for these technologies.

Making this job easier was the fact that PCs (including Macs), the Windows operating system, and the Internet environment greatly lowered the technology learning curve and provided a number of development tools. The open source movement has also been a significant factor, making many more development tools available in an environment that encourages exploration. We now have the opportunity to customize general technologies to suit specific library needs. Adding to the systems librarians' pressure to customize and develop new applications is the fact that the users of library technology, both library staff and end users, have become increasingly sophisticated. They demand much more of library technology. As a result of all these changes, the library systems department is increasingly involved in developing custom solutions and creating new technologies.

None of these responsibilities—management, maintenance, and development— is mutually exclusive. One or more are often part of a system librarian's job. However, the skills needed for each type of responsibility can be very different. For example, the skills needed to maintain an existing system are relatively easy to define and are not as sophisticated as those needed to customize and develop new technologies. Development skills need a deeper understanding of the underlying technology, usually some sort of programming or scripting ability, and an enjoyment and a desire to learn and imagine new technical possibilities.

In addition to all the systems-specific responsibilities, the systems librarian is often expected to participate at a broader level in the life of the library. As a librarian, she may be expected to take on other library duties, such as providing reference services or developing collections in a particular subject area. As a department manager, she may sit on committees and contribute to planning and governance of the library as a whole. In an academic library, she may be expected to contribute to service activities and committees in both the library and the university. If she is in a faculty position, she may also be expected to conduct research and publish. While these activities may come from a systems perspective, the competencies needed for these responsibilities are generally the same as those expected of any librarian in a similar institution and are not discussed here.

Core Competencies for Systems Librarians

The responsibilities and competencies needed by the systems librarian have been studied since the late 1980s, often by analysis of position announcements. Two of the most quoted studies were conducted by Margaret Foote (1997), who studied job ads from 1990 to 1994, and by Hong Xu and Hsin-liang Chen (2000), who studied ads from 1996 and 1997. Comparing the studies conducted by Foote and by Xu and Chen is particularly interesting because they represent the state of the library systems position during the time period before and after (respectively) the World Wide Web became a major factor in libraries.

Because the data in these position announcement studies are over a decade old, I also conducted a brief analysis of positions advertised in print issues of *College & Research Library News* (*C&RL News*) from January 2006 through December 2007. However, the data from this study can only be considered a cursory summary of job characteristics. Unlike the sources used for the earlier studies, print job advertisements these days only represent the tip of the iceberg. Many announcements are very brief and expect the reader to go to the employer's Web site for a detailed job description. Because this information is usually removed after the position is filled, it is difficult to find data for a retrospective study. Also, many employers are choosing to advertise only online, so their announcements may not appear in the print listings at all. Nevertheless, the data from this brief study provide a useful snapshot of current expectations and corroborate that most of the findings from the earlier studies still hold true today.

Overall, I found 13 print advertisements for systems librarian positions. Of these, three announcements did not provide enough information to be useful, so my conclusions are based on ten advertisements. In addition, I found nine positions advertised for upper administrators who were responsible for oversight of the systems department, usually in conjunction with one or more other departments. All of these administrator positions had some sort of responsibility for trend spotting and for providing direction to the library in taking advantage of new technologies. While it is interesting to see how much systems- and technology-related management has penetrated higher levels of library administration, details from these positions are not included in my results.

Another source of data used to identify competencies for systems librarians comes from the other authors of this book. During spring 2008, I surveyed their opinions on the importance of over 50 technology competencies in four areas: general computer technology, Internet-related competencies, computer hardware peripherals, and library-related automation competencies. Appendix 3-1 includes a complete list of the competencies along with the authors' survey responses. I used the survey instrument created by Diane Neal; it is described in detail in the appendices in Chapter 2.

Finally, I've included information from a variety of other sources, two of which are included in the tables provided later in this chapter. The Association of Research Libraries (ARL) conducted several surveys of member libraries' systems departments since 1990; information from the 2002 survey is included here. I've also included information from Tom Wilson's (1998) book *The Systems Librarian*. His book, which contains extensive lists and competency descriptions, is widely referred to in the literature about systems librarianship.

Basic Competency Categories

Authors writing about systems librarianship typically group the responsibilities and skills needed for the position into several categories. These categories can provide a useful framework for defining job responsibilities and identifying competencies at their broadest level.

Foote analyzed job announcements published from 1990 to 1994. She concluded that systems librarians "must be able to work equally well with technology and with people and above all facilitate between the two" (Foote, 1997: 524). She used the following categories to organize systems position requirements (percentages represent the number of announcements she identified that referred to each category):

- Technology experience (75 percent)
- Library or systems experience (61 percent)
- Communication skills (57 percent)
- Management skills (33 percent)
- Interpersonal skills (34 percent)
- Library organization or service knowledge (19 percent) (Foote, 1997)

Xu and Chen (1999) looked at systems librarian position announcements published between 1996 and 1997. They also conducted a follow-up study that surveyed recently hired systems librarians and directors in libraries from the first study. One of the particularly useful findings in Xu and Chen's study is the different levels of importance that various types of libraries place on the skill groups. For instance, interpersonal skills were mentioned in 25 percent of the academic library ads but in only 2 percent of the public library ads (Xu and Chen, 1999). They grouped the job responsibilities listed in these announcements into the following knowledge and special skills grouping:

- Technology-related
- Management-related
- Human-related (Xu and Chen, 1999)

Tom Wilson's book *The Systems Librarian* provides an extensive discussion of responsibilities and skills for systems librarians using the following groups:

- Library
- Library automation
- Computing
- Networking
- Management
- General
- Qualities, approaches, and attitudes (Wilson, 1998)

It is clear from these lists that technology is only one category of responsibilities or competencies that systems librarians need. People- and management-related skills are also important. Wilson (1998: 21) states that the position "represents a blend of library science, computer operations, and management." Although the categories come from literature from the late 1990s, these types of abilities are still commonly referred to in more recent sources. These seem to form the "classics" that have enduring value.

Because the dividing line between job responsibilities and personal skills can be fluid and hard to define, I've ignored the distinction in the competency lists that follow. Based on the categories used thus far, I have grouped systems librarian competencies into five areas:

- Technology
- Library
- Management
- Interpersonal
- Personal characteristics

Figures 3-1 to 3-7 list the responsibilities and skills identified in some of the articles and books on systems librarians. Percentages are included for those studies and surveys that quantified the responses or indicated the amount of importance placed on specific skills. For instance, the percentage may represent the number of employers listing that requirement in a position announcement or the number of survey respondents who rated the skill highly. Where detailed information is not available, a simple "X" indicates that the author believed this was a desirable skill for systems librarians.

Technology Competencies

Technology competency is key to the systems librarian, but it is also one of the most complex set of competencies to describe. I've tried to list the most relevant technology competencies for today, but it is not a comprehensive list and I will undoubtedly have missed some. Also, it is important to bear in mind that appropriate competencies are different for each position. Specific technologies in the list may quickly become dated, but the basic types of technology functions should continue to be relevant for some time to come.

Library-Specific Technologies

The core technology for libraries is the ILS. Traditionally, this technology has been the raison d'être for the systems librarian's position. The ILS continues to play a very important role in most systems librarians' jobs but it is rare these days to be the only or even the most important responsibility. It is also worth noting that the level of ILS support can vary greatly from basic maintenance (e.g., backup, update, and troubleshooting) to function-specific processes (e.g., defining loan rules, downloading bibliographic records) to customization and programming (e.g., creating scripts to automate processes, setting up load tables). It is in supporting the ILS that most authors mention the usefulness of a library background.

Library-specific technologies include more than the ILS and are a growing area of responsibility. Additional software is often needed to handle a variety of other library processes. Examples include bibliographic utilities such as OCLC, interlibrary loan (e.g., ILLiad), electronic reserves systems (e.g., ERes), link resolvers (e.g., SFX, ArticleLinker), and federated search tools (e.g., MetaLib, WebFeat). Most of these additional technologies need to work with the ILS, but integrating these disparate systems is often complex and a skill in and of itself. Some of these technologies involve rather large systems that may be supported outside the systems department. For example, acquisitions or serials staff may oversee the electronic resource management system, or a new department may be formed for digitization projects or for the institutional repository system. In addition, the library may be part of a consortium and share technology that needs to work with local systems and processes. Interestingly, these non-ILS library technologies are often not mentioned, at least in any detail, in the systems librarian literature.

Library-related technology skills go beyond actual computer systems to include knowledge of relevant protocols and standards and an understanding of information science theories and practices. Mark Jordan (2003), in his article "The Self-education of Systems Librarians," provides a good overview of some of these ancillary areas of knowledge, including XML, metadata (MODS, METS, OAI-PMH, and Dublin Core), search and retrieval protocols (z39.50 and XML-based standards), and messaging protocols (ISO ILL, NCIP, SOAP). Figure 3-1 shows the library-related technology competencies expected of systems librarians.

Computer, Server, and Network Technologies

Computer knowledge, from desktop systems to servers and networks, is one of the most commonly required competencies for systems librarians (see Figure 3-2).

Figure 3-1. Library Technology Competencies

LIBRARY TECHNOLOGY	FOOTE (1997)	WILSON (1998)	XU AND CHEN (1999)	MUIR AND LIM (2002)	C&RL* (2006–2007)	AUTHOR SURVEY (2008)
Integrated library system	82%	X	95%	91%	90%	100%
Function-specific (ILL, OCLC, e-reserve)			X			75%
Digitization					20%	75%
Electronic resource management					20%	63%

*College & Research Libraries News

Responsibility for "computers" seems obvious, but what is included is not always clear. Is anything with a computer attached to it part of systems' responsibilities? After a recent building project at my library, our systems department was surprised to find itself responsible for the microform readers, university ID card system, and the public announcement system all because they have computers attached. For the purposes of this chapter, computer knowledge includes knowledge of networks, telecommunications, the Internet, operating systems, system installation, hardware, and microcomputer applications. In addition, peripherals, such as printers and bar-code scanners, may be part of systems' responsibility. Typical equipment responsibilities include procuring new systems, managing warranties and maintenance contracts, troubleshooting problems, and performing upgrades. The actual amount of physical repair and customization of computers is less than it has been in the past thanks to more reliable equipment and more inexpensive computers that are often easier to replace than repair.

At a 2006 meeting of the Heads of Library Technology (HoLT) interest group, the one technology that all 22 of the systems managers around the table agreed their departments should and do support was desktop computers (Thompson, 2007). Desktop systems include both the computer hardware and the software applications on personal computers. At the software level, the participants' systems departments differed as to which applications were supported. Most commonly supported were library-related applications, and many also supported productivity applications such as Microsoft Office. Less commonly supported were multimedia, digitization, and course management or other specialized applications. Related to desktop support were responsibilities for troubleshooting, security, software license control, and print management systems. However, because this chapter is concerned with "systems librarian" competencies it is important to note that responsibility for supporting these technologies often fell to other, non-librarian, staff in the systems department.

Figure 3-2. Computer Technology Competencies

COMPUTER TECHNOLOGY	FOOTE (1997)	WILSON (1998)	XU AND CHEN (1999)	MUIR AND LIM (2002)	C&RL* (2006– 2007)	AUTHOR SURVEY (2008)
Desktop support	67%	X	20%	100%	60%	97%
Network/server support	27%	X	70%	100%	30%	90%
Operating system			62%			100%
Installation and troubleshooting		X	39%			100%

*College & Research Libraries News

Some of the most sophisticated systems work revolves around the care and feeding of the network and server technologies. Key is the level of responsibility that library systems itself has for the network. Often the network server and physical infrastructure are controlled by the broader organization's IT department. The parent IT department may also control enterprise systems such as e-mail. Security, reliability, and access issues are particularly important for network and server technologies. Support for these systems often requires a fairly sophisticated level of technology competence. As a result, these technologies may be allocated to specialized staff other than the systems librarian. Nevertheless, systems librarians are expected to understand the principles if not the day-to-day operation of server and network technologies.

Web Technologies

The one technology area that has changed most over time is support for the library's Web site. This responsibility often didn't appear in the systems librarian's responsibilities in the 1990s, when many of the systems librarian job studies were done. It was also not uncommon for this technology to evolve in other areas of the library, such as reference, particularly early in its development. Nevertheless, at least some knowledge of the Web is now considered an essential skill for any systems librarian (see Figure 3-3).

Just what constitutes appropriate Web knowledge, however, can be very different from one library to the next. It is important to realize that there are actually several types of Web work that require different competencies. The World Organization of Webmasters (WOW, accessed 2008) identifies three areas of specialization: Web design, which creates images and designs; Web development, which creates Web site structure and interactivity; and Web site administration, which includes responsibility for the hardware and software infrastructure supporting Internet communications. Certainly the ability to create Web pages and understand HTML at some level should be required for anyone in the systems field. In Figure 3-3, I

91

Figure 3-3. Web Technology Competencies

WEB TECHNOLOGY	FOOTE (1997)	WILSON (1998)	XU AND CHEN (1999)	MUIR AND LIM (2002)	C&RL* (2006– 2007)	AUTHOR SURVEY (2008)
Internet	10%	X	30%			85%
Web (page editing)			27%	94%	50%	72%
Web 2.0 (blogs, wikis)						85%
Web techniques (XML, programming)		X	20%			75%
Web soft skills (usability, evaluation)						75%

College & Research Libraries News

have included both "Internet" and "Web" because some authors distinguished between the two terms. Interestingly, more of the early authors refer to the "Internet," whereas later authors appear to use the "Web" to describe what seem to be similar skills. Later authors who do refer to the Internet are usually clear that it is the telecommunication protocols to which they are referring.

The Web is one of the most exciting and dynamic technologies in the library. The possibilities are constantly growing and changing beyond the basic skills to create a Web page that we're familiar with. Under the rubric "Web 2.0" lie a number of technologies that can significantly enhance library services and interactions with users. These technologies include blogs, wikis, podcasts, and RSS. In the results of my author survey, it is notable that almost all of these Web 2.0 technologies are rated higher than the more traditional Web skills. I would hope any systems librarian would also meet the requirements given for the Librarian 2.0 described in Chapter 1, which revolve around Web 2.0 technology. If anyone is spotting trends and advocating for new technologies in the library, it should be the systems librarian no matter what her portfolio. The Web also has a number of related "soft" skills, including user studies and usability testing, ADA accessibility, and various legal and ethical considerations. Rhyno (2003) details how Web technologies have impacted the role of the systems librarian. She now needs to use a wide variety of mainstream Web technologies, including XML, scripting, link resolvers, and Web services, to develop library-specific applications and integrate local and remote resources into the library's Web offerings.

And There's More . . .

A wide variety of technologies fall outside of the basic categories discussed, including multimedia, digitization, databases, and instructional technologies, to name a few (see Figure 3-4). These can require quite a sophisticated level of technical knowledge, but responsibility for maintaining and developing these technologies may or may not fall within the purview of the systems librarian. Like the Web 2.0 technologies, it is worth tracking current trends and determining which are appropriate for your library and whether responsibility for them will be part of the systems librarian's portfolio.

Systems librarians also should add development skills to their portfolio. The need to know programming faded away with the advent of vendor-supported turnkey library systems, but it has come roaring back over the past few years. The Web and open source software movement have encouraged building and customizing applications and have provided a number of tools to facilitate this development. Xu and Chen (2000), in their survey of newly hired systems librarians, found that, while it was usually not mentioned in the job ads, new systems librarians reported frequently having programming responsibilities (half of academic and a third of public library positions). Scripting languages, such as JavaScript, Perl, and PHP, are particularly accessible to library technologists, because they have a lower learning curve than traditional programming languages and are often available at no cost. Database knowledge, particularly SQL, is very desirable and often works together with other development tools such as PHP. Thanks to the open source movement and to standards such as OpenURL, application programming interfaces (APIs), and Web services such as Google gadgets, libraries can access and customize applications at a level unheard of only a few years ago.

Library Science Competencies

It is not clear how critical traditional library knowledge is regarded for the systems librarian position. It is often not listed directly; however, many authors mention the

Figure 3-4. Other Technology Competencies						
OTHER TECHNOLOGY	FOOTE (1997)	WILSON (1998)	XU AND CHEN (1999)	MUIR AND LIM (2002)	C&RL* (2006–2007)	AUTHOR SURVEY (2008)
Programming/scripting		X	14%		40%	66%
Database design		X			20%	72%
Digitization/imaging			1%	93%	20%	75%
Standards (Z39.50, SGML), and ADA			5%			81%
Systems design/projects		X		83%		

Note: Fifty-eight percent of recent hires in Xu and Chen's (2000) follow-up study reported programming duties.
College & Research Libraries News

93

benefits of understanding the library and its operations in carrying out systems work. It may also be that some degree of library knowledge is assumed from a systems "librarian." However, a number of position announcements do explicitly specify experience working in libraries, knowledge of the library's mission, and commitment to library service (see Figure 3-5). Wilson (1998: 10) stated that "In an ideal environment, systems librarians would have a solid understanding of the operations of most, if not all, units within libraries. . . ." A systems librarian often must know some library science to be viewed as a colleague at a professional level.

General knowledge of library functions such as cataloging and reference can be very useful for designing and supporting technology to meet library needs. Cortez, Dutta, and Kazlauskas (2004: 137) point out that the interviewing skills librarians learn as part of the reference interview's information negotiation process are extremely valuable for systems librarians to be able to ask the right questions to clarify users' expectations and requirements when developing technical projects. Cataloging teaches critical skills in information organization, bibliographic data structures, and record formats. Lessons learned in areas such as information literacy, Web usability studies, and information architecture can improve the systems librarian's understanding of how users search for, evaluate, and use information. This can be invaluable for developing effective user interfaces. Finally, a library background can assist in researching and evaluating solutions to technical problems.

Whether it is learned from cataloging or from some library or information science coursework, the systems librarian should be knowledgeable about basic protocols and infrastructures used by library-specific technologies. In particular, knowledge of the various bibliographic utilities and format protocols is important, including MARC and metadata standards. Knowledge of these protocols is often predicated on an understanding of the underlying information structures and bibliographic formats used in the organization of information in libraries. Wilson (1998) lists a variety of information science "theoretical" requirements, including library-specific data structures, knowledge organization and classification, information retrieval and access technologies, database design, and information policies.

Aside from knowing traditional library functions to better perform systems work, some positions, especially in smaller libraries, combine the systems librarian function with other library duties—most commonly reference. Systems librarians may also value the opportunity to work in the "real world" in order to see firsthand how well the library's technology actually meets the needs of users and staff. Foote (1997) found that nonsystems duties were included in a small number of ads, with about 10 percent expecting reference or bibliographic instruction work, 8 percent collection development, and 3 percent cataloging. In my brief study of systems positions, 40 percent expected some sort of reference knowledge. About the same number also expected either teaching ability or support for instructional technology. Several positions also expected some collection development. Because this group of position announcements came from a publication aimed at academic libraries,

Figure 3-5. Library Competencies

LIBRARY	FOOTE (1997)	WILSON (1998)	XU AND CHEN (1999)	C&RL* (2006–2007)
Master of library science desired	62%	X	66%	80%
Knowledge of library	19%	X		30%
Library experience	61%	X	62%	50%
Bibliographic utilities		X	29%	
Reference/instruction	12%			40%
Collection development	8%			20%
Cataloging/metadata	3%	X	16%	
*College & Research Libraries News				

College & Research Libraries News, the ability to meet tenure requirements, particularly research and publication, was mentioned in 40 percent of the ads.

Management Competencies

Systems librarians are expected to possess a number of management skills. While this is often because she is responsible for managing the systems department, even systems librarians without departmental management responsibilities are usually involved in management-related activities such as procurement, coordination, and project management. Four types of management activities are frequently expected of systems librarians: supervision, planning, coordination, and leadership.

Supervision

Systems librarians who are department heads usually supervise the other technical staff in the department. Muir's 2002 ARL survey found that, at least among research libraries, the sizes of systems departments are growing and can have from 4 to 30 employees. With the breadth of technologies used in libraries today, systems librarians may find that effectively managing a team of experts is a more valuable skill than attempting to master all aspects of the technologies themselves. However, systems managers who come from a library background may find that supervising technical personnel can be different from managing other, more traditional, library personnel. Brian and Doralyn Rossmann (2005) discuss the psychology of "techies" versus the psychology of employees in traditional library departments. Among other things, IT personnel tend to be more analytical and logical, practical, and somewhat inflexible in their approach, and they are often socially reserved. The level of the systems librarian's technical knowledge can be a factor, because techies tend to respect people with real technology know-how, although they may be more accepting of people who admit that they don't know.

Planning

A large amount of the systems librarian's duties revolves around planning, both for her department and for technology in the library in general. In Xu and Chen's (2000) follow-up study, they found that all of the newly hired systems librarians were involved in planning. Almost 90 percent were involved in purchasing decisions, although this was an area usually not mentioned in the ads. All of the authors in this book have stated that library technology planning is important. Planning ranges from developing policies and procedures to prioritizing work within the department to developing strategic, long-range plans. Creating a formal technology plan is perhaps the most critical responsibility of the systems librarian. The technology plan documents the existing state of technology in the library, outlines the role or purpose of technology in meeting library goals, and lays out an approach to future growth.

Second to personnel and collections costs, technology is likely to be a significant part of the library's budget. In addition to ongoing repair and replacement of existing technology, the systems librarian should include in her technology planning how to acquire large new technologies or make major upgrades to existing technology. Large-scale technology procurements require further skills, including understanding how to put together a formal request for proposal (RFP).

Project management is a special kind of planning and management competency that is important for successful development of new technology initiatives. It may involve many of the management elements discussed in this chapter but applied on a one-time project scale. Project management responsibilities include selecting appropriate personnel to work on the project, determining the goal of the project, identifying resources—including funding—needed to carry out the project, and, of course, outlining the steps or tasks required to accomplish the project. Project management is increasingly recognized as a crucial skill that most systems personnel, not just department heads, should have. Benefits include the ability to manage large (or small) projects and get them done within the expected time and avoid scope creep.

Coordination

It is critical that the systems librarian be able to work effectively with units and personnel outside the systems department. Because of the interrelated nature of systems work, technology may cut across several organizational units or involve personnel in other areas of the library, the broader organization's IT department, external vendors, consortium, and so forth. It is often important not to work on systems projects in isolation. For instance, systems often maintains the ILS that stores the bibliographic records that catalogers create, that reference librarians help users search for, and that circulation clerks use to track who borrowed which book. While it's possible for the systems librarian to change the cataloging module, the search interface, or the loan rule tables without consulting the various departments involved, it is not a very wise or constructive approach. On the other hand, requests from one of these other departments to change something such as the search interface can impact work in another area of the library, and it can impact library users. Rather than simply responding to independent requests, systems librarians should be able to see these connections and work proactively with all the various library units involved to ensure that the entire system works together.

Leadership/Change Agent

The systems librarian is usually expected to lead the library's technology initiatives (see Figure 3-6). She is responsible for spotting technology trends and understanding their potential impacts on library processes. She represents the technology needs not just inside the library, but also outside—to the larger parent organization, consortiums in which the library participates, and vendors or external IT departments. What's more, she is responsible for advocating for emerging technology and helping move her library into the future. In my brief look at *C&RL* position announcements in 2006 and 2007, I found that 80 percent of the ads described leadership responsibilities and attributes, with descriptions such as "future-oriented leadership," "vision and leadership" and "anticipating future needs and trends."

Interpersonal Competencies

> The systems librarian is a unique breed. The position requires someone who not only understands libraries and computers but someone who can put both fields into context.
>
> —Ingersoll and Culshaw (2004: 25)

Historically the systems librarian' mission, according to Morgan (1999: 36), was to "serve and protect" the library's automation system. In other words, it was the

Figure 3-6. Management Competencies				
MANAGEMENT	**FOOTE (1997)**	**WILSON (1998)**	**XU AND CHEN (1999)**	**C&RL* (2006–2007)**
Supervision/dept. head	27%	X	48%	50%
Planning	33%	X	78%	60%
Coordination	68%	X	57%	30%
Leadership/change agent				80%
College & Research Libraries News				

computer rather than library staff or end user that was seen as the primary duty of the systems librarian. When computers were hidden away in back rooms and were difficult to use, the systems career typically attracted people who didn't have a lot of people skills. Today this is no longer the case. Morgan (1999: 37) argues that systems administrators need to "communicate with the people they serve and learn what their needs are." The literature and potential employers agree. Almost every advertisement for systems librarians in my recent review listed interpersonal skills, sometimes even if they did not specify technical skills. The categories listed in Figure 3-7 are some of the most commonly required interpersonal skills, although often just the term *interpersonal* is used to imply at least part of this range of skills (where this is the case in the sources used for Figure 3-7, I combined the collaboration and liaison category). Michelle Robertson's Chapter 5 is also a good resource for social and communication competencies needed by systems librarians, particularly in the small library environment.

Communication

The first and most basic interpersonal skill is effective communication. It is the foundation on which other interpersonal skills are built. Often both oral and written methods of communication are specified. Communication is critical for the systems librarian to function effectively in the one-on-one and group activities that form so much of her work. Unlike conventional programmers, systems engineers, or some of the other IT people, the systems librarian rarely works alone but must constantly communicate with other people to accomplish her work. In order to determine the needs of users and departmental staff in the library, it is particularly useful to have prior training in conducting reference interviews—listening to the requestors' objectives and helping them describe what they really need.

When providing support, it is important to be careful not to intimidate the user. The systems librarian should actively listen to the user's problems and needs and keep the user informed on the resolution process. She should provide on-the-spot

Figure 3-7. Interpersonal Competencies

INTERPERSONAL	FOOTE (1997)	WILSON (1998)	XU AND CHEN (1999)	C&RL* (2006–2007)
Communication	27%	X	48%	50%
Collaboration	34%	X	25%	40%
Liaison				
Training	59%	X	64%	30%
*College & Research Libraries News				

training as needed or identify other sources of training (formal or informal) where appropriate. Her ultimate goal is to empower the end user.

Collaboration and Teamwork

Beyond the basic communication level, the systems librarian needs to collaborate with colleagues in and out of the library—share solutions, identify needs, solve problems, negotiate funding for new purchases, and so forth. Computer technology usually doesn't operate in isolation. The systems librarian needs to talk to vendors to purchase, configure, update, and maintain equipment and applications, including determining appropriate agreements. She needs to know who manages various parts of the network and work with other departments, possibly not in the library, that are responsible for network infrastructure, security, and so forth. She needs to be able to collaborate and communicate with staff and end users to solve problems, configure systems appropriately, and plan new advances.

It is very important to understand how the library works. What are the needs and priorities of the various functions in the library? Politically, who is responsible for what, and who is best to work with to accomplish tasks? Many libraries, especially academic libraries, arrive at decisions using a collaborative process. The systems librarian frequently works with others in a team environment to accomplish her work. It is not always the most technologically adept colleagues who are needed on project teams; sometimes a management or function-specific viewpoint is just as valuable (Thompson, 1999). She needs to speak in the language of each. Project teams benefit from multiple skills that other team members bring to the table. A unique reality for many systems librarians is the need to accomplish projects using staff who are not necessarily under her direct management control. Planning and carrying out cross-departmental projects requires skills in negotiation, organization, and priority setting with the goal to obtain buy-in from all involved.

Liaison

A major duty of the systems librarian is to serve as a liaison between the library and the technical experts, often outside the library. One of the earliest recognized interpersonal skills was for the systems librarian to act as an intermediary between regular library staff and IT techies. She needs to translate technology terms and realities to library staff and end users as well as interpret the library's needs and priorities to vendors and other technology providers.

In my cursory study of position announcements, liaison skills were mentioned less often in current position descriptions than in earlier ones. Perhaps this is due to a growth in comfort and sophistication in using technology. However, I believe there is an increasing need for a new kind of liaison relationship, one that helps the library relate existing technologies and ways of doing things to new, emerging technologies. Almost all the announcements I examined (see Figure 3-6) were

99

looking for the ability to identify emerging technologies and advocate or help the library understand their significance.

Training

It is often the role of the systems librarian to identify what technical skills are needed both within the systems department and in the rest of the library and then to provide training. The ability to teach technology effectively requires skills beyond knowledge of the technology itself. Learners are often intimidated by the technology and embarrassed by their lack of knowledge, so it is important that the trainer be able to create a comfortable atmosphere in which it is safe to express ignorance and try new things. The systems librarian should be able to break learning tasks down into digestible units and explain the technology in the staff's language.

While training may in some ways seem ancillary to the systems librarian's other duties, anecdotally it's been shown that a higher staff knowledge and comfort with technology can significantly reduce and improve the systems department's support efforts. Managers should encourage and support IT skills across the library. The less skilled library staff are in general, the harder it is for them to help systems personnel identify problems and the more time it takes for the systems department to solve them. Of course, technology proficiency in regular staff also increases effective use of technology by the library.

Training is a very special skill, and to some extent a great trainer is "born," not "created." Enhancing the technology or management skills of a really good trainer may be easier than taking a general technology librarian and adding the training component. Donna Hirst (e-mail communication, June 4, 2008) points out that this area more than most highlights that the systems librarian can't be all things to all people.

Attributes

Many discussions of skills and competencies for systems librarians go beyond the description of specific job skills to identifying desirable attributes and personal characteristics. The idea is that these traits predict an individual's ability to adapt to changing job requirements—certainly a vital consideration in a dynamic field like library systems. While less precise than a list of specific skills, these "soft" skills represent the essence of those personality traits and attributes important for success today and in the future. Roy Tennant (1998: 102) has one of the most often-quoted list of personality traits for digital librarians:

- Capacity to learn consistently and quickly
- Flexibility
- Innate skepticism
- Propensity to take risks
- Abiding public service perspective

- Good interpersonal skills to work well with others
- Skill at enabling and fostering change
- Capacity for and desire to work independently

It is notable that, while Tennant's list is now a decade old, it remains true today, suggesting that systems professionals with these attributes will also hold up well in the long run. A number of other authors recognize the value of soft skills. Muir and Lim (2002) recommend that systems staff need to remain flexible, knowledgeable, and open to change. Wilson (1998) has another excellent list of qualities that contribute to the success of the systems librarian that includes attributes such as sound judgment, persistence, perspective switching, resiliency, and technical aptitude. Most of the position announcements I reviewed included attributes as well as specific skills and responsibilities, which indicates employers also recognize their importance. Some of the attributes mentioned in these announcements included analytical skills, problem-solving and critical thinking abilities; organizational skills; the ability to multitask and set priorities; and creativity in various contexts. One of the most significant attributes mentioned over and over was vision—the ability to serve as a change agent, providing leadership and an idea of where the library should go next in technology. Wilson (1998) also mentions "fire in the belly," which seems to get at this ability to inspire and influence others.

When I think of these attributes, I imagine someone able to surf each new wave—skillful enough to keep her balance and use the power of the existing technology while keeping a weather eye out for the next big technology wave.

Conclusion

Systems librarianship has grown into a specialty with broad technology responsibilities and a role in library decision making. History has shown that the position has expanded from its original focus on the ILS to a broad range of modern technologies and from maintenance responsibilities to development of customized and unique solutions. The systems librarian's role has evolved from that of support technician to manager of systems operations and a visionary library leader.

While there does appear to be a common set of core technology competencies, including the ILS, desktop support, and advanced Web technologies, there is a much larger set of competency needs that vary considerably from library to library. Each job more or less defines a unique position, and the local environment determines the skills and competencies needed. For example, a systems librarian in a smaller library will probably be less specialized than one in a larger library. Or, if the library is embarking on implementing new technologies, such as an electronic resource management system or Web 2.0 initiatives, her responsibilities will be different from one in a library that is not implementing those technologies or that puts the responsibilities in a different unit of the library.

Technology competency expectations also depend on the systems librarian's role. A department manager may need only a basic level of knowledge of a wide range of technologies with just a few areas in which she is a technical expert. A more hands-on position requires a much deeper level of technical competencies, including development and programming skills. Nevertheless, it remains important for all systems librarians to understand the theoretical underpinnings of library science and information structures as well as computer science.

I believe a critical difference between library systems and other types of IT support organizations is the role of the systems librarian. She is a member of the library rather than an external service provider. She has the opportunity to directly influence library technology services through her intimate understanding of the library mission and through her ability to anticipate future technology capabilities. She must be able to work in a team environment, often coordinating the work of others over whom she has little direct control. As a result, competencies key to her success include communication and interpersonal skills, and, indeed, these are the most commonly cited requirements in advertisements for this position.

Although it began with an expectation of superior technical knowledge, the systems librarian has evolved into a position that also requires good people skills and knowledge of the mission of the library. There is every reason to expect that the systems librarian will continue to be a position defined as much by vision and leadership as by technical competence.

102

References

Chan, Graham K.L. 1987. "The Systems Librarian." In *Personnel Management in Polytechnic Libraries*, edited by D.H. Revill. Aldershot, England: Gower: 175–199.

Childers, Scott. 2003 "Computer Literacy: Necessity or Buzzword?" *Information Technology and Libraries* 22, no. 3 (September): 100–104.

Cortez, Edwin M., Sanjay K. Dutta, and Edward John Kazlauskas. 2004. "What the Library and Information Professional Can Learn from the Information Technology and Project Management Areas." *Portal: Libraries and the Academy* 4, no. 1: 131–144.

Foote, Margaret. 1997. "The Systems Librarian in U.S. Academic Libraries: A Survey of Announcements from *College & Research Libraries News*, 1990–1994." *College & Research Libraries News* 58, no. 6 (November): 517–526.

Gordon, Rachel Singer. 2001. "A Course in Accidental Systems Librarianship." *Computers in Libraries* 21, no. 10 (November/December): 24–28.

Gordon, Rachel Singer. 2003. *The Accidental Systems Librarian*. Medford, NJ: Information Today.

Ingersoll, Patricia and John Culshaw. 2004. *Managing Information Technology: A Handbook for Systems Librarians*. Westport, CT: Libraries Unlimited.

Jordan, Mark. 2003. "The Self-Education of Systems Librarians." *Library Hi Tech* 21, no. 3 (2003): 273–279.

Lavagnino, Merri Beth. 1997. "Networking and the Role of the Academic Systems Librarian: An Evolutionary Perspective." *College & Research Libraries News* 58, no. 3 (May): 217–231.

Morgan, Eric Lease. 1999. "Systems Administration Requires People Skills." *Computers in Libraries* 19, no. 3 (March): 36–37.

Morgan, Eric Lease. "Technical Skills of Librarianship." *LITA Blog* (August 7, 2005). Available: http://litablog.org/2005/08/07/technical-skills-of-librarianship/ (accessed May 30, 2008).

Muir, Scott P., Comp. 1995. *Library Systems Office Organization. SPEC Kit 211.* Washington, DC: Association of Research Libraries.

Muir, Scott P. and Adriene Lim, Comp. 2002. *Library Systems Office Organization. SPEC Kit 271.* Washington, DC: Association of Research Libraries.

Rhyno, Arthur. 2003. "From Library Systems to Mainstream Software: How Web Technologies Are Changing the Role of the Systems Librarian." *Library Hi Tech* 21, no. 3: 289–296.

Ross, Mary and Dan Marmion. 2000. "Systems Librarians and the Client/Server Environment." *Library Hi Tech* 18, no. 2: 151–157.

Rossmann, Brian and Doralyn Rossmann. 2005. "Communication with Library Systems Support Personnel: Models for Success." *Library Philosophy and Practice* 7, no. 2 (Spring). Available: www.webpages.uidaho.edu/~mbolin/rossmann.htm (accessed May 30, 2008)

Tennant, Roy. 1998. "The Most Important Management Decision: Hiring Staff for the New Millennium." *Library Journal.com* (February 15). Available: www.libraryjournal.com/article/CA156490.html (accessed May 30, 2008).

Thompson, Susan. 1999. "Riding into Uncharted Territory: The New Systems Librarian." *Computers in Libraries* 19, no. 3 (March): 14–20.

Thompson, Susan. 2005. "LITA Heads of Library Technology Interest Group." *Technical Services Quarterly* 23, no. 1: 71–75.

Thompson, Susan. 2007. "Strategies for Managing Desktop Support." *Technical Services Quarterly* 24, no. 4: 77–84.

Wasserman, Paul. 1965. *Observations on the Applications of Machines in Administration of College and University Libraries.* Detroit: Gale Research.

Wilson, Thomas Carl. 1998. *The Systems Librarian: Designing Roles, Defining Skills.* Chicago: American Library Association.

World Organization of Webmasters. "Get WOW Certified." Available: www.webprofessionals.org/certification/ (accessed May 21, 2008).

Xu, Hong and Hsin-liang Chen. 1999. "What Do Employers Expect? The Educating Systems Librarian Research Project 1." *The Electronic Library* 17, no. 3 (June): 171–179.

Xu, Hong and Hsin-liang Chen. 2000. "Whom Do Employers Actually Hire? The Educating Systems Librarian Research Project 2." *The Electronic Library* 18, no. 3: 171–182.

Appendix 3-1. Survey of the Importance of Technology Competencies for Systems Librarians

GENERAL TECHNOLOGY COMPETENCIES	NOT AT ALL IMPORTANT	NOT VERY IMPORTANT	SOMEWHAT IMPORTANT	VERY IMPORTANT	RATING AVERAGE
Parts of a computer and their function (CPU, hard drive, RAM)	0%	0%	0%	**100%**	4.00
Computer operating systems (Microsoft Windows, Mac OS)	0%	0%	0%	**100%**	4.00
Office productivity software (Word, Excel, PowerPoint)	0%	0%	0%	**100%**	4.00
Computer security (antivirus, anti-spyware software)	0%	0%	0%	**100%**	4.00
Basic PC troubleshooting (determining why the printer won't print, why a computer locked up, etc.)	0%	0%	0%	**100%**	4.00
Advanced PC troubleshooting and maintenance (fixing or replacing hardware, installing software)	0%	0%	**50%**	**50%**	3.50
Wired and/or wireless networking configuration and troubleshooting	0%	0%	**50%**	**50%**	3.50
Special needs/adaptive technologies for ADA patrons (JAWS, ZoomText)	0%	17%	**33%**	**50%**	3.33
Server administration (Web servers, ILS servers, network drives)	0%	17%	**33%**	**50%**	3.33
Database construction and maintenance (Access, MySQL)	17%	0%	**50%**	**33%**	3.00
Digitizing/scanning of printed resources	0%	**33%**	**33%**	33%	3.00
Photo editing/digital imaging software (Photoshop)	0%	33%	**67%**	0%	2.67
Scripting languages (Perl, PHP, JavaScript)	0%	33%	**67%**	0%	2.67
Gaming software (Second Life, instructional games)	17%	50%	33%	0%	2.17
Object-oriented programming languages (Visual Basic, Java)	17%	67%	17%	0%	2.00
Total rated important by at least 60% of respondents: 13 of 15					

(Cont'd.)

104

Appendix 3-1. Survey of the Importance of Technology Competencies for Systems Librarians *(Continued)*

INTERNET-RELATED COMPETENCIES	NOT AT ALL IMPORTANT	NOT VERY IMPORTANT	SOMEWHAT IMPORTANT	VERY IMPORTANT	RATING AVERAGE
Blogs	0%	0%	**17%**	**83%**	3.83
RSS	0%	0%	**33%**	**67%**	3.67
Wikis	0%	17%	**17%**	**67%**	3.50
Electronic database searching (e.g., using complex Boolean searches in EBSCO databases)	0%	17%	**50%**	33%	3.17
Evaluating Web sites for validity, authority, etc.	0%	17%	**50%**	33%	3.17
Internet protocols (HTTP, FTP, SMTP)	17%	0%	**33%**	**50%**	3.17
Podcasting	0%	0%	**83%**	17%	3.17
Social networking sites (MySpace, Facebook)	0%	0%	**83%**	17%	3.17
XML	0%	0%	**83%**	17%	3.17
Web page creation with FrontPage or Dreamweaver	0%	33%	**33%**	33%	3.00
Web page creation with hand-coded XHTML and CSS	0%	33%	**33%**	33%	3.00
Online metadata schemas (Dublin Core, EAD)	0%	0%	**100%**	0%	3.00
Virtual reference service using instant messaging or a product such as QuestionPoint	0%	0%	**100%**	0%	3.00
Creating online information literacy tutorials	17%	33%	17%	33%	2.67
Thin clients	0%	50%	50%	0%	2.50
Total rated important by at least 60% of respondents: 13 of 15					

HARDWARE PERIPHERALS COMPETENCIES	NOT AT ALL IMPORTANT	NOT VERY IMPORTANT	SOMEWHAT IMPORTANT	VERY IMPORTANT	RATING AVERAGE
Office printers	0%	0%	0%	**100%**	4.00
USB drives	0%	0%	0%	**100%**	4.00
Bar-code scanners	0%	0%	**17%**	**83%**	3.83
CD/DVD writable media	0%	0%	**17%**	**83%**	3.83

105

(Cont'd.)

Appendix 3-1. Survey of the Importance of Technology Competencies for Systems Librarians *(Continued)*

Hardware Peripherals Competencies	Not at all Important	Not Very Important	Somewhat Important	Very Important	Rating Average
Color printers	0%	0%	**33%**	**67%**	3.67
Projectors	0%	17%	0%	**83%**	3.67
Digitization scanners	0%	0%	**50%**	**50%**	3.50
Digital cameras	17%	0%	**50%**	**33%**	3.00
Pay-for-print printers	0%	33%	**50%**	17%	2.83
Digital camcorders	17%	17%	**67%**	0%	2.50
MP3 players (iPod, Zune)	17%	17%	**67%**	0%	2.50
Personal digital assistants (Palm, pocket PCs)	0%	50%	50%	0%	2.50
e-Book readers	0%	67%	33%	0%	2.33
SmartBoards	17%	33%	50%	0%	2.33
Tablet PCs	17%	33%	50%	0%	2.33
Total rated important by at least 60% of respondents: 11 of 15					

Library Technology Competencies	Not at all Important	Not Very Important	Somewhat Important	Very Important	Rating Average
Integrated library systems (Voyager, Horizon, Innovative Millennium)	0%	0%	**17%**	**83%**	3.83
Library technology planning	0%	0%	**17%**	**83%**	3.83
Federated search tools (WebFeat, MetaLib)	0%	0%	**33%**	**67%**	3.67
Link resolvers (SFX, ArticleLinker)	0%	0%	**33%**	**67%**	3.67
Request for Proposal (RFP) writing for purchasing technology products	0%	0%	**50%**	**50%**	3.50
Electronic resource management (Verde, Innovative ERM)	0%	0%	**67%**	**33%**	3.33
Institutional repository software (DSpace, EPrints)	0%	0%	**67%**	**33%**	3.33
Interlibrary loan management (ILLiad, Ariel)	0%	17%	**50%**	**33%**	3.17
Digital asset management (Digitool, ResourceSpace)	0%	17%	**50%**	**33%**	3.17

(Cont'd.)

Appendix 3-1. Survey of the Importance of Technology Competencies for Systems Librarians *(Continued)*

Library Technology Competencies	Not at all Important	Not Very Important	Somewhat Important	Very Important	Rating Average
Public access systems (PC reservation software, printing control software such as GoPrint or Pharos, filtering software)	0%	33%	**33%**	**33%**	3.00
RFID/self-check hardware and software	0%	33%	**33%**	**33%**	3.00
Magnetic bar-coding hardware and software	0%	33%	**50%**	**17%**	2.83
Total rated important by at least 60% of respondents: 12 (all)					

Note: The survey respondents consisted of the eight authors of this book, who are all managers of library technology departments. Respondents were asked the following question: How important do you think it is for systems librarians and heads of library technology to possess the following technology competencies? Boldface indicates competencies ranked high in importance.

Chapter 4

Core Competencies for Non-Librarian Systems Managers

Kevin Herrera

Overview

Library systems departments can vary greatly in key areas such as number of staff, local expertise, and variety of technologies supported. These factors make the system manager's responsibilities essentially unique in each library. With widely varying duties, there is no single list of competencies that forms a clearly defined, one-size-fits-all skill set for every systems manager position. While a master's degree in library science (MLS) is a traditional job requirement for the position, it is widely acknowledged that MLS programs do not teach all of the skills necessary to be an effective systems manager. In fact, non-librarians have been fulfilling the systems manager position quite successfully for many years. Although there is no definitive list of competencies, many systems positions will share similar responsibilities; librarians and non-librarians alike will face many of the same challenges and need many of the same skills. This chapter explores competencies the non-librarian systems manager may need while examining some of the issues affecting non-librarians in these roles.

Introduction

Libraries are complex organizations with increasingly complex staffing needs. Large libraries may have volunteers, paraprofessionals, human resources and development officers, Webmasters, information technology specialists, and, of course, librarians. As the roles of various library departments become more specialized, the need for specialized talent also increases. Accordingly, libraries are now seeing an increase in the number of non-librarian managers. But what is a non-librarian manager? Essentially this is a person without a library degree who serves as the manager of one of the library's functional areas.

In this chapter, I explore the roles of non-librarians as systems managers. I consider the various responsibilities that may be encountered in systems manager positions and the skills that are required to meet these responsibilities. After having been employed in an academic library for a number of years, I completed a library degree and transitioned from a non-librarian manager to a manger with a library degree. Because I have had the opportunity to see the job from both sides of the MLS fence, I also examine my experiences and the differences (if any) for each role.

Non-Librarians versus Librarians

For many library positions, the American Library Association–accredited master's degree is a significant first qualification criterion. Degree holders are considered to have core knowledge and a standard level of education that prepares them for a variety of library positions. This long-standing requirement still appears in the majority of job descriptions for library openings, and it has merit for many library functions. Reference, serials, collection development, interlibrary loan, and catalog librarians are all positions that can benefit from coursework in a library school.

There are some perceived advantages to having librarians as managers. If all managers are librarians, there is a sense that they all speak the same language. Their common educational backgrounds make them all more immediately conversant in the same terminology and with the same issues. There is also a sense that the library degree places employees on equal footing with their colleagues. This idea was expressed in a 2007 blog discussion on Ross Singer's *Dilettante's Ball* (Singer, 2007). In response to Singer's question about why a particular job description required an MLS, one visitor replied, "Requiring that the person have an M.L.S means they're putting the position on a par ('professionally' speaking) with the other library departments. This can be handy in certain situations" (Klein, 2007). Karen Coombs (2007) agreed with this perspective in a related post on her *Library Web Chic* blog. The unspoken implication here is that those without an MLS are subpar when compared with degree-holding colleagues, or, to paraphrase George Orwell, "Some library employees are more equal than others."

Susan Martin (1997: 222) acknowledged this problem in strikingly candid terms:

> It is discomforting to note that frequently librarians (often young librarians) behave in a condescending manner to these senior and capable people, who believe that they are just as professional in their responsibilities as are the librarians. As if the mantle of the MLS degree suddenly turns a person into a different kind of creature, these librarians make it clear to paraprofessional staff that there is a real and significant difference between the two, and "I am better than you."

She goes on to note that librarians sometimes disregard colleagues who are not librarians, feeling perhaps that they will not be able to understand libraries and their plans and priorities (Martin, 1997: 222).

However, libraries are increasingly in need of employee skills that fall outside the traditional library education. For example, a library's administrative office might need a person with a human resources background. A background in public relations and fundraising might be the best combination for the development officer. The Webmaster position requires yet another skill set.

Just as librarians are specialists in classifying, organizing, navigating, and preserving information, other roles demand equally specialized training. The Webmaster is a specialist in online content presentation and delivery. The accountant is the expert when it comes to planning and managing budgets, and the information technology (IT) professional is the expert on technology matters. These diverse roles highlight just a few of the non-library-based skills now in demand in the library world. In analyzing this diversity, Julia C. Blixrud (2000: 7) observed, "as libraries create new types of positions, especially for those with significant technology components, library directors and personnel officers have begun to questions whether the M.L.S. degree is as necessary as other degrees or experiences."

The reality of the twenty-first-century library is that library school programs simply do not teach all of the skills that are needed in the workplace, and rightfully so. Imagine trying to combine a thorough library education with extensive marketing, information technology, accounting, and human resources education. Such a program would either be diluted to the point of uselessness by offering only a cursory treatment of important subject areas or bloated into a four- or five-year master's program that would frighten away all but the most determined. The literature shows the efforts of library education programs to expand the scope of coursework. These efforts to provide a more diverse background, while laudable, must not be mistaken for in-depth training or education. Simply put, a one-semester course in management does not a manager make. Similarly, a course in current Web 2.0 trends or how to write a Web page does not make one a systems manager. At some level, these diverse offerings in library schools may actually serve to further confound the question of which educational path is most appropriate for a person interested in systems work. Wilson (1998: 54) addressed this problem by noting, "There appears to be significant confusion over what every librarian should understand about technology and the specialization and in-depth training needed for those who wish to devote their careers to this role within the profession."

Nevertheless, libraries need diverse skills, and the skills have to come from somewhere. There is no doubt that a strong library background can give anyone a better understanding of how the organization functions. From the public relations officer to the IT department, every employee can gain a greater understanding of libraries' challenges and roles through a library education. In an ideal setting, all libraries would be able to hire IT professionals, marketing experts, and accountants who also have library credentials. However, it is not always realistic to expect employees to hold master's degrees outside their primary field of study. Indeed, in noting the expanding and diversifying numbers of professional positions in academic libraries, James Neal (2006: 44) states that "other degrees and thus different expertise are typically favored and recruited." John Berry (2003: 34) also points

111

out that this extends to the highest level of library administration: "For decades, however, we've watched great research libraries hire scholars over librarians as their directors." With the great diversity of roles currently found in libraries, an MLS may no longer be the one-size-fits-all solution to finding the best employee.

Non-Librarians versus Librarians in Systems Positions

"Jack-of–all-trades"—To many people, this phrase sums up their feelings about and expectations of their local systems manager. The other part of this old saying, "master of none," simply doesn't apply, because the systems manager is expected to be the guru of all things technological. Depending on library size, complexity, and staffing, the person in this role may manage and provide support for any or all of the following:

- Integrated library system (ILS)
- Additional library application servers
- Remote authentication for access to library resources
- Desktop computers (purchasing, set up, support)
- Software installation and troubleshooting
- Peripheral equipment such as bar-code readers and network printers
- Windows/Novell/Macintosh network
- Network hardware such as switches, firewalls, routers
- Library's Web pages
- Public computer lab spaces
- Public wireless network
- Public printing system

In addition to this direct in-the-trenches type of support, the person in this role is usually also responsible for a host of management functions, such as the following:

- Tracking current and evolving trends
- Forecasting technology needs
- Evaluating new technologies
- Acting as liaison to related campus, city, or county IT offices
- Providing training
- Developing in-house documentation
- Working with vendors for planning, purchasing, and technical support
- Planning, budgeting, and implementing major new technology initiatives

Although these lists are admittedly very general and do not exhaust all of the intricacies of a systems manager's responsibilities, most duties will fit neatly into one of these broad categories. A quick glimpse over these lists reveals only a single item, the integrated library system, that is the exclusive domain of the library world. All of the other support and planning functions are common to information technology roles in other organizations and businesses.

Lists compiled by others exploring the roles of systems managers further expose the diverse nature of the job. Thomas Wilson's 1998 (pp. 37–42) examination of this topic describes six specific skill categories that facilitate systems management:

- Library skills
- Library automation skills
- Computing
- Networking
- Management
- General

Wilson's discussion also includes a number of detailed examples for each category type. From examination of various areas of responsibility, he also suggests a number of training areas for consideration by those in systems. Excerpts from this list (Wilson, 1988: 65–66) include the following:

- Basic administration and management
- Library administration and management
- Basic accounting and auditing practices
- Communication
- Personnel management
- Project management
- Information technology management
- Computing industry structure and relationships
- Classification theory
- Data structures (MARC and non-MARC bibliographic formats)
- Software and hardware engineering process
- Operating systems
- Programming
- Integrated library system management
- User applications
- Network architecture and management
- Network protocol analysis
- Security and authentication.

While both lists include library-specific skills, the majority of functions might be handled by information technology managers in many non-library settings.

An investigation by Hong Xu and Hsin-liang Chen of job advertisements for systems librarians yielded similar sets of responsibilities. After reviewing over 100 job advertisements posted during a two-year period, their resulting list of knowledge areas begins to look very familiar (Xu and Chen, 1999: 176):

- Library system
- IT technology
- Bibliographic utilities

113

- Cataloging tools
- Telecommunications
- Internet
- World Wide Web
- HTML
- CD-ROMs
- Microcomputer applications
- Installation,
- Operating systems
- Programming languages
- Imaging technology
- SGML
- Z39.50

Rachel Singer Gordon (2003: Chapter 2) outlines a suggested list of "technical areas you may need to master":

- Microsoft software
- Macintosh
- Open source software
- Networking
- Web design
- Integrated library system management
- Troubleshooting
- Programming
- Antivirus and workstation security
- Miscellaneous issues

All of these lists are similar in that they contain a mixture of standard information technology responsibilities and library-specific job functions as well as assorted other duties. It is worth noting also that in each list there are more IT responsibilities than library-specific responsibilities. (While this should not be taken to mean that all systems managers will spend more time on general IT duties than on library-specific ones, this may very well be the case in some institutions.)

Ingersoll and Culshaw offer an interesting spin on systems responsibilities in their examples of daily and periodic systems office operations. Their list (Ingersoll and Culshaw, 2004: Chapter 8) includes the following:

- Prototype, test, configure, deploy
- Hardware maintenance
- Printing issues
- CD-ROMs and DVDs
- Software upgrades and monitoring
- License control

- Server management
- Data protection and backups
- Security
- Departmental procedures
- Logs and record keeping
- Inventory
- Statistical reports and analyses
- Programming
- Link checking

Noticeably absent from this list is anything that sounds library-esque. These daily and periodic operations might well represent any of thousands of IT departments around the globe.

Although the titles "systems manager" and "systems librarian" are commonly used, they can be a little misleading in terms of the technological complexity in today's library environments where a vast array of information technologies are employed. In one sense these titles sound like holdovers from the days when the library primarily had one major automation "system," usually the ILS and its associated online catalog. The computing environment of the twenty-first-century library uses a combination of integrated and independent systems to provide services to the public and a multiplicity of tools to employees, and it is this environment that the systems manager supports. Jordan (2003: 274) describes the systems librarian as one "who is responsible for managing the information technology used in a library." To return briefly to the guru analogy, Seadle (2003: 268) states, "Systems librarians exist to handle all things dealing with computers."

With so many general IT functions and relatively fewer library-specific functions, do systems managers need to be librarians? The answer is an unqualified "maybe." Individual systems manager positions can be as diverse as their libraries, and responsibilities can vary greatly from one library to another. In trying to determine whether the position requires a background in librarianship, a straightforward albeit simplistic approach is to estimate the percentage of the job that focuses on library-centric tools.

If 80 percent of a position is dedicated to supporting the ILS, then a library background might be considered essential. It will be much easier to work with the details of MARC records, serials management, and collection development practices and tools with a solid conceptual background. Most organizations employ their own "jungle rules" based on local practices and available technology, and these can be learned in the field. However, the learning curve will be much easier to surmount with the appropriate educational background. On the other hand, if 80 percent of the job responsibilities focus on hardware, software, and network maintenance with ILS duties splitting time between managing a public lab and long-range planning, then a library background becomes far less important.

The question then becomes, "How much time will this position spend supporting traditional library-specific technologies?" Or, if one prefers the inverse, "How much time will this position spend supporting standard information technologies?" Again, this is a simplistic approach, but it can give libraries meaningful insight into what skills their organization needs at that time, and thoughtful, open-minded consideration of these questions will lead to a very good assessment of whether the position requires an MLS or not. This approach also needs a word of caution. It is important to consider not just what the job will entail on the start date but also three to five years down the road. Technologies and technology needs will change. Personnel changes in the organization will introduce new interests and skill sets, and the systems manager's job may be a very different one in five years as the local computing environment changes. Nevertheless, it is important to know what the job is supposed to be at its outset. John A. Lehner (1997: 200) cautioned, "One of the fundamental shortcomings of library practices is the failure to develop careful, detailed job descriptions, much less engage in genuine job analysis." He also adds, "Job analysis should not be confused with simply having a supervisor draft a description of the job. Job analysis is much more thorough, detailed, and systematic in its approach" (Lehner, 1997: 201).

The complex nature of library systems means that different services, options, local implementations, and relationships to other units will combine to make each library setting unique, and these differences can require vastly different skills. For example, if a library chooses a turnkey ILS implementation, then the vendor typically manages the server operating system and OS updates. Alternatively, in software-only implementations, the library is responsible for managing the server platform. In some cases, this responsibility is also handled by the systems manager or another person in the systems department. On some campuses a central data center may be responsible for managing all Windows servers, while on others the responsibility falls to the individual units or departments. In some systems the library may be responsible for maintaining employee and public computers and software, while in others this may be managed by another unit such as a city or county IT unit. As if these major areas weren't enough, the myriad choices of software, public print systems, authentication tools, online databases, digitization projects, and specialized services combine to make every library setting truly unique.

Then and Now: The Evolution of Our Systems Support Roles

I started working as a full-time staff member in the University of Mississippi Libraries' Systems Department in late 1994. In this position, some of my responsibilities included desktop hardware and software support, support of Internet and World Wide Web technologies, and assisting in supporting and troubleshooting the libraries' online catalog. I provided support to the main library and four branch libraries. As with any library IT job, duties are subject to change as the library's array of technologies changes. Within a few months we added our first self-checkout machines and a lab full of new Macintosh computers. During this time construction was underway on an addition to our building, and I worked with the systems librarian as we planned network and telephone drops for the new facility. Although I had an undergraduate degree in English, it is interesting to note that a college degree was not required for this senior computer operator position. According to the human resources requirements in place at the time, it was determined that a high school diploma and two years postsecondary education or related work experience was sufficient for this position (Appendix 4-1).

The new building opened in May 1995 with a number of technological changes. Prior to this we had a handful of computers with Internet access. In the new building we had more Internet-capable machines and direct access to the network hardware in the communications room. We moved many of our dumb terminals from dedicated data circuits to Ethernet connections. Because of a personnel transition, the systems department inherited a Novell CD-ROM network from reference. This also marked the first time that each library employee had a computer at his or her desk. Prior to this, many areas relied on shared departmental computers. This change added a new dimension to end-user support and training. In addition to our five libraries, we added two temporary off-site work areas. During this time the university began its initiative to develop an Internet presence on the World Wide Web. I was drafted as a member of the committee that developed the libraries' initial Web site, and I served as Webmaster for many years thereafter. This initiative required yet another new set of skills.

117

Everything changed radically in late summer when our systems librarian took a new position at another university. I went through a quick crash course on the ins and outs of our ILS, and soon I was responsible for user accounts, troubleshooting, configuration, batch loading records, and software updates. Following the opening of our new building, we began preparing for the renovation of the old building. I was working with the building architects, contractors, and our campus telecommunication department to plan network and telephone drops as well as electrical outlets for our public spaces. Another person was hired as my assistant, and suddenly I was managing a full-time employee as well as student workers.

These responsibilities continued for the next four years, gradually evolving over time as the libraries' needs changed. New technologies were introduced, and older ones were phased out. Many of the changes were gradual and subtle, such as the slow migration from floppy disks to Zip drives and then to writeable CDs/DVDs and USB flash drives. Other changes, such as the introduction of a Web-based OPAC and online databases, were of a grander scale. They caused everyone to rethink the way we delivered information to patrons, they greatly changed the libraries' technical support needs, and the influence of those technologies is still felt in libraries today. My position title also underwent a number of changes during this time. As part of a human resources reclassification initiative, the Senior Computer Operator position (see Appendix 4-1) was upgraded to a Network Administrator position (see Appendix 4-2). Later the Dean of Libraries appointed me Acting Head of Library Systems. Throughout these title changes, there were no significant changes in the fundamental daily duties. In all three positions, I managed the full range of systems responsibilities in our libraries.

From 1995 until 1999 I managed the libraries' systems needs—sometimes with help and sometimes as a one-person department when we were between assistants. A couple of important changes took place in 1999. At the encouragement of our Dean of Libraries, I enrolled in an MLS program that spring and began my first semester of coursework. During the summer we hired a new librarian to join our systems team. This hire led to a revision of support roles within the department.

Our new librarian came from a position in which she had gained significant ILS and electronic resource experience. Although I had been supporting the ILS for several years, the nature of our local computing environment was such that other core technologies required more routine support than the ILS. As a result my own expertise had grown most in those areas. This led to a very natural division of responsibilities in which the librarian handled the bulk of the support calls related to cataloging, acquisitions, and serials within our ILS. Additionally, she handled some of the requests for hardware, software, and network support. Because librarians at the University of Mississippi have faculty status, she was also doing research to meet publication requirements. Conversely, while I handled most of the calls for hardware, software, and network support, I also provided support for the circulation module of our ILS and self-checkout units as well as managing ILS updates and hardware. We shared Webmaster responsibilities for the library's Web site, and we both provided support for our OPAC.

In retrospect, this division of support roles seems very clear cut. However, at the time it seemed very fluid and informal. There was often overlap between these roles during busy times, and we routinely covered for each other during conference and vacation times. We continued this informal distribution of responsibilities as the libraries added new technologies, such as the proxy server, Uniprint (public print system), ILLiad, and digital library systems including ContentDM and MetaData Builder.

As the library and our personnel evolved over the years, our support roles evolved to match the needs of the libraries and the strengths of our personnel. As we moved through these personnel and technology changes, the ebb and flow of responsibilities was, for the most part, a series of subtle changes handled internally among IT department members. Over the next few years, some notable events occurred. I completed a master's degree in information resources and library science in 2001, but this did not immediately translate into a faculty librarian position. However, in 2002 I moved into a newly created tenure-track librarian position, Head of Library Network Services (Appendix 4-3). At various times in the past I had served as a member of the libraries' management group, and I rejoined this group upon beginning this new position. However, as with my previous title and position changes, my daily responsibilities were essentially the same in the new position.

In 2003, the other department member moved into another newly created position: Assistant Dean for Technical Services and Automation (see Appendix 4-4). With this transition, the division of ILS responsibilities remained largely unchanged. She continued to support many of the traditional technical services automation modules, using her expertise to streamline workflows and explore previously untapped system features. ILS hardware, circulation, and digital library functions were still supported by the IT department. As the complexity of the ILS and the base of installed modules continue to grow, others within Technical Services and Information Technology are being trained to manage specific components of the system. Troubleshooting complex issues related to the ILS often remains a joint effort.

In the Trenches: Daily Operations and Management

A systems manager has many responsibilities related to long-range planning. With rapidly changing technology and the desire to introduce new and innovative patron services, this is a formidable challenge. However, one of the most critical aspects of the systems manager's job, while seemingly commonplace, can be just as challenging: maintaining a stable local computing environment. Indeed the local computing environment could be considered the foundation upon which all new technologies and services are built. Supporting and maintaining the array of currently installed technologies is no small task. In fact, there is a very delicate balance of technologies and support personnel. With too many technologies and/or too few personnel, a library systems department will be inadvertently locked into a cycle of just trying to maintain the local environment with little or no time for long-range planning and new deployments. In this section I describe my experiences and the trends I have observed in my university library setting. Because of the widely varying nature of systems manager positions, there is no one-size-fits-all list of competencies that guarantees success as a systems manager. However, there are a number of technical and nontechnical areas that deserve emphasis. A combination of some of these areas will appear in any systems position, and the effectiveness with which they are handled can be a determining factor in gauging overall success as a systems manager.

Integrated Library System

When I became the de facto systems manager in 1995, I also assumed responsibility for supporting the ILS. Of all the technologies in place at that time, I found the ILS to be the most intimidating. In retrospect, I think that this was simply because at that time I had less experience supporting the ILS than other technologies. In actual practice, supporting the ILS was fairly painless. Our ILS was a turnkey solution, and we had very solid vendor support. The result was that solving many of our ILS problems was actually easier than solving the more traditional IT problems.

In working with the ILS, my experience has been that understanding the technology is often easier than understanding the workflow. When I first began supporting this system, I worked closely with our department heads of circulation and technical services. When users reported problems, it was essential that I understood the process and order of events that led to the problem. This was important for a couple of reasons. First, I needed to be able to replicate the problem while I was troubleshooting. I also needed to be able to reproduce this problem if I reported it to our vendor. Understanding the individual processes also helped me gain greater familiarity with the overall function of the ILS, and it helped me understand the interrelationships among the various modules. I still use this approach with some of the ILS problems I investigate. Those who use a specific module or function on a daily basis are the ones who have the most detailed knowledge of the workflow. I often ask them to guide me through their steps, particularly when I have not used that module in quite some time.

In our institution an exhaustive knowledge of the ILS was not necessary. However, a strong general overview of the total system functionality is important, because many aspects of the system rely on shared data and processes. As with any large and complex system, the manager needs an overall understanding that will facilitate troubleshooting. The manager also needs to be conversant with that system's terminology. This will be helpful in bridging the gap between the end user and the vendor when investigating a problem. While a library science background may be useful in understanding the concepts upon which the system is based, there is no substitute for practical experience in actually using the system.

Operating Systems

In supporting employee and public computers, the desktop operating system will probably be a significant area of responsibility for at least one member of the systems team. Whether a library uses Microsoft's Windows, Apple's Macintosh OS, or Linux, the operating system will require periodic updates and patches. These sometimes take the form of "critical" updates that are necessary to maintain the security of the computer and the local network. Others extend the functionality of the operating system by introducing new features.

Over the years our experience has been that we are always supporting multiple versions of desktop operating system software—the most current version, at least one prior version, and sometimes the upcoming version. When supporting the OS, systems managers must constantly think in both backward-compatible and forward-compatible terms. When a new or updated operating system is introduced, there is no guarantee that all of the libraries' applications will immediately be completely compatible with the new system. In some cases it may be many months before another vendor's software is updated to work with the new operating system. When considering the various operating system choices, the systems manager must consider several questions. Will current applications be compatible with the new operating system? Is existing hardware sufficient to effectively run the new operating system? How easy or difficult will it be to migrate data to the new operating system platform? Will my antivirus, disk imaging, and other software work with the new operating system, or will I have to buy new versions? Because systems managers are responsible for charting the library's technological course into the future, the questions of data and application migration are key components of both short-term and long-range planning.

Systems personnel may also be called upon to support a number of handheld devices such as PDAs or smartphones. In some cases these may be library-owned devices, or they may be owned by library employees who want to synchronize calendar, contact, and other data between the handheld and their office computer. This introduces yet another range of operating systems that the systems manager must consider.

Server Operating Systems

When I first started supporting technology in our libraries, the ILS server was our only server. Although I managed software updates and hardware/software troubleshooting, ours was a turnkey system with the operating system managed by the vendor. Like many libraries we have added a number of specialized applications that provide specific patron and internal employee services. Many of these require a Windows-based server platform. They also typically require SQL database software and Microsoft's Web server, Internet Information Services (IIS).

In this area as well we find that we are frequently supporting multiple operating systems. Just as it is important to monitor changes in upcoming desktop operating systems, it is equally important in the server environment for many of the same reasons. New and updated versions of the operating system and associated software services may or may not be compatible with existing applications that rely on those servers. In some cases software updates may be required. In other cases, certain applications simply may not run on the new platform.

Our department's current server knowledge focuses heavily on Active Directory, IIS, and Microsoft DNS. The Active Directory and DNS components reflect our desktop computer and user account management coupled with resource sharing across our organization. IIS is a required component for several key technologies deployed in our library: ILLiad, ContentDM, and SharePoint.

Libraries are increasingly turning to open source software as tools for specialized employee and patron services. With tools and services such as DSpace, Greenstone, MySQL, and Apache, many libraries are choosing to deploy these in a Linux environment. This opens up yet another potential area of server-related knowledge. While some libraries choose to have all servers housed and managed

121

by a central campus IT department, many prefer having direct access to their own hardware and software when needed. In today's library computing environment, it is highly likely that the systems manager will be responsible for multiple servers, and those machines may be running different operating systems with vastly different services.

Server-Side Software

In our libraries we use a number of server-hosted applications. Some provide specific employee services, others provide patron services, and some do both. Uniprint is used to manage the public pay-for-print system. ILLiad is used for employee and patron interlibrary loan functions. ContentDM is one of the digital library solutions currently used by the libraries. Microsoft SharePoint is used for internal communications and collaboration across the organization. The need for these services has been the driving force in the acquisition of Windows-based servers, as well as subsequent training, ongoing support, and server migration.

Not every library will have this exact combination of services. Some libraries may use more or less, while others may use entirely different suites of applications. Regardless, in the current library technology realm, most libraries will at some time need to use a special application that resides on a server. As libraries continue to offer new and innovative services to employees and patrons, it is to be expected that the numbers of server-based solutions will grow. Deployment of these new solutions requires a still more detailed knowledge of the server platform (Microsoft, Linux, etc.) as well as an understanding of how the application works with the server. It also points to a need for the systems manager to have a working knowledge of these specialized products and how they will integrate with existing systems. Last, but certainly not least, the manager must understand the needs of the client base who will use the products.

Management Tools

Libraries are often in the position of deploying new technologies without corresponding increases in the number of support personnel. In these cases, the systems manager often looks for ways to streamline certain processes or to centralize some management functions. As we have increased the number of office and public computers in our libraries, a number of server-based management tools have proven to be very helpful. In listing the tools that we use, it should be noted that there are other similar applications that will do the same job; I am merely listing the ones in use at our location. Rather than focusing on a specific product, it is more helpful to emphasize the functions performed and ways in which they can streamline deployment and simplify the management of large numbers of computers. Whether or not these are essential tools may be debated, but the time-savings they offer in the long term have certainly been worth the initial setup time.

Disk Imaging

Symantec Ghost has been an invaluable tool in preparing computers for deployment. When we acquire a number of new computers, we install software and configure a single machine as we want it. The imaging software allows us to take a snapshot of that hard drive with the operating system, application software, and other applications already configured. After capturing this image, we can then push the image out over the network to multiple computers simultaneously. This eliminates the need to individually configure each additional computer and greatly reduces initial setup time. Once the imaging is completed, only a few steps are required to add the computer to the local network before it is ready for deployment. This has often proven to be a great time saver after deployment as well. If we subsequently encounter software or operating system problems, it is sometimes quicker to simply re-image a computer than to spend extensive time in troubleshooting.

Central Antivirus Management

For many years we have used Symantec products as our antivirus solution. This company's management console offers several important tools for systems administrators. One of the most basic is a remote deployment function that can install the antivirus software on multiple computers simultaneously. Once the software has been deployed, administrators can modify software settings on all clients from the console. The console also provides a central location for monitoring virus activity, scheduling automatic virus scans, and making sure that virus definitions are up to date. In addition to alerting systems personnel about virus risks, the management console has a number of report options to help the systems manager identify high-risk areas and evaluate the effectiveness of installed antivirus solutions.

Security Update and Patch Management

Most operating system developers routinely issue sets of software updates and security patches. In many cases these updates are designed to correct potentially serious security flaws in the operating system, and it is important to install them on all computers as soon as they have been tested and verified to work properly in the local computing environment.

A patch management tool such as Microsoft's Windows Server Update Services (WSUS) can help automate this process. Using the WSUS console, administrators can quickly see what new updates are available and select the ones they want to deploy. The product console also shows which computers are missing updates. This type of tool can greatly simplify the installation of patches and updates, and it helps administrators stay apprised of patch status without having to physically visit each computer.

Public Computer Security

Maintaining public computers is a significant responsibility of most library systems departments. Because these computers are very heavily used, maintaining the integrity of the operating system and application software poses an important challenge to the systems manager. Consistent look and behavior are important aspects of patrons' experiences using library computers. If the desktop of each public computer in the library looks a little different, then patrons may think that the computers have different options or access different resources. (In some cases this may be desirable, especially when computers do in fact have different options or programs available.) Similarly, if the same computer looks different each time a patron uses it, the computer experience changes a little each time, and less technologically savvy users may find it difficult to adapt to a constantly changing computing platform. In some cases, critical system files may even be missing. In order to guard against this, a number of security tools are available to prevent accidental or intentional system changes.

Our tool of choice, DeepFreeze, uses a stored disk image to help safeguard the desktop platform. If users make any changes to the computer, these are erased upon reboot when the computer reverts to the saved image. This also has implications for protecting patron privacy. Because all changes are erased when the computer restarts, Web browser histories and temporary Internet files on the computer are also erased.

The Web and the Internet

The Internet and the Web have been radically changing the face of libraries since the early 1990s. In the early days of the Web, systems managers' responsibilities often focused on Web browser software, telnet, FTP, and TCP/IP protocols. HTML coding and the use of scripting languages also gained importance as libraries began creating their own Web presences. Web trends, including those currently grouped under the "Web 2.0" heading, are consuming ever-increasing amounts of time in library systems departments, and they are claiming increasing levels of importance as systems managers watch the horizon.

The current crop of freely available Web 2.0 tools includes a number of customization and personalization features. Users can easily create and interact with Web content. They can create their own social communities around this body of content. The Application Programming Interface (API) found in many Web applications allows users to combine data from several tools under a new interface. These hybrids, also known as *mashups*, continue to gain prominence as users explore new ways to manipulate and deliver information.

It is significant to note that major library automation vendors are now introducing tools and features already widely available in the Web 2.0 environment. However, it is equally significant that librarians are not only using existing free tools in their libraries, they are also building their own tools and mashups to extend services and meet user needs.

In this environment, the systems manager may be involved in an array of technologies that is at once fascinating and overwhelming. Although individually many of these tools are easily configured and managed by users, the systems manager may be responsible for integrating them into the larger library technology environment. Evaluating and selecting future Web technologies presents an even greater challenge. In such a dynamic environment, it is difficult to know which technologies to invest in, and it is almost impossible to guess which ones will gain popularity with users. Nevertheless, this is an increasingly important area for systems managers and one that illustrates the need to stay informed about new and emerging technologies.

Management

In the modern systems department, management assumes a number of roles: management of services, management of people, and management of projects. These roles are at once independent and interrelated, and they may be thought of as combinations of technical and nontechnical competencies. Management of services relies heavily on technical skills with some elements of nontechnical skills. Management of people focuses on nontechnical skills, although in a systems setting there will, of course, be technical aspects as well. Project management requires both technical and nontechnical skills. Among these key nontechnical management skills are communication, interpersonal skills, good analytical skills, and decision-making abilities.

Communication

In some ways communication may be more important for the systems manager than for almost any other position in the library. In examining systems manager positions, it is widely documented that one of the most important roles in this position is that of translator. In many projects the systems manager serves as the "information conduit" (Goddard, 2003: 286). The systems manager may facilitate discussions between the library and vendors, between the library and other campus IT units, between vendors and campus IT, or among various other groups. Goddard (2003: 286) states, "The ability to talk to a vendor in their language, and translate this information to librarians helps provide a buffer between the two different cultures and skill sets, lessening the frustrations that can arise from these disparities."

The nature of the position means that the systems manager will be working with every department in the library. As departments evaluate new products or plan new initiatives, the systems manager can help frame the discussion in terms of the larger library technology context. The systems manager must first understand the clients—whether patrons or other library employees—and their skill sets, language, and workflow. This person must be able to communicate the libraries' needs and goals in the technical language of vendors and other IT units. Conversely, he or she must be able to explain technical concepts to nontechnical audiences. This type of open communication, unencumbered by jargon and buzzwords, makes the systems manager a valuable asset to the library.

125

Interpersonal Skills

Communication and interpersonal skills are such complementary traits that they can be thought of as two sides of the same coin. It has been noted earlier that the systems manager frequently plays the role of translator between the library and various other constituencies. This person also plays the equally important part of interpreter for the various systems used by the library. Whether it is deciphering cryptic error messages, providing training, or explaining the concepts on which a system operates, a good systems manager demystifies technology and makes it more accessible to users by becoming the human face of the technology.

Several qualities typify a systems manager with strong interpersonal skills. This person is approachable and fosters a nonthreatening environment in which others feel comfortable asking questions. The use of plain language goes far in helping shape this environment. With a certain comfort level established, the systems manager will likely find that information flows more freely throughout the organization. When seeking input from other library departments, one is likely to find that this atmosphere of openness encourages others to offer suggestions and share ideas.

However, strong interpersonal skills do not ensure that the systems manager will find smooth sailing on every project. In fact, the vary nature of the position is so politically charged that it may sometimes be difficult to offer dissenting opinions. As Janet Guinea (2003: 329) points out, "When systems offer practical objections to implementation requests, the systems librarian may be seen as obstructive. The expectations of library staff sometimes exceed the limitations of the library system, or indeed the capabilities of the systems team."

Analytical Skills and Decision Making

At its foundation, much of systems work is based on logic, analysis, and critical thinking. These are invaluable tools for troubleshooting problems, investigating new systems, and planning deployments. They also have implications for many other areas under the systems manager's responsibility. Budget planning, weighing the pros and cons of new technologies, allocation of fiscal and personnel resources, and long-range planning are all areas that rely on these tools. But this is not to say that systems managers are locked into methodical, machinelike thinking. The ingenious, creative solution to a problem often yields far more satisfaction and utility than the one that proceeds inevitably and inexorably from long cogitation, and many systems managers revel in this creative approach.

Unfortunately, far too often libraries lock systems personnel out of the creative aspects of the organization. People with technical skills are relegated to the role of mere mechanics who exist to keep the machinery running. This situation leaves a number of additional viewpoints and ideas potentially untapped. Moreover, most employees seek creative outlets within their workplace, and feeling locked out of those venues and opportunities can be demoralizing to the person who genuinely wants to participate.

How Do I Get There from Here?

How exactly does one become a systems manager? Lisa Tyson (2003: 318) observed, "The methods for becoming one still vary and are in many ways unclear." Library literature documents the limited educational opportunities for those wishing to pursue careers in systems-related areas. Although MLS programs abound, their ability to produce systems managers is extremely limited. Michael Seadle (2003: 268–269) described the state of library school education for systems in the editorial of a *Library Hi Tech* special issue on systems librarianship:

> The focus tends to be on Web-programming and human–computer interaction, rather than the basics of operating system administration, network management, database design, or languages like Java, Perl, or C++. This fits with a trend in library schools to provide a broader and more intellectually-based education, rather than train students to step immediately into a specific library job like cataloging or reference.

Currently, no MLS programs prepare the systems manager as thoroughly as other library employees are prepared for their respective positions. A newly graduated systems librarian will step into an intimidating array of systems offered by different vendors and boasting multiple modules that may or may not interface with other technologies at the local, state, or regional level. This person is expected to know how all of these modules work independently and in concert and to know them well enough to provide training and user support. No wonder library schools can't prepare systems librarians!

Setting aside the logistics of training students on numerous proprietary systems, the complexity and uniqueness of each systems job could almost require its own dedicated, individualized course of study. The sheer number and complexity of services supported combine to form a very high learning curve for systems work—perhaps the highest of any library specialty. Systems personnel face another challenge: In many cases the systems manager may be the entire department! In most institutions a reference or catalog librarian will have peers to whom they can turn for instruction and advice. In contrast, the systems manager may be the only systems person at all.

If library schools do not provide appropriate training, then how does one learn to do the job? The systems manager, perhaps more than any other library person, relies on self-education and on-the-job training to learn the intricacies of all the systems he or she will support. Moreover this type of independent learning is essential when working with new, cutting-edge technologies. Mark Jordan (2003: 273) states, ". . . the ability to learn new technologies independently lies at the foundation of the systems librarians' professional life, because they often have to use technologies, or make planning decisions about specific technologies, before they become common enough to be the subject of formal training sessions." Tyson (2003: 318) echoes this sentiment: "Many systems librarians grow into the role without formal training, yet are expected to have technical knowledge equaling formal qualifications." In fact, independent learning is so important to the systems manager that it constitutes an essential core skill.

Notes from the Field: Before and After the MLS

In 1988, Susan K. Martin wrote:

> Over the years the library world has argued whether systems librarians should be librarians who have learned information technologies, or computer experts who have learned about libraries. The argument appears to be fruitless. Now, as two decades ago, the systems librarians we employ are a mix of librarians and computer scientists. Now, as then, it does not appear to make too much difference where the emphasis is placed, as long as input from both professions is made available to the library. (Martin, 1988: 61)

Twenty years after Martin's writing, the debate continues, and it appears to be just as fruitless.

Having acknowledged that perhaps library schools do not produce full-fledged, job-ready systems managers, is there any advantage to pursuing a library school program? Does an MLS really make any difference? The answer, as before, is "maybe."

Prior to enrolling in a library school program, I had gained extensive practical experience working in a library setting. While pursuing undergraduate degrees, I worked for almost eight years as a student assistant in the university library. I was employed in the reference department throughout this time, and as part of my duties I regularly assisted patrons at the reference desk. I also worked at various times in interlibrary loan, administration, and in the music library. Additionally, I worked for a number of years in a scientific library at a local government facility. By the time I enrolled in library school in 1999, I had been managing the systems department full time for over three years. In essence I had worked through a very thorough apprenticeship before enrolling in the master's program. Additionally, the systems work in particular gave me valuable insight into the roles of the various departments.

After completing my library degree in 2001 and in the years since, I have often considered the implications of the educational program and specifically what it did and did not do for my career. Unfortunately, I am sorry to say that my master's program did not teach me anything that helped me do my daily job better. Some of the classes generated interesting discussion topics but nothing that helped me better manage or understand any of the technologies I supported. In fact, at the outset of my library education, a number of colleagues warned me that this would be the case. These librarians, who came from a variety of departments and who had been in the profession for a number of years all echoed the same sentiment: "Library school is fine for theory and background, but you actually learn what you need to know on the job." I had secretly suspected that this might be the case for the systems position, but I was genuinely surprised to hear them express this as a broader and more universally applicable viewpoint. In short, although the program gave me the right to call myself a librarian, it gave me no tools to help me perform better on the job.

However, there were some benefits. Through a program administered by my university's staff council, almost immediately I received a salary increase for completing a job-related master's degree. And of course the MLS opened the door to professional positions requiring an American Library Association–accredited degree. After completing the degree I was able to move into a tenure-track faculty position with professional development funding, and that in turn opens the door to further advancement in academe.

There were other, more intangible benefits as well. As expressed earlier, there is occasionally a sense that librarians and non-librarians do not meet on equal terms. In certain environments there is an unspoken sense that librarians form a class that is somehow above other non-librarian employees. Prior to completing my library degree, there were a number of times when I personally felt the condescending manner Martin (1997) described. In fairness, I must state that this attitude was shown by just a few people, but it persists in libraries, and it is easily promulgated with only miniscule effort.

In some libraries there remains a sense that non-librarians simply cannot grasp the complexity of library work. They cannot speak the language, and they cannot share the same goals. I disagree with this assessment. In disagreeing, I suggest that there is more than one way to become conversant with the issues of libraries, and the MLS may not necessarily be the best way.

Lisa Tyson (2003: 320) writes, "For those without a background of working in libraries in a client services or technical services area, it can be very hard to obtain the necessary understanding of the details of tasks in these areas to allow for effective technological support." I agree with this observation, and I'll point out that the emphasis here is on working in libraries. The emphasis is on the practical experience.

Conclusion

Over the past 13 years, my essential job responsibilities have broadened as would normally be expected through expanded technology initiatives, additional systems deployments, and increased systems staffing. These changes would have happened with or without a library degree, and I would have felt equally prepared to meet these challenges with or without a library degree.

As stated before, systems is not a one-size-fits-all profession, and my experience might not necessarily mirror that of others in similar positions. My library school education was decidedly overshadowed by practical experience and by the many close working relationships I already enjoyed in my library. Martin (1998: 61) noted, "One attribute of systems work is that those involved inevitably gain an unusually strong perspective of the library and its operations as a whole. . . ." I definitely feel that this has been the case in my systems work, and I have found the practical day-to-day experience in the library to be invaluable in understanding the organization as a whole.

Many systems departments can be successfully managed by either librarians or non-librarians. In some cases, depending on the exact mixture of technologies and support personnel, there may be a slight preference for one over the other. However, given the current array of technologies deployed in modern libraries, the deciding factor often seems to be local practice or personal preference rather than a true needs-based qualification derived from a careful job analysis. Regardless of whether the systems manager is a librarian or not, the list of competencies required will be strikingly similar, leading to the conclusion that perhaps there really isn't that much difference after all.

References

Berry III, John N. 2003. "But Don't Call 'em Librarians." *Library Journal* 128, no. 18 (November): 34–36.

Blixrud, Julia C. 2000. "The M.L.S. Hiring Requirement." *SPEC Kit 257*. Washington, DC: ARL Office of Leadership and Management Services.

Coombs, Karen. 2007. "Why Require an MLS for Library Technologists?" (July 18). Library Web Chic. Available: www.librarywebchic.net/wordpress/2007/07/18/why-require-an-mls-for-library-technologists/ (accessed March 2008).

Goddard, Lisa. 2003. "The Integrated Librarian: IT in the Systems Office." *Library Hi Tech* 21, no. 3: 280–288.

Gordon, Rachel Singer. 2003. *The Accidental Systems Librarian*. Medford, NJ: Information Today.

Guinea, Janet. 2003. "Building Bridges: The Role of the Systems Librarian in a University Library." *Library Hi Tech* 21, no. 3: 325–332.

Ingersoll, Patricia and John Culshaw. 2004. *Managing Information Technology: A Handbook for Systems Librarians*. Westport, CT: Libraries Unlimited.

Jordan, Mark. 2003. "The Self-Education of Systems Librarians." *Library Hi Tech* 21, no. 3: 273–279.

Klein, Leo Robert. 2007. Response to "Union Card." Dilettante's Ball (July 9). Available: dilettantes.code4lib.org/2007/07/09/union-card/ (accessed March 2008).

Lehner, John A. 1997. "Reconsidering the Personnel Selection Practices of Academic Libraries." *Journal of Academic Librarianship* 23, no. 3: 199–204.

Martin, Susan K. 1988. "The Role of the Systems Librarian." *Journal of Library Administration* 9, no. 4: 57–68.

Martin, Susan K. 1997. "Clinging to 'Status:' The Attitude of Librarians to Non-MLS Staff." *The Journal of Academic Librarianship* 23, no. 3: 222.

Neal, James G. 2006. "Raised by Wolves: Integrating the New Generation of Feral Professionals into the Academic Library." *Library Journal* 131, no. 3: 42–46.

Seadle, Michael. 2003. "The Status of Systems Librarians." *Library Hi Tech* 21, no. 3: 267–269.

Singer, Ross. 2007. "Union Card." Dilettante's Ball (July 9). Available: dilettantes.code4lib
.org/2007/07/09/union-card/ (accessed March 2008).

Tyson, Lisa. 2003. "Library Systems Teams—More than Just Peripherals." *Library Hi
Tech* 21, no. 3: 317–324.

Wilson, Thomas C. 1998. *The Systems Librarian: Designing Roles, Defining Skills.*
Chicago, IL: American Library Association.

Xu, Hong and Hsin-liang Chen. 1999. "What Do Employers Expect? The Educating
Systems Librarian Research Project 1." *The Electronic Library* 17, no. 3 (June):
171–179.

Appendix 4-1. Position Description: Senior Computer Operator

Position: Senior Computer Operator
J.D. Williams Library, University of Mississippi
January 1995

Occupational Summary

Assist systems department by performing complex technical duties that support the use of computers in the library

Report to a librarian/manager

Work Performed

Maintain and support microcomputer hardware and software for DOS and Macintosh computers in the University of Mississippi libraries (J.D. Williams Library, Chemistry Library, Music Library/Blues Archive, Government Publications, and Pharmacy Library)

Troubleshoot problems related to microcomputers and peripherals used by library staff and patrons

Facilitate the use of microcomputer hardware, software, and related equipment by library staff and faculty

Assist with support and troubleshooting for library's online catalog

Assist with management, support, and troubleshooting of the library's computer network

Support the use of the Internet and tools such as the World Wide Web, gopher, telnet, and finger by library staff

Document and maintain inventory of computer equipment

Supervise student assistants

In absence of librarian/manager, assume responsibility for operation of a library unit, as assigned

Qualifications

High school diploma or equivalent

Two years postsecondary education or substantive work experience with computers and computer applications

Experience with microcomputer hardware and software, including word processing, spreadsheet program, MS-DOS, Windows, and Novell Netware

Abilities to function as part of a team, to work independently without supervision, and to use independent judgment and interpretative and decision-making skills

Excellent written and verbal communication skills, organizational skills, and ability to establish priorities

Ability to interpret technical documentation

Supervisory skills

Mechanical aptitude to handle computer equipment

Appendix 4-2. Position Description: Network Administrator

Position: Network Administrator
J.D. Williams Library, University of Mississippi
February 1998

Occupational Summary

This is a nonsupervisory position in which the incumbent assists in the development and maintenance of network systems at the school and/or unit level. Incumbent provides technical support to network users.

Work Performed

Work with manufacturers and vendors to determine costs, specifications, and functional requirements of network equipment

Process necessary paperwork for equipment purchases

Maintain interface with department and office personnel to determine local area network (LAN) needs and requirements

Monitor network systems to ensure that networks are functioning within design standard; make adjustments as necessary to optimize performance or repair a fault

Administer a school or unit's LAN, including analyzing, selecting, and installing hardware and software programs related to departmental computer needs

Diagnose and correct computer software and hardware problems and failure

Provide advice as to upgrades and maintenance of existing equipment

Provide faculty, staff, and students with training and support in the use of hardware and software

Assist faculty and staff in facilitating distance learning education and videoconference meetings

Supervise student workers in a computer lab environment

Monitor Internet Web server; design, maintain, and update Internet page(s)

Perform database programming and maintenance for the assigned unit

Perform related or similar duties as required or assigned

Functions

The essential functions include, but are not limited to, the following. Additional essential functions may be identified and included by the hiring department.

1. Develop and install computer programs and network systems for individual schools and/or units
2. Monitor operations and perform necessary maintenance to network systems
3. Provide technical assistance to faculty and staff regarding network operations and capabilities

Minimum Qualifications

The minimum qualifications have been agreed upon by Subject Matter Experts (SEES) in this job class and are based upon a job analysis and the essential functions. However, if a candidate believes he or she is qualified for the job although he or she does not have the minimum qualifications set forth below, he or she may request special consideration through substitution of related education and experience, demonstrating the ability to perform the essential functions of the position. Any request to substitute related education or experience for minimum qualifications must be addressed to the University of Mississippi's Department of Human Resources in writing, identifying the related education and experience that demonstrates the candidate's ability to perform all essential functions of the position.

133

(Cont'd.)

Appendix 4-2. Position Description: Network Administrator *(Continued)*

Physical Requirements

The physical requirements are not exhaustive, and additional job-related physical requirements may be added to these by individual agencies on an as-needed basis. Corrective devices may be used to meet physical requirements.

Physical Exertion: May be required to lift up to approximately 50 pounds

Vision: Requires the ability to perceive the nature of objects by the eye

Near Acuity: Clarity of vision at 20 inches or less

Midrange: Clarity of vision at distances of more than 20 inches and less than 20 feet

Far Acuity: Clarity of vision at 20 feet or more

Field of Vision: Ability to observe an area up or down, left or right while eyes are fixed on a given point

Depth Perception: Three-dimensional vision; ability to judge distance and space relationships so as to see objects where and as they actually are

Accommodation: Ability to adjust focus

Color Vision: Ability to identify colors

Speaking/Hearing: Ability to give and receive information through speaking and listening

Motor Coordination: Frequently required to sit, talk, or hear and use hands to finger, handle, or feel objects, tools, or controls; occasionally required to stand, walk, climb, or balance and reach with hands and arms

Experience and Educational Requirements

Education: Bachelor's degree in business, computer science, engineering, telecommunications, or a related field from an accredited four-year college or university AND

Experience: One (1) year of experience related to the above-described duties

Substitution Statement

Related education and related experience may be substituted on an equal basis.

Appendix 4-3. Position Description: Head of Library Network Services

Position: Head of Library Network Services
University of Mississippi Libraries
April 2002

Occupational Summary

Reporting to the Dean of Libraries, this person assists in the planning and integration of new network systems as well as the daily operation and troubleshooting of existing network and library technologies. The incumbent will be expected to work collegially with library faculty and staff to assess and address changing technological needs in a rapidly expanding library environment. This person will also coordinate overall Web design and maintain the libraries' Web presence. This person works closely with the Head of Library Technology to oversee and maintain currently installed technology and develop additional means to maximize library resources. Incumbent also participates in planning, evaluation, selection, and implementation of library automation. Incumbent provides technical support and training for multiplatform library microcomputers and peripherals, as well as sharing responsibility for supervising one FTE (full-time equivalent) staff member and student assistants.

Qualifications

American Library Association–accredited Master of Library Science degree

Excellent organizational, analytical, interpersonal, written, and oral communication skills

Academic library experience with integrated automation systems and knowledge of emerging trends in information technology

Knowledge of HTML

Web site management experience preferred

Experience supporting networked technologies in an academic library setting preferred

Responsibilities

Webmaster for library Web pages

Maintain and troubleshoot existing network and library technologies

Maintain and support the libraries' Innovative Interfaces Incorporated

integrated library system

Provide consulting to library personnel regarding new technology initiatives

Assist library departments in hardware/software evaluation, selection, andpricing

Provide technical expertise, support, and training for library automation planning and development

Plan and implement new technologies

Manage IT department, including overall library IT planning and supervision of network administrator, temporary employees, and student workers

135

Appendix 4-4. Position Description: Assistant Dean for Technical Services and Automation

Position: Assistant Dean for Technical Services and Automation
University of Mississippi Libraries
August 2004

Responsibilities
- Manage and provide leadership for Technical Services
- Oversee the accounting unit regarding the library materials budget and serve as signatory
- Manage and provide leadership for library automation, monographic ordering and receiving, as well as electronic resource products and services
- Provide long-term and short-term planning for Technical Services and automation investments by keeping current with trends and standards in addition to assessing resources
- Coordinate vendors providing outsourced services and library materials
- Directly supervise and evaluate seven full-time employees
- Provide feedback for Technical Services staff, committee, and team members as well as Subject Librarians

Chapter 5

Social Survival Skills for the Lone Information Technology Librarian

Michelle Robertson

Overview

The lone information technology (IT) librarian needs to be everything to everyone. Technical skills are essential in this role, but so are social survival skills. Other chapters focus on technical competencies; this chapter addresses the social and communication competencies required for systems work in a small library environment. As our case study, I shall describe my role at the small library at Anne Arundel Community College (AACC) where I work.

In the fall of 2006, AACC had about 5,000 full-time credit students and almost 10,000 part-time credit students. Our students include both traditional- and nontraditional-age students. We have associate's degree students who will transfer to a four-year college or university after completing their work at AACC, as well as individuals working on career-related certificates and those wishing to brush up on their skills with just a class or two.

The Andrew G. Truxal Library at AACC has over 135,000 books and multiple online resources and serves a wide variety of patrons, including students, parents, faculty, staff, and community patrons. The library is small, with six librarians, ten full-time staff, student workers, and a longtime volunteer. Occasionally there are additional volunteers as well. The library departments include the following:

- Library Administration: one librarian, one full-time staff
- Access Services (circulation, reserves, stacks maintenance, copyright compliance, media services): one librarian, three full-time staff (one shared with Systems), one part-time staff, five to nine student workers
- Information Resources (cataloging, interlibrary loan, distance learning services): one librarian, three full-time staff, one volunteer
- Instruction: one librarian
- Reference: one librarian, three full-time staff, three part-time staff
- Systems: one librarian, one full-time staff shared with Access Services

The library systems department consists of two people and is the primary point of contact for computer support in the library. As the Automated Services Librarian, I represent more than two-thirds of the library systems department and am responsible for maintaining library-specific software and services, including the library catalog software, the Web interface to the catalog, the authentication service for access to library databases, and some of the library's Web pages. I communicate with database and library software vendors and install and maintain library-specific software. I also help staff the reference desk two hours a week and provide library instruction. The full-time Library Media Technician, classified as staff, splits her time between the circulation and systems departments. Her systems-related duties include front-line PC troubleshooting and maintaining the computers in the library reference area. Problems and requests regarding library computing equipment and software are first brought to the systems librarian and library media technician. If a problem needs to be referred to the campus help desk, library systems acts as the intermediary for all campus help desk requests.

Introduction

A systems librarian must handle a wide variety of problems and be able to assume a number of different roles. Dealing with people can be one of the biggest challenges a systems librarian faces, regardless of the size of the library. Systems and IT jobs tend to draw technophiles, who are not renowned for their extroversion or people skills. Strong communication skills are an essential competency of the effective IT librarian. This chapter identifies a number of specific competencies based on this overarching concept.

To fully understand a user's need or understand how technology is failing the user, the systems librarian must be able to synthesize the nontechnical information a user provides, identify areas where additional information is needed, and determine the ramifications of the request. Then the systems librarian must communicate the requested change and its effect to all individuals who could be affected and solicit feedback. This process requires clear, strong communication skills and an enthusiasm for initiating conversations. This can present a challenge to the introverted systems librarian.

This process is especially important for the lone systems librarian and for anyone who provides IT services in a small library context. There may not be anyone else in your library who is comfortable dealing with communication issues and who has a solid understanding of technical issues.

Communication with the patron or end user is also important. Systems librarians may not have the patron constantly in mind as they go about their behind-the-scenes work, but they directly affect everyone who uses library services. The library's Web presence is essential to the effective day-to-day operation of the library, especially for remote users who may not ever set foot in the library building. Fortunately, increasing acknowledgement of the importance of usability testing is helping to sensitize us to designing Web pages for the users' needs rather than the librarians'.

In library systems, we tend to hear about the most annoying problems or from the most vocal complainers. It is easy to assume that if no one is complaining, everything is fine. Learning about the problems that library users are encountering, and maintaining communication with those users, is one of the challenges inherent to library systems work. It requires working effectively with staff as well as finding ways to get information directly from patrons.

In a small academic library, the lone systems librarian may have little control over the technology environment. Campus IT often manages the network and makes decisions about most equipment purchases. They may house the servers, maintain the operating system, and handle backups. The systems librarian's ability to install programs on library machines may be restricted.

As a systems librarian you must consider your customers, your environment, and your own personality and skills when determining how best to go about dealing with a problem or pursuing a project. Whom do you need to work with in order to do your job effectively, and how knowledgeable are they about technical issues? The different customer groups the academic systems librarian regularly interacts with include librarians and library staff, patrons, and a variety of other college employees. Each provides a number of challenges and opportunities. This chapter discusses these customer groups and describes 14 character types reflective of the individuals with whom an IT librarian might work. These character types are then used to illustrate the communication challenges the lone IT librarian may encounter, recommendations for dealing with them, and relevant skills. The benefits to the library if these skills are practiced effectively are also addressed. Effective social interaction skills are a core competency for all systems librarians, especially in a small library setting.

Customer Groups

Library employees have a wide range of technical and interpersonal skills. They may have job duties that include excellent analytical ability and advanced computer skills, or they may only use a small number of specific programs in their work.

Staff

The largest group of employees in most libraries is the staff. Because of their wide range of technical skills and knowledge, they present a variety of challenges for the lone IT librarian. A sampling of qualifications for library staff positions in Truxal Library include the following:

- *Required:* Working knowledge of computers and ability to type accurately at a moderate rate, use computer for e-mail, and word processing

- *Required:* Willingness to learn new technical skills in order to enhance performance and maintain currency with developing technologies
- *Required:* One year of experience in data entry or working in a library
- *Required:* Ability to keyboard accurately at a moderate speed using a word processing program
- *Preferred:* Working knowledge of word processing, databases, and/or computerized software

These requirements involve fairly minimal technical skills. However, all AACC employees must complete an online tutorial on information security, and the college offers regular software training on a variety of topics to employees. Members of the library staff are often long-time employees with knowledge of the library's institutional history. Expectations of an ability to analyze and synthesize information are commonly listed in librarian job descriptions but not for staff positions.

Interaction with staff requires a great amount of flexibility on the part of the systems librarian. Different staff members may need different explanations of the same technical problem in order to understand a situation. Staff who are not treated courteously and collegially, or who have not been treated respectfully by a previous systems librarian, may be reasonably reluctant to report problems if they are not urgent.

Librarians

Librarians may or may not have significant technical skills and knowledge. The librarians should have a solid understanding of the procedures that staff are following as they go about their daily work, in addition to having some experience using the integrated library system (ILS). They also may be able to help the systems librarian better understand and answer the more challenging questions brought up by the staff. Some librarians may act as the staff's initial go-to person for questions, before coming to you. Engage the librarians to interpret problems and questions that staff have about the ILS. Librarians who fall into one of the more challenging character types may cause more of a headache if they have a decision-making or gate-keeping role or are able to influence others.

Boss

In a small library environment, the systems librarian's direct supervisor may also be the library director. At AACC, the library director was previously responsible for the ILS and has a solid understanding of technical issues as well as institutional history. Regardless of the library director's grasp of systems concepts, you need to get along with this individual, and ideally you will make it easier for her to do her job, just as she helps you to do yours.

The boss holds the purse strings and is a gatekeeper for approving library projects and directing the systems librarian's work. Her ability to justify projects to the administration can be a deciding factor in whether a project is enthusiastically received and lauded, quietly budgeted, or rejected. She sets the tone for the library's attitude toward technology and for the library's interaction with other departments across campus. She may also be on technology-related administrative committees that determine or advise the technological direction of the institution as a whole. The boss can make the systems librarian's job very easy to do or nearly impossible.

Patrons (Students and the Public)

Sometimes the patron can be the systems librarian's most invisible user even though the library exists to serve the patron. The patrons are ultimately the ones the systems librarian most needs to serve successfully. As a systems librarian, the most likely contact I might have with patrons is through Web form comments or e-mailed complaints and perhaps through face-to-face interaction during an hour spent on the reference desk.

Truxal Library's patrons have widely differing levels of technology skills and needs. Many of our students are traditional-age students who will complete an associate's degree and go on to transfer to a four-year university. Our patrons also include high school students getting a jump start on their college careers, community members who are not affiliated with the college, returning students who may be IT professionals or novices at using a computer, and everything in between.

Campus IT Department

Library systems and centralized IT's roles and responsibilities vary depending on the size of the institution and other factors. The systems librarian at a small library understands library-specific software and hardware needs better than central IT but may not have the expertise or resources in-house to maintain the library servers, much less the building's network infrastructure.

AACC's campus IT department, Information Services (IS), manages all servers that run library-related services and maintains the campus network. It also maintains all computer-related hardware and non-library software for all PCs.

Institutional Factors (College Administration, the Budget)

College administration and the budget can seem remote and not very relevant to the systems librarian's day-to-day work, but they still need to be kept in mind. Hardware and software are expensive. Pay attention to the big picture of technology and systems health. Don't be afraid to envision the possible results of catastrophic server failure. Plan for ways to deal with such a disaster, including developing budget estimates, a technology plan, performance statistics, purchase specifications, political arguments of necessity, and so forth, that the administration may require to make money available.

One of the realities of a community college is that during an economic downturn in the community, adults often decide to go back to school. Community colleges may see significant fluctuations in the types of students who are enrolling and in the programs that are attracting students because of the community college's focus on serving the educational and training needs of the local population. This focus on serving the community's needs can result in quick and innovative changes to the curriculum. The in-house and remote services that the library must provide to students can be greatly affected by these changes, and they may affect the library's budget, purchasing decisions, and focus as well.

Finally, the library's next ILS migration may not be as far off as you might think, given how quickly the current ILS marketplace is changing. If you are concerned that you may need to move to a new ILS soon, make sure the library director is aware and considerations are being taken into account in the administrative budget planning process.

Character Types

Certain challenging behaviors may be exhibited by any of the types of customers you have contact with, including library staff, librarians, student workers, administrators, and library patrons. In Figure 5-1 I detail some of the different behaviors you may encounter. Be assured that not all of these examples draw on real life or reflect individuals at my institution, now or in the past. These "character types" are offered because they are common to the experiences of systems librarians in many places.

Social Survival Competencies for the
Lone Systems Librarian

This section describes the different types of challenges that the lone systems librarian may encounter, strategies for dealing with them, and specific competencies that are key to success. Some challenges are universal, regardless of the particular situation you find yourself in. Others are rare and may be encountered with just a few people.

Communication

Challenges

Maintaining effective communication with diverse groups can be a huge challenge. Pay attention to where communication failures are happening. This is your job, like it or not.

Different people need information explained to them in different ways. Nelly Know-Nothing just wants to know what's broken and when it will be fixed. Polly Power User, on the other hand, is curious about the details and might be able to help. When composing an explanation of a problem that affects a number of

Figure 5-1. Character Types

CHARACTER TYPE	CHALLENGES	STRATEGIES
Nelly Know-Nothing: technologically challenged because of lack of knowledge, insecurity, or fear of technology	Needs to know what information to provide when reporting a problem; may need more help to understand and figure out a workaround for a problem; may need one-on-one time to explain or demonstrate a problem or question	Provide simple, nontechnical explanations to illustrate a problem; expect different learning styles; be patient; reassure her that a problem isn't "just her"; let her know that technology can fail the user in many ways; set expectations and follow through
Secret Sue: won't tell you about problems	Can inconvenience patrons, coworkers and herself; may claim everything is fine; may be unwilling to provide feedback when asked	Address issue directly and explain difficulties that arise in the absence of information; establish regular mode of communication and set expectation for contributions from Sue
Friendly Frank: has trouble with boundaries between colleague and friend; may impose on work relationship inappropriately	Has trouble distinguishing between friendship and a good working relationship; appearance of friendship may lead to perception that Frank receives special treatment or favors; "but I thought we were friends . . ."	Explain that friendship can be a barrier to fair treatment of coworkers across the board; sensitize Frank to concerns and implications, both for the workplace and for him
Larry Luddite: change averse and proud of it	Skeptical of new technology; may slow adoption of necessary upgrades; may become disciplinary problem for supervisors if job performance suffers because of reluctance to adapt	Provide information Larry needs about why a change would be helpful; don't waste time trying to convince him to be enthusiastic about the change; work with him on changes to procedures
Ned Says No: Creates roadblocks for projects not his own; never agrees that other people's projects are important	Will not agree to anything; determined to squash everyone else's projects; resents IT librarian's time spent on others' projects; gets power trip from saying NO; uses influence to derail projects; may repeatedly refuse to comment on a project until very late, and then claim to have disagreed with it from the start	Requires patience and determination; provide opportunities for agreement by presenting projects in small phases; reward cooperation; identify underlying cause of resistance; document his input (or lack thereof)

143

(Cont'd.)

Figure 5-1. Character Types *(Continued)*

CHARACTER TYPE	CHALLENGES	STRATEGIES
Eddie Expert: tries to fix things himself	His attempts to jump in and fix things himself may cause headaches for systems librarians; ego problems; may lead to communication gaps, inappropriate solutions	Ensure procedures are known to Eddie and to rest of staff; provide an avenue for Eddie's suggestions and input; respect the limits of his position and ask for the same consideration
William Wants: wants what others have and tries to get it	Complains about not having everything he wants or needs (especially if someone else has it); may want nonessential software or hardware, or both; at worst, may lie or bully others to get what he wants; may sabotage others	Keep track of what he has and what he requests; document his requests and your answers and double check on changes once they've been made; behavior may be about power rather than resources
Wanda Wannabe: Thinks she knows the systems librarian's job and how best to get things done	Provides too much detail about problems; researches problems, recommends her own solutions and demands that they be provided; cares about the process and insists that her process be used to get results	Get support from higher-ups and colleagues; if not possible, may just have to suffer through; if she repeats past arguments, have her restrict her comments to new ideas
Polly Power User: has grown beyond the typical technology support provided	May push beyond current, standard technology or need advanced technology; has expertise in her own area; may need access to additional resources.	Work with Polly to make sure she has what she needs to do her job; be ready to do additional research if needed; keep her in mind as a possible resource (e.g., she may be able to point you to useful tools or solutions rather than having to find them yourself); take advantage of her expertise
Mother's Helper: asks for things she believes that others want or need	Leaps to conclusions about what others want and need; especially troublesome if individual is highly placed in organizational hierarchy; can lead to lots of wasted time for systems librarian	Recognize that some third-party requests may have merit; ask for details about the need and go directly to the source to confirm, if possible; explain appropriate procedure to Mother's Helper

(Cont'd.)

144

Figure 5-1. Character Types *(Continued)*

CHARACTER TYPE	CHALLENGES	STRATEGIES
Ellen Emergency: everything is an emergency!	Asserts that every problem is urgent; reports same problem multiple times; "forgets" time line for solution that has been provided; unwilling or unable to comprehend institutional bureaucracy that may control timing; circumvents established procedures in the name of emergency; cries wolf	Explain that multiple requests slow response time and create unnecessary work; recognize that some things reported by this individual might really be emergencies; request details immediately if it is unclear whether the problem is really urgent; provide guidelines for reporting problems
Thoughtless Ted	Forwards urban legends and chain letter e-mails; unintentionally installs malware	Be kind but clear; requires more than pointing him to the institution's computer usage policy; emphasize personal responsibility; if you strike the wrong tone, he may turn into Secret Sue
Donald Dumb-Down	"The databases don't work"; does not provide sufficient details to figure out what the problem is	Let Donald know what kind of information to provide; give him alternatives (e.g., either type up the error message or provide a screenshot)
Iris Ideal	Needs to be kept adequately informed about things that could affect her in the future; knowledgeable, reasonable, appreciative, has sense of humor; supplies chocolate	Almost anyone can become Iris Ideal, and any Iris Ideal can fall into the other categories; clear, consistent communication, a willingness to listen, and demonstrated knowledge and concern on the part of the systems librarian will go a long way toward keeping Iris ideal

145

library staff, there is a trade-off between providing minimal information that takes little time to prepare but that will seem inadequate to the technically savvy staff and providing a detailed explanation that will confuse the less technical staff. It may be best to take the time to provide both a simple and a more detailed explanation for these different groups.

Communicating your expectations of others' behavior can be challenging with certain character types. It isn't always going to be possible to convince Larry Luddite of the need for change, regardless of how good your rationale is. Even "this software is being discontinued and will no longer be supported, and if the system crashes we could lose all our data and have no way of getting it back" may not be sufficiently persuasive.

Strategies and Competencies

Strategies that are key to technology-related communication fall into several broad categories: organization, teaching and documentation, planning, consultation and change management, and providing feedback and follow-through.

ORGANIZATION

- Have an established method for questions and problems to be reported to you, and track them. This can be helpful when dealing with Ellen Emergency or if multiple people report the same problem in a public area. Provide guidelines on what information is needed when reporting a problem, and how best to report it.
- It is impossible to keep one step ahead of William Wants, but you can come close. Keep track of what he has and what he requests, have him document his requests, document your answers, and double-check on changes once they have been made.
- There are many opportunities for a misunderstanding when something is communicated secondhand. Be careful when you hear about a problem from Mother's Helper. Make sure you know who wants a change and why. Document the request and send it out to all appropriate parties to confirm the details. These kinds of communication issues can be less politically challenging in a small library than in a larger library setting, where hierarchy often is more formal.

TEACHING AND DOCUMENTATION

- Provide appropriate training and document step-by-step instructions when needed (e.g., for an essential but rarely used ILS procedure when the vendor's documentation is inadequate). You may need to figure out what steps the staff member will need to take, document the steps, and get feedback on what doesn't work. It may be necessary to sit down with Secret Sue or Nelly Know-Nothing and walk through the new process together. Put her at the keyboard and have her show you what she does. This will help identify any problems with the documentation. Checking your work this way is time-consuming, but it ensures that you and the user will both understand the process thoroughly.
- Polly Power User is likely to create her own documentation.
- Sympathize with the user. Software that does not meet the user's needs is not the user's fault, nor is it evidence of faulty procedures. Procedures may need to be adapted to accommodate the software that is available, but never give the impression that you think the software is right and the user is wrong.
- Most staff will appreciate a brief explanation of things in nontechnical language. Don't overload them with information they don't want or need; this wastes your time and theirs. It may be useful to provide a simple version of a problem, followed by a "stop reading here if that's all you want to know" statement and then a more detailed explanation of the problem. If

this seems likely to only create confusion, consider sending separate messages to different groups.

- When a system won't do what the staff member wants and you don't have the ability or resources to fix it, a brief explanation is often preferable to a simple "it won't do that." If you can figure out why the system might be designed the way it is, it may help if you can describe a situation where it would be appropriate for the system to work the way it does. This can help demystify the software design, even if it doesn't solve the staff member's immediate problem. If you take this approach, be sure to emphasize that the designers did not accommodate your site's needs and that their oversight is a flaw in the software.

- Maximize direct communication with patrons via Frequently Asked Questions (FAQs), informative Web pages (e.g., troubleshooting guides for the databases), feedback links for e-mail, and so forth.

- Provide Larry Luddite with the information he needs about why a change will be helpful, without wasting time trying to convince him to be enthusiastic about the change. Listen to his complaints about the change; they may be valid.

- When Eddie Expert is solving problems for himself and others, differentiate between the behaviors that create work for you and the behaviors that are frustrating to you only in principle. It may be necessary to discuss issues with Eddie on more than one occasion and to bring in his supervisor.

- Provide checklists for your coworkers to work from when testing a software upgrade if they have trouble understanding what you want them to test. If the software is new to you, you may be able to get a testing checklist from a similar library that uses the same software and modify it to suit your local needs.

PLANNING

- Warn everyone who might be affected in advance about anticipated downtime so they can plan around it. Ellen Emergency may still report the downtime despite having been warned in advance about it.

- Keep library staff informed of any changes that are coming that may affect their work, without burdening them with useless information. Coordinate downtime with all areas of the library. Communicate with others outside the library to be sure you're not planning to take the system down at the same time the president is bringing notable guests for a tour.

- Keep your boss informed and solicit feedback on the progress of your projects. Ask about campus-wide projects outside the library that could affect you. If your boss has trouble identifying relevant projects, ask to see the minutes of IT-related committee meetings.

CONSULTATION AND CHANGE MANAGEMENT

- Be able to explain how a change will make life better; if this isn't the case, briefly explain why it is necessary. Your customers still might not like the change, but they will better understand why it is happening. Do not pretend that a change will benefit them directly if it isn't true.

- Consult public services staff on changes that will affect the public. Give them time to think about their options and provide feedback, especially during busy times of the year.

FEEDBACK AND FOLLOW-THROUGH

- Provide feedback. If you can't fix the problem now, let them know and explain why (in nontechnical language). If you can fix it, let them know when it has been fixed!

Learning About Problems

Challenges

You can't realistically expect your coworkers to report problems completely and accurately. You will need to get more information from them, let them know your assessment of the problem, and keep them up to date on your progress in solving the problem.

Secret Sue will not tell you if she doesn't understand something. You have to ask if she has questions. Donald Dumb-down will report problems but provide insufficient detail, even if you specify exactly what kind of information you need. People who don't want to provide the information you need can't be forced to talk to you. If you can't get the information you need and this makes it difficult or impossible for you to do your job, you must try to address this issue directly, indirectly, and any other way you can think of that seems workable.

Assess others' strengths and weaknesses. This is essential to know who is likely to need your help and who is likely to be able to help you. Most types of customers will do some of both. Know who is good with spreadsheets, who is good with your e-mail client, and who is good at communicating what they know to others.

Strategies and Competencies

An excellent way to learn about common problems patrons encounter is to work on the reference desk a couple of hours every week. You will learn even more if you treat your interactions with patrons as though you are conducting a usability session. When patrons want help, walk them over to a computer and have them sit down and try a search. Let them do the driving. If it is necessary for you to point at the screen to show them where to click, your interface needs some work. You will see what problems people are having firsthand, and most of them will be problems that no one would ever think to report to you. This can also be helpful in identifying problems with article database design, which can then be reported to the vendor.

If working for two or three hours a week on the reference desk is not an option, make a point to stop by the desk occasionally when it is not busy and chat with the staff there. You will hear and see things that you would not know about otherwise.

Also, regardless of whether you work on the reference desk, consider doing some usability testing to evaluate the design of your resources. This does not take a lot of time and can provide very useful information.

Have the user show you what's happening if you can't reproduce a problem. They may be going about it in a different way. It may be necessary to go to Donald and Sue, sit down with them, and ask them to walk you through the problem on their computer. Donald and Sue may find it impossible to reproduce a problem during a meeting, though, even if it is reliably reproducible. It may be something they encounter only at a certain point in their workflow, for example. Encourage customers who are having an intermittent problem to immediately come and get you the next time they see it. Sometimes this is the only way to understand a problem.

Be proactive by making yourself available. Ask your coworkers what they need and what kinds of problems they are running into. Volunteer to come to library department staff meetings to discuss how things are going, technology-wise. If general questions aren't getting results, ask about specific applications and services, for example, the library catalog or article databases.

Another important way to be available is to have an open-door policy. I sometimes have to drop whatever project I'm working on if there is a systems-related emergency at the circulation desk or in the reference area. It is essential to try to refrain from giving people the impression that you are annoyed or frustrated at the interruption when an actual problem is brought to you. Staff who view you as having a strong commitment to patron services will have more trust in you and will be more likely to notify you of problems. On the other hand, when William Wants, Wanda Wannabe, or Friendly Frank takes advantage of an open-door policy and begins to interrupt your work constantly, it may be necessary to establish some guidelines regarding what kinds of problems are appropriate to bring to you on a whim and what are not.

One of the advantages of working in a small library is that, with such a small number of employees, it is easy to informally get most people's input. If a librarian or other type of supervisor prefers that all official communication go through him or her, it should still be possible to get individuals' input informally as you see them in the library or on campus.

Core competencies that are key to learning about problems include being proactive and anticipating problems.

Time Management

Challenges

Getting it all done is a major hurdle for any systems librarian. It can seem especially overwhelming for anyone who works more or less alone.

Sudden additions to your schedule are unavoidable. They may be relatively insignificant, or they may have a substantial impact on your other projects.

When dealing with Ellen Emergency, it can become very difficult to assess and prioritize problems. It creates unnecessary work for you to analyze a situation and provide feedback on the same problem multiple times.

Strategies and Competencies

Be responsive . . . but don't be too hasty, especially when you have incomplete information about a situation or are dealing with an individual for whom everything is an emergency. Have regular meetings to discuss new problems, ongoing projects, and so forth. Solicit agenda items and send out a tentative agenda ahead of time. Work with your boss and consult others in the library to determine your priorities. If other librarians have projects that require your involvement, you need to know about them ahead of time. If your boss doesn't watch for these kinds of projects for you and let you know about them in advance, ask others regularly about projects they have in mind for the future. If you are having regular meetings as a group and setting your goals as a team, unexpected requests should be brought to the group. "Here are the priorities we agreed on. What do we want to move lower on the list?" If necessary, have a process for dealing with emergency requests.

It can be difficult to keep in mind that some things reported by Ellen Emergency actually are emergencies. Don't take for granted that everything she reports is overblown. However, don't let her rule your schedule.

Ned Says No may wait until the last minute to object to a project, which can throw its time line off track. Try to work with him throughout the project and figure out what he wants. If this fails, do what you can to work around him. Making decisions based on consensus may be the best way to handle this. Do what you can to prepare for his arguments, if they are relevant to the project, but don't let him become a time sink.

Improve your project management skills if you find that you have a serious problem with allocating your time. This can protect against "scope creep" and pin down expected responsibilities, accomplishments, and time lines. Document what you're working on and what you and others have agreed on. Send out the documentation and regular updates to all interested parties, including the library staff.

The core skills relevant to time management include responsiveness, planning, diplomatic skills, organization, political awareness, and an ability to prioritize.

Troubleshooting Problems

Challenges

Diagnosing where things are going wrong can be complicated, especially with non-technical users who may not be able to describe what is happening accurately. Many individuals do not know what information to provide when reporting or describing a technical problem. This can be especially true when the problem is with an off-campus resource; the problem could be occurring anywhere along the line, perhaps with the originating server, their Internet service provider (ISP), your ISP, your network, or the individual's computer. Lack of knowledge can be compounded by time pressures, for example, if a remote user calls the reference desk about a problem accessing the databases at a time when reference is swamped with patrons. When a service that is largely taken for granted suddenly stops working, it can be difficult for a nontechnical person to analyze the problem accurately.

Donald Dumb-Down finds it nearly impossible to provide useful information about a problem, regardless of the situation. He may feel that it is not his responsibility to provide such information, or he may not have the knowledge or confidence to express what he is seeing and doing in appropriate terminology. Continuing to press Donald for information may result in him saying that he has already supplied you with all the information he has.

Strategies and Competencies

Focus on resolving the problem, not the person. I once had a difficult discussion with a patron who was unable to access our article databases from off campus, and after many questions I was able to determine that she was referring to her DSL modem as "Internet Explorer." Once I understood what she meant, I was able to help her resolve the problem. I did not tell her that she was using the wrong term, because that could have embarrassed her and made her feel less comfortable with continuing the troubleshooting process.

Be responsive and understanding about the problems you hear about; this should help encourage staff not to be Secret Sue. If necessary, get at Sue through other people. Ask a coworker in that area or a supervisor to discuss a question with Sue, if you suspect that others might have more success in communicating with such an individual. Take baby steps. Ask: "What problems are you having now?" Find and implement ways to fix these problems or at least to improve things. This will help build trust.

Explain to Donald Dumb-Down that the more information you have about a problem, the quicker you will be able to fix it. However, in most cases you are going to have to go to Donald and have him show you the problem.

Essential skills relevant to troubleshooting include focusing on the problem itself and being able to follow a logical step-by-step process in the face of panicked customers.

Making Decisions and Building Consensus

Challenges

Getting consensus on technical issues and making decisions can be one of the greatest challenges facing the lone systems librarian. As the individual who is most affected by the implementation of technical projects, the systems librarian is often

151

the one who ends up facilitating the decision-making process during planning and implementation.

If a decision about something can't be reached, the systems librarian is stuck in a difficult position; either she must go forward with a project despite a lack of consensus, or she drops the project even though some people support it. This can result in lack of trust and can be damaging to relationships with coworkers. It falls to the systems librarian to make sure that everyone has had a chance to provide input and to respond to the concerns. This can strengthen relationships with others if she takes their concerns seriously, even if they have worries that aren't technically valid or aren't reasonable given the scope of the project. Addressing the concerns in a respectful way will help build consensus.

Ned Says No and Wanda Wannabe can be major roadblocks for making decisions and building consensus. Ned may be selective in the projects he attempts to thwart, or he may disagree with everything you work on. He may even protest projects that were originally his suggestion. He may not complain until work is well underway and many other people are on board with a project. Often he will claim that he disagreed with a project from the beginning, despite never having expressed such an opinion. If his participation is crucial, Ned can derail a project, leading to wasted days or months of work.

Where Ned objects to the direction or final outcome of a project, Wanda Wannabe focuses on the process. She may not like the way decisions are being made or may feel that her perspective is not being given appropriate attention. She may attempt to monopolize meeting time by rehashing how a decision should have been made and by asking repeated questions about whether appropriate procedure is being followed. She also may repeat long-winded arguments about why things should be handled differently.

Being asked to do the impossible is another challenge. Sometimes customers want changes that a given system just can't accommodate or that aren't possible to implement without additional funds and staff.

Strategies and Competencies

Staff-requested changes to library software, especially to the ILS and how it works, can be a major challenge. A change that facilitates workflow for one department may create enormous headaches for another area of the library. The systems librarian must take a leadership role in these situations. If you don't understand the ramifications of a change, you must investigate exactly what is desired and bring that proposed change to both policymakers and practitioners in other areas of the library. Any individual who requests a change without running it by other areas of the library is unlikely to understand the wider impact of the change they're asking for. Tact and diplomacy are required to negotiate the exact change that will do the most good while causing the least amount of inconvenience to other areas.

Talk to individuals in all possible affected areas, let them know the details of the request, and find out their concerns. Ask questions. "What problems do you see with this?" It may help to attend a departmental meeting and talk to them as a group, or it may be better to speak with them individually. It can be very helpful for you to hear what the staff have to say when they discuss this. Attending their meeting or discussion of things that are relevant to your work will make you better informed about the issues of concern, and you will get a better feel for the personalities involved. However, some individuals may feel more comfortable expressing themselves when you are not present, especially if they think you are looking for a particular outcome.

Work with everyone—staff, librarians, and supervisors—to try to get consensus on changes. Wanda and Ned may be motivated by a perceived loss of power or a concern that if a project goes forward it may somehow reflect badly on them. With Wanda, it may be necessary to preemptively ask her to contribute only new thoughts and ideas so that the team can move forward (and remind her immediately when she brings up old issues).

It isn't always going to be possible to convince Larry Luddite of the need for change, regardless of how good your rationale is. You need to provide him with the information he needs about why a change would be helpful, without wasting time trying to convince him to be enthusiastic about the change.

Essential skills in making decisions and building consensus include leadership, diplomacy, and understanding others' interests and needs.

153

Customers' Expectations

Challenges

It can be difficult to keep track of others' expectations of you, but these expectations determine what information your customers provide you, what questions they bring to you, and what things you will never hear from them. Librarians who have a personal stake in your projects can complicate your work, especially if you agree on a project but then priorities shift and the project gets delayed as a result. Know what others expect of you; everyone you work with, including your coworkers, campus IT, your boss, and the administration, may have different expectations of you.

Even in small libraries, territory can be an issue. Who talks to whom and whether or not a librarian wants to be the liaison between you and his or her staff can be a challenging issue, even in situations where all relevant information is effectively communicated.

Friendly Frank may use your friendship to request unusual services or allowances. He may invoke your "friendship" as a way to avoid doing things that others must do; "but I thought we were friends" may be his objection if you bring up concerns about his behavior, and his feelings may be genuinely hurt. Questions along the line of "can you help me with this problem I'm having with my home computer" are also commonplace. It might be a temptation to cave in to Friendly Frank, especially if he is genuinely upset about perceived changes in your relationship.

Another challenging character type is William Wants. William may suddenly "need" a larger flat-screen monitor after someone else in the library gets one or request privileges to override overdues in circulation even though he has no circulation-related responsibilities. His requests for equipment and software may be relevant to his job or may not. He sometimes attempts to circumvent the normal procedure for requests, especially if he knows the request is likely to be denied, and can even resort to belittling and intimidating others to get what he wants.

It is important to be aware that sometimes an individual with a legitimate need for additional resources does not get support from his or her supervisor and will make requests informally because of this. Not everyone who attempts to circumvent established procedures is a William Wants . . . and sometimes even William's requests are reasonable.

Strategies and Competencies

Look for others' motivations, which inform their expectations of you. If your colleagues' goals require that you set up and/or maintain a new service that they will provide, make sure that you don't lose sight of that need. Be able to balance internal needs with projects that may be mandated at higher levels of your organization.

Analyze the motivation behind each request. Be aware of interpersonal dynamics within the library so that you will be aware of the individuals who clash with their supervisors. When an employee and supervisor have communication difficulties, addressing the user's needs appropriately requires tact and diplomacy.

You need to know what your boss wants and what she expects from you. This is helpful in accomplishing your day-to-day work and will be invaluable when you want to argue for new resources, for or against proposed projects, and so forth in the systems area. If supporting the mission of the institution is very important to your boss, consider how your activities are supporting that mission, and use that information to make your decisions about priorities (and to justify them). Being aware of the political situation at your institution will be even more helpful if your boss is not very politically savvy.

Work with William Wants' supervisor to determine what he genuinely needs for his job. Insist that he follow the established procedure for requesting additional resources or permissions. Do not let William be the go-between on discussions with others regarding his requests. Be firm in your handling of his requests.

Some requests aren't technically possible or practical to implement. William or Nelly Know-Nothing may keep bringing up a request after you have explained that it can't be done or that you don't have the resources to make it happen. If your say-so isn't enough, it may be helpful to get confirmation from others . . . or it may not be worth the time. If an old request does become possible to implement in the future, revisit it and find out whether it would still be useful.

Be sure to report software design flaws to the manufacturer or vendor, and identify clearly how the software fails to accommodate your needs. Systems librarians at small libraries may not feel that they have the time to pursue such issues, but you should not allow only large libraries to influence a product's development.

Managing Library Technology

Challenges

Factors that can affect your ability to manage library technology include campus IT, the administration, and the budget. The greatest challenge here is learning about your parent organization and maintaining awareness of issues affecting it. Keeping track of the politics involved as well as the technological trends on campus can be difficult. It can be a challenge to learn what motivates others across your institution. Some of the character types are likely to be present in other areas of your institution as well.

Establishing and maintaining a good relationship with other areas of campus may be a major challenge, especially if the relationship has been bad historically or where personality conflicts are an issue. This kind of work can be frustrating, with very little apparent reward over time. Deciding how much effort is worthwhile in this kind of situation may require regular reassessment.

Strategies and Competencies

Establishing and maintaining a good working relationship with campus IT is essential. Whenever you work with campus IT, try to make the experience a positive one for them. You want them to respect you and to enjoy working with you, and when you call with a problem you want them to be glad you're the one calling about it.

Build trust with them as well. Be careful not to break things, especially things that they will have to fix. Don't be their Eddie Expert. The less often they have to bail you out of a problem you created, the happier everyone will be. However, if you do break something, let them know about it ASAP.

Keep in touch with campus IT about projects of yours that are in the works, and try to keep informed about their projects as well, especially when they are in the planning stages.

If they don't respond, be persistent. For a project, let them know your time constraints. Ask them to let you know what their schedule looks like. If that does not work, you may need to get the library director involved.

The library's relationship with campus IT is critical; if you do not have good support for the library's infrastructure, software, and hardware, it can become extremely difficult and even impossible to serve your users well. Don't schedule your big upgrade when they are in the middle of a big project. Work with their schedule. If you don't know what their schedule is, ask about it.

155

The systems librarian should strive to be an effective liaison between the library and campus IT. Establishing and maintaining this relationship is an essential competency that will help make things much easier when you need to interact with them. IT politics are likely to be different from those in the library. Becoming familiar with the individuals, their skills, and their priorities will help you prepare for discussions with them and report emergencies more efficiently and accurately. Know whom to call about a problem. Go through the channels when appropriate; when you don't, have a good reason.

In your liaison role, be helpful. If someone in your area is having trouble with campus IT, intercede on their behalf and negotiate a resolution, calmly and collegially. This will make things easier for both parties. If you are responsible for front-line troubleshooting of library computer problems, have library staff come to you first and you be the primary contact for campus IT. This will make it possible for you to provide appropriate details about a problem when it is reported, so IT will have better information to begin with.

At AACC, the library was eager to be involved in the implementation of a new content management system (CMS) and began working on moving library Web pages into the CMS much sooner than other areas of campus. The library was recognized for reporting more bugs in the new CMS than any other department on campus. The Web developers appreciated our effort to help improve the CMS interface and have included the library in all subsequent pre-release testing of upgrades.

If campus IT is managing your servers, make sure the appropriate IT people know everything they need to know about the ILS and more, if possible. A data migration is an excellent opportunity for this kind of education. For example, the AACC library's DEC Alpha server running DRA Classic had been kept in a wire closet in the library and was the only system of its type on campus. When the library migrated from DRA Classic to Sirsi Unicorn in 2005, the new server's operating system was AIX, which campus IT was already supporting and maintaining for the college's student information system. As a result, the new library server was housed in the central IT server farm and maintained by IT. The library advocated to have the campus IT database administrator included in all relevant meetings and phone calls with the Sirsi migration consultant and arranged for him to participate in library training both in server-side management and day-to-day use of the software. This was done despite the fact that it made a training slot unavailable to library staff in every training session. The library benefited because it ensured that our IT contact would have an understanding of our processes and work and would hear firsthand our discussions with the trainer about the extent to which the delivered software would need to be customized in order to meet our needs.

Pay attention to budget updates and to the campus IT planning documents you receive; this information may not be fascinating reading, but it has a lot of useful information in it, and it does have a direct impact on your work and the resources that are available to you. It also provides information about the direction of the institution. Where is money being added, and how is it being justified?

Plan ahead, and keep the big picture in mind. Your boss may do this for you . . . or may not. If not, you need to be informed about what is going on at the institutional level. Read the strategic plan; look through any long-term planning documents. Are there campus IT or facilities projects that would affect the library on the five-year plan? On the ten-year plan? How much are your public workstations being used? What about your Web resources? Do you have the data to back up what you know is true?

Your Personal Attributes

Challenges

Being the only technical library person at a small institution can make you feel isolated and can make it difficult to get informal advice on communication issues from other technical people who have had similar experiences. How can you get it all done? Even if no one is making unreasonable or unexpected demands on your time, it isn't possible to do everything your library needs or wants you to do.

Taking the time to understand problems thoroughly is another challenge. This can take some time to research, and it can be difficult to stay on track. Prioritizing the things that you need to follow through on can be very difficult. Making change happen can be both the most frustrating challenge to struggle through and the most rewarding success when it all comes together.

Strategies and Competencies

Evaluate your strengths and weaknesses. Recognize things that make you uncomfortable, and look for ways to address them.

Agitate for change, and be willing to push people. This may be necessary to get software upgrades done in a timely fashion. However, pick your fights. Be able to support your arguments. Don't push a change unless it has concrete advantages that you can explain to others, and listen to their objections. Avoid being the first to try a new software version; wait until some of the bugs have been worked out to reduce stress on staff. This is especially important in a small library environment, where the systems librarian may not have the time to deal with all the bugs and problems that can crop up in a new software release.

Know as much as you can about all areas of the library. Make appointments to go and sit down with the staff, and have them show you what they do. If you can let them know what you want to see and ask them to set aside a few examples to do with you when you are present so they can walk you through the process, you will learn more than if they simply show you the screens they use without doing the work. The better you understand the work that goes on in your library, the easier your job will be.

It is easy to feel overwhelmed and to imagine that library software vendors don't care what you think if you are from a small library. Get to know your peers at other institutions who can help you with advice and testing when you run into problems or bugs in your ILS. Network with systems people at other libraries, and attend appropriate conferences and meetings.

Managing your time is an essential part of getting it all done. Even if no one is making unreasonable or unexpected demands on your time, it isn't possible to do everything you want to do. Prioritize your work and don't lose track of your projects as a result of the inevitable emergencies that crop up.

Know how to negotiate and work out a resolution to problems that will work for everyone involved. Be proactive in recognizing when an intermediary is needed.

Conclusion

What social and communication skills does the lone systems librarian need to succeed? Being flexible, eager to learn new things, and interested in ferreting out problems and trying to fix them will help keep your job interesting. You need to be an advocate for change, willing to push others when needed, but also able to identify when pushing will be unproductive or detrimental. You must have strong communication skills; this will help you get the resources you need and will also help you be more effective in your day-to-day work. You need to be able to determine when to get started on a long-term project and when to delay based on the amount of work that you currently have to do and that may be coming your way in the future. Accept that interruptions are unavoidable.

Get input from your customers—staff, librarians, the library director, students, teaching faculty, and your users. Listen to what your customers tell you, and look for things they are not telling you. Take their concerns into account. Make room to deal with problems as you find out about them; if one customer is having a problem, others probably are having that problem too. Provide others with the tools they need to help you do your job.

Finally, keep your sense of humor. If all else fails, make friends by bringing doughnuts.

Part III

SUCCESSFUL
COMPENTENCY
IMPLEMENTATION
PROGRAMS

Reinventing Information Technology Support at the Public Library of Charlotte and Mecklenburg County, North Carolina

Kevin Moderow

Overview

During the 1990s, the Public Library of Charlotte and Mecklenburg County in North Carolina experienced a period of rapid growth. To support the resulting increase in new technology, individual library branches hired their own technical support personnel. However, by the year 2000, economic reality set in, and the existing model of technical support could no longer be sustained. A new technical support infrastructure was needed. I helped the library system develop a new model that centralized technical support and developed a standard set of technological competencies for all librarians and staff.

Introduction

My first adventure in technical support was in the seventh grade when I was pulled out of Social Studies class to set up a new computer lab. Being an awful student and one who was particularly bored to tears with classroom work, this method of escape became a habit. I also learned that if I never quite finished what I was doing in the lab they would have to keep pulling me from class.

My junior high school had just purchased TRS-80 personal computers. The faculty didn't know what to do with them, but computers were obviously important. They must do something.

That was 1981, and the curriculum at Springman Junior High was a bit prophetic. We didn't use the new computers to learn typing, which was the norm back then. We were actually taught (or, rather, taught ourselves) the science of programming. We wrote BASIC programs, and basic they were indeed. The little

Radio Shack wonders were some of the earliest color computers, and they opened up (to us at least) endless possibilities. I learned the TRS-80. By that I mean I could set it up. I could program it, and I could teach others (including my elders) the same. I was technical support.

Later came the Apple II and the Apple IIe (uppercase capable) upgrade. We learned hexadecimal coding so we could crack open the locks on our favorite games. We were inquisitive—an ingredient in technical support that probably is the greatest predictor of one's success.

Our school dropped the TRS-80 as it and other schools in our district were standardizing on the Apple product line. This was my first experience with an industry standard, and it was one that lasted until Super Bowl XX, when a blond jogger in skimpy shorts threw a hammer into the eyes of oppression.

That year was 1984. The Mac was supposed to change the world. It did, and it altered the course of my life.

Two decades later I'm still doing the same things in many ways. I'm a hacker and a cracker. My current business card says Senior Information Technology Manager for the Public Library of Charlotte and Mecklenburg County, but that's a title. What I and my staff do and how we do it is just like junior high. We're inquisitive.

In the typical public library during the 1990s, being inquisitive was just about enough to qualify a person to provide technical support (to be a "techie "). Library applications were not terribly complicated, and user demands were miniscule by comparison to today. So it was common for technical support staff to be picked from library staff if they were inclined and if they were, well, inquisitive about computers.

The Technical Support Problem

The Public Library of Charlotte and Mecklenburg County has over 20 branches serving a 500 square mile region. During the 1990s, funds were plentiful, and much of it was spent on computer technology. Computers grew from 50 personal computers (PCs) in the mid-1990s to over 500 by the year 2000. However, it was relatively difficult for staff to adjust to the new PC technology. The computers were not as reliable as terminals, and patrons were bringing more and more technology issues to the library staff, which is not what the library staff had gone to school for.

During this time, a model of technical support was based on hiring techies at local branches. A library branch would produce a "techie," or, if it was a library of sufficient size, several techies would be "born" as new technology was added. These techies weren't computer science majors in college and probably did not carry a single industry certification, but they were chosen, or they themselves chose, to be the computer person based on their enthusiasm and comfort with technology. These local techies reported to the local branch manager and sometimes were also expected to perform other, non-information technology (IT)–related duties. There was no central authority or consistency.

This model worked well while there was sufficient funding to purchase computers and hire techies to get them out there on the floor for our patrons. Regular library staff were not typically involved very much at this point because the PCs were "over there" and staff were still accessing the OPAC through a TTY (teletype) terminal.

Problems arose, however, because the size of our PC fleets grew by leaps and bounds. The local techie model of support was being strained. Patrons and staff began using a variety of different applications and came to expect reliable access to the technology. Exacerbating the problem was the fact that this model of technical support had created a dependency on the techie. Library staff were not motivated to learn about these new technologies, because the techie had always been there to take care of problems.

I call this dilemma of hiring a techie and then handing all technical problems off on him the Dump 'n' Run model (see Figure 6-1). Staff who were dependent on the computer guy to solve technology-related problems and deal with patrons with technology-related questions were the recipients of the Dump. Having always been dependent on the techie in previous years, library staff were accustomed to doing the Run, and after leaving their issue with the techie they would move onto real library business.

Our library was faced with the Dump 'n' Run model at the end of the 1990s but did not identify it as a problem until years later. Those years were very good to the Charlotte, North Carolina, metropolitan area, and rising tax revenues were a guarantee. With increasing budgets and a technical support model that appeared to work, more and more techies were added each year.

Our staff's dependency on the techies grew as well. When growth in revenues waned for a few consecutive years, everything changed. The techies no longer grew in number. Library staff became frustrated that there was never enough technical support staff around. In fact, after several dry years, talk began of reassigning the techies to other areas of the library.

163

Figure 6-1. Dump 'n' Run Support Model

| Step 1 | Step 2 | Step 3 |
| Break Computer | Get Supervisor Involved | Call Techie |

This sent shockwaves through our library system. Just the mere suggestion of removing the techies from branches throughout the system was enough to burn holes in the grapevine.

As the manager of the library system's central IT department, I was summoned to several secret meetings. We discussed the unthinkable with senior library administration officials. They wanted to know what would happen if a day came when the techies weren't there. We were sworn to secrecy and dismissed but not before it was made clear to us that something would have to replace the Dump 'n' Run techie model.

Creating the Solution

In the old technical support model, techies did not report formally to the IT department. The techies were part of the library's public services apparatus. This by itself was a broken system. Conflicts between public services' techies in the branches and the central library system IT staff were endless.

As Senior Technology Manager it was not as though I was to lose any staff as a result of the proposed reductions, because the techies were not part of my department. This perhaps provided me some comfort to think freely, outside the box as they say.

When summoned by the library administration for what I felt had to be the last secret meeting on this subject (it wasn't), I presented my findings. "What if we said technology is part of everyone's job?" I asked. The looks were stern to say the least. Daggers were being stared right through me by senior library officials most of whom had cut their teeth in the public services wing of the organization. "What is this punk talking about?" they thought to themselves, and some even said it out loud later.

What I was talking about was "core competencies," although that term was coined later by the bureaucracy after audacious youths like me had been dismissed from the process. What I had in mind was to develop a set of skills in technology that we would expect all of our staff to have or to learn. I felt this approach had several advantages:

- it would empower staff,
- reduce calls to our help desk,
- increase up time, and
- reduce the "technology gap."

My proposed solution had four key components. First, it would reduce, centralize, and mobilize frontline technical support. We would be able to get all technical staff on the same page and standardize procedures. Second, it would allow us to develop specialized back-end support. The existing expert staff in central IT would be able to deepen their skills and focus their efforts on several key areas: network infrastructure, Windows clients and servers, the integrated library systems, and emerging technologies. Third, an online ticket tracking system would be used to manage deployment of techies to remote locations and let staff know who is doing what. Finally, at the heart of the new technology support structure was the development of a list of core competencies that would enable all library staff to better understand and control their own branch computers.

I was, not surprisingly, charged with developing the first set of core competencies. The next section represents my thinking and development of the initial concepts used to formulate these competencies. The framework I discuss got us through our transitional years. Those were the critical times, specifically when our library moved from a model of dependency on techie staff to a more decentralized and collaborative form of technical support. Later this list was refined and improved by other staff in our library; but the final form of the competency checklists is highly specific to our organization (see Appendices 6-1 through 6-5).

Appendix 6-1 outlines the four core sets of competencies in their final form. Core I (Appendix 6-2) are technology competencies expected of all library staff. Core II (Appendix 6-3) are competencies directed at public services staff. Core III (Appendix 6-4) and Core IV (Appendix 6-5) list competencies that apply to specialized technologies that may not be available at all branches. These competency checklists are used as a part of the personnel performance review process. Both employees and supervisors can view the checklists on the library's intranet. When a skill has been demonstrated (usually to a Level I technician) it is checked off.

However, for libraries interested in developing their own core competency list, the conceptual framework that follows is likely to be more helpful than the detailed checklists. When I first sat down to write the competency list, I drew heavily on what I had seen in how technology was supported over the past two decades. If I could have designed or controlled the staff I had been supporting, what would I have wanted them to know? These competencies focused on three areas: infrastructure, library technology, and online collaboration.

Infrastructure Competencies

Before we can help our staff understand higher levels of specific technical services and applications knowledge, they have to know what they are looking at. Think in terms of your help desk or call center: what do you want the users to know when they are asking for help?

First and foremost, you would want staff to know the correct technical terminology so they can describe what they are looking at and you can guide them to a solution. Infrastructure knowledge falls into three areas: hardware, printers, and network.

Hardware Knowledge Core

Originally, I would have been happy if callers to our help desk could just identify whether they were using a public PC or a staff PC. When our technology trainers worked out the details of our core competencies they developed more detail. You will see from Appendix 6-2 that this competency branched out into the identification of all of the hardware components in our libraries.

Under the hardware competency, we want staff to know which PC model they are calling about. We want them to be able to power up and recycle the power on the machine. We want them to identify a CRT versus a flat-panel display. As part of this competence, you might also want to consider including in this core some knowledge about the benefits of the two display types. For example, you may want staff to understand that the elderly or the visually impaired often prefer the CRT display, because they find the flat panels, particularly older models, difficult to stare at for great lengths of time. Just by including this fact in the Hardware Knowledge Core you may have made your library a touch friendlier to this growing part of your community.

Obviously, library staff had better know a mouse from a keyboard. You may laugh, but if you don't put it in your core you may be asking for trouble.

Printer Knowledge Core

If we could just eliminate printers from this world we could probably cut our help desk calls by a third or more. We would also be doing a tremendous service to our environment.

In reality, people print. Our patrons expect this service, as do our staff members. Before calling the help desk, however, we need library staff to know some basics about printers. In particular, is this a dedicated printer for one individual or a shared network printer? This is critical in terms of triage, so our help desk staff understand the scale of the problem.

In the Printer Knowledge Core we included the ability to identify the printer type as well. We want staff to know the difference between toner versus ink printers (including the type "impact printer" for bonus points). This core competency also includes some knowledge of the costs associated with printers. Introduce staff to the concept of cost per page—CPP. When people understand the costs associated with ink-based printers they often are more receptive to the notion of sharing a larger, networked and toner-based printer. You may then find that your CPP is reduced system wide.

Network Knowledge Core

No, we are not going to ask staff to become Cisco Certified. We do, however, want them to understand some basic networking concepts. These are easier for non-technical people to learn than you might think.

First, require that library staff can identify some basic components. The Ethernet device on their desktops and the Ethernet cable are good starting points, because the help desk person is going to have to ask, "Are you plugged into the network?" For bonus points you may consider adding the ability to identify whether the connectivity light is lit on the Ethernet device, although be careful here as not all manufacturers include this feature.

We also want them to understand concepts that will help the help desk personnel determine where on the network the problem is located. Is the problem the caller is experiencing limited to his or her desktop? Does it affect all desktops? Does it affect the branch as a whole?

Specifics about the connection proved to be difficult to cover in the Network Knowledge Core. My staff developed a Web site called *Helpdesk* to assist with this. It displays to the user his or her network IP number, the name of the proxy server being used, and some other key information. So, rather than having this core require that staff understand these concepts, we can merely require that they be aware of the *Helpdesk* page and can read the information displayed about their connection there.

In conclusion, technical support staff and other members of the library staff need to have some basis for successful communications concerning infrastructure issues. Help desk staff understand that technical problems affect the library's staff and patrons, and they are eager to help, but staff must be able to communicate with them using terminology that puts both parties on common ground.

I'm reminded of a call that once came into our help desk. The caller reported that her PC was off. After being asked to check around her branch she added that all of the PCs were off and would not power on. She informed the help desk that none of the monitors would power on either.

"Let me ask you," the help desk said. "Are the lights on in your branch?"
"Oh no," she replied. "They've been off all morning too."

So you can see that nothing is too basic.

Library Technology Competencies

Staff should know what the library offers in terms of technology. Once they have an understanding of the overall technological landscape for the entire library system, which I shall refer to as "enterprise level services," the core competencies should then specify what services are available at their specific location. Core II (Appendix 6-3) addresses many of the competencies specific to local branches, particularly technology services for the public.

Enterprise Level Services

First, let's look at the enterprise level of knowledge here. Put yourself in your patron's shoes for a moment. You have just been relocated by your company and are walking into your local branch for the first time. You approach the information desk. What do you want your contact to know?

Does the library have a Web presence? Where is it located, and what services are available online? Is the OPAC available? Can I reserve books online? Are branch locations and contact information available on the library's Web site?

This is enterprise level information. It's not the sort of technical information about library services that technology folks are concerned with, but that level of detail isn't needed on the front line. In terms of core competencies, when we speak of enterprise level information we are talking about what the library system as a whole offers in technology services.

Location-Specific Services

Once competencies in enterprise level services are mastered, the front-line public service staff can answer the newcomer's questions regarding what the library system is all about and what services and technologies the institution has invested in. For instance, all locations share common technologies such as the OPAC and access to the Internet. However, not all branches are the same. We also wanted staff to understand the specific technologies in use at the location level. For example, not all locations in our library system have wireless networks.

The variations in local services have as much to do with floor plans as they do with funding. Wireless just doesn't make sense in a location where there is no place to sit. In this section of the competencies we wanted a list of those specific services available in the branches. We also wanted the staff to understand why certain technologies may or may not exist so they can pass that information on, rather than just telling our patrons that a particular technology hasn't been funded yet.

Another example of location-specific services is the software available under the local user profile. If we don't have adequate staff to support the public's use of something like a programmable database application, we simply aren't going to offer it in the local user profile on the public desktop PCs.

The purpose of Core II is not to list all of the required knowledge to support the location-specific services but rather to explain to the newcomer at that location what is available, and perhaps a bit of the why as well (see Figure 6-2).

Catalog Skills

All staff should be able to find materials for patrons. At a time when we seem to be forever short staffed, we simply cannot limit this competency to professional librarians.

The intricacies of our OPAC are going to require a set of competencies a bit more detailed than simply understanding how to search. Paraprofessional staff may feel they have this skill already because they are familiar with Google; but, we know that our OPAC systems have peculiarities that they do not share with Google and that it therefore requires training to use them with proficiency.

The core competencies in catalog skills we want staff to have are simply the skills we want patrons to have. We want them to be able to locate materials of course, but we also want them to understand how to place items on hold and how to specify a pickup location. We want them to understand how to access the catalog

Figure 6-2. Example of Core II Competencies for Local Branch Services

✓	N/A	A.	BASIC BRANCH TECHNOLOGY KNOWLEDGE
☐	☐	1.	Knows levels of service that are available under each login (e.g., Internet access versus online resources only, what kind and version of word processor is available, etc.).
☐	☐	2.	Knows which computers/logins have full versus restricted Internet access.
☐	☐	3.	Has basic understanding of how a computer has full versus restricted Internet access.
☐	☐	4.	Can explain the purpose and benefits of the borrower self-sufficiency initiatives, including receipt printers, Express Check, self-holds, and can use the system as a borrower.

remotely if we've made that service available. We want staff and patrons to have a basic understanding of Boolean logic to facilitate their searches.

Application Skills

The core competencies for application skills is perhaps the most wanting in libraries I visit. Library techies are very quick to add applications to PC profiles but are not nearly as quick to empower staff to understand the applications. As a result, patrons often do not get the assistance they need.

In our system, applications are determined by the different types of user profiles created for each computer. To understand what applications are available, we started by creating an inventory of what the local user profiles offered. Once we had a list of these applications, we could move on to create the basic and necessary skills.

Examples of what might appear in the applications inventory include the word processor, Internet browser, media plug-ins, and other so-called office applications. Of course you are never going to fully empower all staff to completely facilitate the deployment of these applications, but there are some obvious essentials.

One application recognized as essential in our Core II is the résumé. Using our word processor, staff must have the ability to manipulate various résumé formats. If we offer spreadsheet access, then staff should be trained in producing a simple expense report.

Basic application skills such as these lead to further learning. One reason staff expertise in applications is minimal and remains dormant is that there is little opportunity or desire to explore and expand on these skills. In addition to helping staff meet the requirements of this core, staff training is often the little push that is needed to generate some intellectual curiosity, which in the end will produce better service for our patrons.

Internet and Emerging Technologies Competencies

The Internet Community

The Internet community is no longer limited to insomniacs staying up late for all-night chats. Our patrons who would otherwise lead rather normal lives are involved in the emerging socialization of the Internet.

Examples include not simply chat rooms with reading and messaging but also virtual reality, gaming, and online communities. Our libraries offer facilities for these activities, but our staff thus far lack the awareness to be engaged and supportive of patrons in these areas. We need to begin requiring our staff to learn more about these emerging technologies.

New Demands on Library Systems

The Internet community in turn places demands on our systems. The tip of this spear is network bandwidth. Adding network circuits to the Internet is a lot like expanding lanes on a busy road. You can't build them fast enough.

While network administrators have their hands full with bandwidth issues, staff need to be able to visually identify problems. If staff are versed in the emerging technologies of this community, such as bit torrent, peer-to-peer sharing, and whatever the latest mp3 music platform is, then they can identify problem users without requiring technical support.

Often this quick identification of a problem user is enough to solve a network slowdown. There are tools to assist as well. Packet sniffers such as NTOP's WWW interface (www.ntop.org) can be used to allow staff to see who the top users are of network resources. The interface is simple enough that the ability to read NTOP's charts requires little training.

The Changing User Base

A librarian once told me that the worst thing to happen during his career was the invention of the Web browser. This graphical tool for the Internet opened the technology up to the masses.

As the Internet faces growing demands, so do our libraries. Our computer labs are now a reflection of all of our communities. Users are no longer traditionally Caucasian, male, and young. Our staff have an enormous task facing them now, because they must become knowledgeable of so many different types of users and their wide-ranging needs.

The constantly changing technologies of the Internet are a challenge for staff to learn and keep up with. There simply is no checklist that can cover the demands placed on library staff by the changing Internet technology environment. It is as diverse and as rapidly expanding as the communities we serve.

The only strategy therefore is lifelong learning. We will have to align emerging Internet technologies with the performance review of the librarian. Many libraries have a healthy approach to setting goals toward changing Internet technologies that make the continuous learning intriguing if not enjoyable even for nontechies on staff.

Realigning the IT Staff

Empowering our library staff with core competencies caused us to reexamine our IT staff. We have lifted front-line library staff up to what was our first level of technical support. They are now finding their own Web sites, clearing their own printer jams—perhaps even formatting their own résumés after updating them with their new skills.

The IT staff have been empowered as well. Freed from the more mundane tasks associated with Level I support, they can now focus on higher level skills development and the higher level technical support associated with them.

IT personnel could now be tiered. Higher level skill sets could be directed toward more complex technology developments, while lower level skill sets could be realigned and Level I support redefined at the same time.

Working from the ground up, we now have higher competencies in our library staff to maintain PCs, printers, and patron questions. Where we once had a group of techies performing these tasks, they are now freed up. With fewer of the more routine tasks on their agenda two things were changed in Level I staff. First, the techie support staff could be reduced in number. Second, they could be mobilized.

These two changes in Level I staff benefit the library strategically. Empowered staff means less demand for quasitechies to solve their more mundane problems. This is a budget analyst's dream. We have achieved higher levels of productivity from our library staff, enabling us to reduce the head count of staff in the higher pay classification enjoyed by techies.

However, because there are fewer Level I techies to support the same number of library locations and maintain an ever-growing PC fleet, we decided the Level I technical staff would have to become mobilized. Rather than work from a fixed location, they cover multiple library locations and departments. Mobilization has had the added benefit of homogenization. To put it another way, PC deployments in libraries have become less proprietary and subject to the whims and quirks of individual techies and more consistent and standardized. Standardized disk cloning, wiring, and software schemes create fewer problems, which makes the overall management of PC assets much less complicated.

Higher level IT staff, sometimes called Level II, were transformed as well. Once burdened with issues of front-line support and training of the myriad of techies, this group can now focus on strategic projects for library technology. Fewer in numbers than Level I and less mobilized, the Level II staff can take on project management in areas that enable library technology to grow, improve, and modernize. Examples of Level II projects in our library include a print management and PC reservation system, Web development, wireless deployments, and voice over Internet protocol.

171

Managing IT

Having defined core competencies allows library technology to grow in breadth and complexity, which is a boon for the library organization but at the same time it can cause headaches for the IT manager. Core competencies allow empowered staff to fix their own computer problems. The core competencies in our library system also created a streamlined and mobile Level I technical staff as well as a focused and more complex Level II project load. How do we manage it all?

The library's information technology department is all about automation, and now it was time to automate some parts of the management of IT. Ticket or job tracking was the key to management of this more complex environment.

Simply put, a ticketing system keeps track of what all these people are doing. Tasks are entered into an online database that issues a ticket tracking number. While this would seem to depersonalize the relationship between users and technical support, the benefits far outweigh the negatives. There are simply too many issues for any person or group to keep track of. Issues such as a network outage tend to be reported to a help desk multiple times because staff are not aware that a colleague has already filed a report. The ticket system can eliminate this. Once a ticket is issued, any future reporting of the issue can be checked for redundancy. Furthermore, staff can verify an issue has been reported without wasting the time it takes to call an issue into the help desk.

Another benefit is that IT staff are always aware of what tasks to do. A good ticket system allows creation of task lists for IT personnel. This reduces the amount of verbal communication that needs to take place between the IT manager and IT staff. The online system has the effect of creating a direct dialogue between the problem reporter (front-line staff) and the problem solver (IT support).

The IT manager can also quickly ascertain the status of projects and issues. This significantly reduces the time the IT manager spends addressing inquiries such as, "Where does my project stand?" and "Why hasn't this been fixed yet?"

An online ticketing system also gives the IT manager a new set of tools for evaluating IT personnel. Working directly with the database, custom queries can be created to look at the workload of each IT staff member. This can quickly identify problem areas and needs for new training of staff.

Conclusion

At first glance the benefits of core competencies appears to be limited to front-line library staff, but in reality the benefits cascade up the technology chain and all the way through the IT support structure to the IT manager. Rather than simply shifting the burden of something like clearing printer jams to librarians, core competency requirements create a paradigm shift for the whole support of library technology.

Our library organization was able to compartmentalize technology issues and refocus our strongest technologists into new and expanding technologies. The efficiencies and effectiveness of core competencies now permeate throughout the organization.

Appendix 6-1. Information Technology Core Competencies: Competencies Outline

Core I

- PLCMC Technology Overview
- Basic Branch/Department Technology Knowledge
- Basic Hardware Knowledge
- Printer Knowledge
- Operating System Knowledge
- Basic PLCMC Troubleshooting
- Basic Application Skills
- Using Internet Explorer/Mozilla
- Basic PLCMC Outlook/Webmail Skills
- Basic Word Processing Skills

Core II

- Basic Branch Technology Knowledge
- Searching HIP (Horizon Information Portal)
- Searching Staff PAC
- Horizon Check In
- Horizon Borrower Records
- Horizon Check Out
- PC Reliance Check Out
- Horizon Other
- Intermediate Word Processing Skills
- Basic Spreadsheet Skills (Microsoft Excel/OpenOffice)
- Basic Presentation Skills (Microsoft PowerPoint/OpenOffice)

Core III

- PC Reservation Staff Software Skills
- PC Reservation Borrower Software Skills
- LPT One Staff Software Skills
- LPT One Borrower Software Skills
- Express Check Borrower Software Skills
- Express Check Staff Software Skills

Core IV

- Audiovisual Knowledge
- PLCMC Intermediate Troubleshooting
- PLCMC Imaging
- Public Technology Training Skills

Appendix 6-2. Information Technology Core Competencies Checklist: Core I

EMPLOYEE			START DATE		COMPLETION DATE	

The following are the foundation Information Technology Core Competencies that are suggested for all PLCMC staff. The employee should check each item as competency is acquired or mark N/A for competencies that are not applicable.

✓	N/A	A.	**PLCMC Technology Overview**
☐	☐	1.	Familiar with basic structure, organization, and function of the Information Technology Department within the PLCMC organization.
☐	☐	2.	Familiar with PLCMC rules of conduct regarding e-mail and computer use.
☐	☐	3.	Familiar with Core Competency Plan for PLCMC and with individual Core Competency Plan.
☐	☐	4.	Can navigate through PLCMC Central and find information pertinent to job duties.
☐	☐	5.	Can log in to and navigate through MyHR. Can enter time sheet via MyHR.
☐	☐	6.	Thorough understanding of PLCMC's Internet Use Policy for the public.
☐	☐	7.	Familiar with CIPA and its implications for the library.
☐	☐	8.	Knows how to complete and submit a request for CIPA block and unblock.

✓	N/A	B.	**Basic Branch/Department Technology Knowledge**
☐	☐	1.	Knows branch (or department) logins and passwords.
☐	☐	2.	Knows location of spare computer equipment (e.g., extra keyboards, mice, and toner cartridges) and how to request more when supplies are low.

✓	N/A	C.	**Basic Hardware Knowledge**
☐	☐	1.	Knows how to turn a computer on and off properly.
☐	☐	2.	Knows how to reboot a computer; knows the difference between a hard and soft boot and under what circumstances to use each.
☐	☐	3.	Knows how to replace a mouse and keyboard.
			Can identify the following the following hardware components:
☐	☐	4.	• CPU (central processing unit)
☐	☐	5.	• Monitor (CRT or flat screen)
☐	☐	6.	• Parallel ports
☐	☐	7.	• Serial ports
☐	☐	8.	• PS/2 ports
☐	☐	9.	• USB ports

(Cont'd.)

Appendix 6-2. Information Technology Core Competencies Checklist: Core I (Continued)

✓	N/A	C.	Basic Hardware Knowledge (Cont'd.)
☐	☐	10.	• Floppy drive
☐	☐	11.	• CD-ROM drive
☐	☐	12.	• Power cord
☐	☐	13.	• Monitor cable
☐	☐	14.	Knows how to clean external PC surfaces including: PC case, monitor, keyboard, mouse.
☐	☐	15.	Knows how to take apart and clean mouse including: ball and rollers.

✓	N/A	D.	Printer Knowledge
☐	☐	1.	Can identify local versus networked printers.
☐	☐	2.	Can identify location of printers for a given PC.
☐	☐	3.	Can print a test page from Windows to identify the printer name, model, and IP address.
☐	☐	4.	Can replace toner or ink cartridges for printers.
☐	☐	5.	Can load paper into paper trays for printers.
☐	☐	6.	Can clear a paper jam.

✓	N/A	E.	Operating System Knowledge
☐	☐	1.	Can identify a computer's operating system and version.
☐	☐	2.	Can identify which user is logged in.
☐	☐	3.	Can log off and on as a different user.
☐	☐	4.	Knows how to use a mouse, keyboard, and function keys.
☐	☐	5.	Knows the functions of the left and right mouse buttons.
☐	☐	6.	Knows how and when to double click versus single click the mouse.
☐	☐	7.	Can identify the active window.
☐	☐	8.	Can print to a non-default printer.
☐	☐	9.	Can cancel a print job (if user permissions allow).
☐	☐	10.	Can clear the print queue (if user permissions allow).
		11.	Can change the default printer (if user permissions allow).

✓	N/A	F.	Basic PLCMC Troubleshooting
☐	☐	1.	Knows how to contact the Help Desk via e-mail and phone. Knows under what circumstances to use each.

(Cont'd.)

175

Appendix 6-2. Information Technology Core Competencies Checklist: Core I (Continued)

✓	N/A	F.	Basic PLCMC Troubleshooting (Cont'd.)
☐	☐	2.	Knows how to identify a PC's proxy server and network settings via helpdesk.plcmc.org.
☐	☐	3.	Knows what information to give the Help Desk when reporting a problem.
☐	☐	4.	Is familiar with the PLCMC Help Desk Ticket System.
☐	☐	5.	Can use helpdesk.plcmc.org to search for tickets for branch and for individual.
☐	☐	6.	Can use helpdesk.plcmc.org to determine status of issues.
☐	☐	7.	Can capture and e-mail a copy of a screenshot to the Help Desk.
☐	☐	8.	Knows how to troubleshoot/fix common branch or department specific technology issues.
☐	☐	9.	The ability to distinguish between and identify the different logons used by PLCMC: e.g., Windows logon user ID, Windows logon domain, Horizon logon, Webmail logon, Outlook logon (if used), PLCMC Central logon (if used).
☐	☐	10.	The ability to determine whether a PC is being logged on using a local login (login box with 2 fields) or a domain login (login box with 3 fields).
☐	☐	11.	Can plug in and unplug a power cord from the CPU/monitor/printer and from the wall.
☐	☐	12.	Can plug in and unplug a network cable and tell whether the terminator is firmly seated or broken.
☐	☐	13.	Can plug in and unplug a monitor cable and tell whether the terminator is firmly seated or broken.
☐	☐	14.	Can plug in and unplug a PS/2 or USB cable or device and tell whether the terminator is firmly seated or broken.
☐	☐	15.	Can tell whether any item is on or off or in power-saving mode (e.g., surge protector, monitor, CPU, printer).

✓	N/A	G.	Basic Application Skills
☐	☐	1.	Can open and save a file to the computer's hard drive and floppy drive.
☐	☐	2.	Can print a file.
☐	☐	3.	Can change the page settings for a file before printing.
☐	☐	4.	Can specify to print in color or grayscale.
☐	☐	5.	Can minimize, maximize, restore, and resize windows.
☐	☐	6.	Can troubleshoot floppy disk problems.

(Cont'd.)

Appendix 6-2. Information Technology Core Competencies Checklist: Core I (Continued)

✓	N/A	H.	Ising Internet Explorer/Mozilla
☐	☐	1.	Can scroll up and down and side to side on a Web page.
☐	☐	2.	Can use navigation buttons in browser (e.g., back, forward, refresh, stop).
☐	☐	3.	Can search for text on a Web page.
☐	☐	4.	Can navigate through the PLCMC family of Web sites.
☐	☐	5.	Can type in a URL and go to a specific Web site.
☐	☐	6.	Can perform a basic Internet search.
☐	☐	7.	Understands what a pop-up window is, how to close out of one, and the tools in place to prevent pop-ups.
☐	☐	8.	Knows how to temporarily and/or permanently allow pop-ups (e.g., when replying to or forwarding messages from PLCMC Webmail).
☐	☐	9.	Can search for images using Google image search.
☐	☐	10.	Can search for information using PLCMC's Online Resources page.
☐	☐	11.	Can print all or part of a Web page.
☐	☐	12.	Can change the text size on a Web page using the menu and/or toolbar options.

✓	N/A	I.	Basic PLCMC Outlook/Webmail Skills
☐	☐	1.	Can log in to PLCMC Webmail (all employees).
☐	☐	2.	Can log in to Outlook (if used by employee).
☐	☐	3.	Can view a message.
☐	☐	4.	Can reply, forward, and delete a message.
☐	☐	5.	Can recover a Deleted Item.
☐	☐	6.	Can view Sent Items.
☐	☐	7.	Can empty the Deleted Items folder.
☐	☐	8.	Can create, edit, and delete appointments (if employee uses Outlook).
☐	☐	9.	Can set a reminder for an appointment (if employee uses Outlook).
☐	☐	10.	Can create, edit, and delete tasks (if employee uses Outlook).
☐	☐	11.	Can set a reminder for a task (if employee uses Outlook).
☐	☐	12.	Can turn on and off the Out of Office Assistant.
☐	☐	13.	Can attach a file to an e-mail message.
☐	☐	14.	Can turn on the junk mail filter and apply appropriate settings as needed in Outlook.
☐	☐	15.	Can create and use a custom e-mail signature (if employee uses Outlook).

(Cont'd.)

Appendix 6-2. Information Technology Core Competencies Checklist: Core I *(Continued)*

✓	N/A	J.	Basic Word Processing Skills
☐	☐	1.	Can create a new document using a template.
☐	☐	2.	Can open a Microsoft Word file using OpenOffice.
☐	☐	3.	Can convert a Microsoft Word XP file for Word 97 (if branch has XP).
☐	☐	4.	Can convert a Microsoft Word file to rich text format.
☐	☐	5.	Can convert a Microsoft Word file to plain text format.
☐	☐	6.	Can select, cut, copy, paste, and delete text.
☐	☐	7.	Can change the line spacing of a document to single or double spaced.
☐	☐	8.	Can insert bulleted and numbered lists.
☐	☐	9.	Can use spell/grammar check to correct a document.
☐	☐	10.	Can insert Clip Art and saved pictures into a document.

Appendix 6-3. Information Technology Core Competencies Checklist: Core II

EMPLOYEE			START DATE		COMPLETION DATE	

The following are the Information Technology Core Competencies that are suggested for all PLCMC staff that work with or support public services. The employee should check each item as competency is acquired or mark N/A for competencies that are not applicable.

✓	N/A	A.	Basic Branch Technology Knowledge
☐	☐	1.	Knows levels of service that are available under each login (e.g., Internet access versus online oesources only, what kind and version of word processor is available, etc.).
☐	☐	2.	Knows which computers/logins have full versus restricted Internet access.
☐	☐	3.	Has basic understanding of how a computer has full versus restricted Internet access.
☐	☐	4.	Can explain the purposes and benefits of the borrower self-sufficiency initiatives, including receipt printers, Express Check, and self-holds, and can use the system as a borrower.

✓	N/A	B.	Searching HIP (Horizon Information Portal)
☐	☐	1.	Can complete authority and keyword searches for items in the collection.
☐	☐	2.	Can find related works by subject heading, author, or title to an item in t he collection.
☐	☐	3.	Can complete cross-index searches for an item in the collection.
☐	☐	4.	Can limit, restrict, and sort searches on items in the collection.
☐	☐	5.	Can determine due date, status, and location of items in the collection.
☐	☐	6.	Can place requests on items in the collection.
☐	☐	7.	Can view borrower information such as: address and other personal information, holds, fines and other blocks.

✓	N/A	C.	Searching Staff PAC
☐	☐	1.	Can complete authority and keyword searches for items in the collection.
☐	☐	2.	Can find related works to an item in the collection by subject heading, author, or title.
☐	☐	3.	Can complete cross-index searches for an item in the collection.
☐	☐	4.	Can limit, restrict, and sort searches on items in the collection.
☐	☐	5.	Can determine due date, status, and location of items in the collection.
☐	☐	6.	Can place requests on items in the collection.
☐	☐	7.	Can place requests on copy-specific items in the collection.

(Cont'd.)

179

Appendix 6-3. Information Technology Core Competencies Checklist: Core II (Continued)

✓	N/A	D.	Horizon Check In
☐	☐	1.	Can check in items on the current date.
☐	☐	2.	Can check in items on the bookdrop date.
☐	☐	3.	Can check in delivery items.
☐	☐	4.	Can check in items on a specified date.
☐	☐	5.	Can check in items in in-house use mode.
☐	☐	6.	Can check in damaged items.
☐	☐	7.	Can print a check-in receipt for a borrower.
☐	☐	8.	Knows why PLCMC does not renew items at check in.

✓	N/A	E.	Horizon Borrower Records
☐	☐	1.	Demonstrates knowledge of all borrower types.
☐	☐	2.	Can create, update, and delete a borrower record.
☐	☐	3.	Can create a non-resident borrower.
☐	☐	4.	Can create a guest card borrower.
☐	☐	5.	Can create a teacher loan borrower and its limitations.
☐	☐	6.	Can create youth borrower types and can limit circ privileges appropriately.
☐	☐	7.	Can view and print what a borrower currently has checked out.
☐	☐	8.	Can add, view, and delete blocks on a borrower's record.
☐	☐	9.	Can check for current blocks.
☐	☐	10.	Can override blocks.
☐	☐	11.	Can add a staff note.
☐	☐	12.	Can add a message to borrower.
☐	☐	13.	Can add a no card block.
☐	☐	14.	Can view a borrower's history.
☐	☐	15.	Can view and print an item record.
☐	☐	16.	Can renew only select items for a borrower and/or all items out for a borrower.
☐	☐	17.	Knows how and when to waive fines for a borrower.

✓	N/A	F.	Horizon Check Out
☐	☐	1.	Can find a borrower record from library card, driver's license, phone number, borrower name, etc.

(Cont'd.)

Appendix 6-3. Information Technology Core Competencies Checklist: Core II (Continued)

✓	N/A	F.	Horizon Check Out
☐	☐	2.	Can navigate the borrower blocks screen.
☐	☐	3.	Can check out items to a borrower.
☐	☐	4.	Can renew items for a borrower using check out.
☐	☐	5.	Can print a check-out receipt for borrower.
☐	☐	6.	Can print a receipt for borrower listing all items out.
☐	☐	7.	Can do a fast add to check out an item that does not have a valid bar code.
☐	☐	8.	Can replace a damaged or missing bar code.
☐	☐	9.	Can accept and apply payment of borrower fines.
☐	☐	10.	Can print a receipt for payment of borrower fines.

✓	N/A	G.	PC Reliance Check Out
☐	☐	1.	Can set the appropriate due date for an item.
☐	☐	2.	Can check out items to a borrower.
☐	☐	3.	Can print a check-out receipt for a borrower.
☐	☐	4.	Can clear PC Reliance workstations of pre-existing data file after successful upload notice and exceptions report are received from Help Desk/IT.

✓	N/A	H.	Horizon Other
☐	☐	1.	Can log in to Horizon, and can log in to a different server in Horizon.
☐	☐	2.	Knows how to use Horizon-specific function keys.
☐	☐	3.	Can change the status of an item.
☐	☐	4.	Can run and fill reports appropriate to work duties.
☐	☐	5.	Can print a Hold Slip.

✓	N/A	I.	Intermediate Word Processing Skills
☐	☐	1.	Can create and edit tables.
☐	☐	2.	Can edit resumes that were created using a resume template.
☐	☐	3.	Can apply a style to a portion of a resume created using a resume template.
☐	☐	4.	Can move, resize, and delete pictures.
☐	☐	5.	Can use the Format Painter button to change the format of text.
☐	☐	6.	Can turn on and off table borders

(Cont'd.)

181

Appendix 6-3. Information Technology Core Competencies Checklist: Core II *(Continued)*

✓	N/A	I.	Intermediate Word Processing Skills
☐	☐	7.	Can adjust margins, tabs, and indents.
☐	☐	8.	Can insert, edit, and delete a text box.
☐	☐	9.	Can use the built-in Help features to locate instructions on how to perform an unfamiliar task.
☐	☐	10.	Can use the thesaurus to change words in a document.
☐	☐	11.	Can add/remove bullets and numbering to a list.

✓	N/A	J.	Basic Spreadsheet Skills (Microsoft Excel/OpenOffice)
☐	☐	1.	Can convert an Excel XP file to Excel 97 (if branch has XP).
☐	☐	2.	Can convert an Excel file to Word.
☐	☐	3.	Can save an OpenOffice file in Microsoft format.
☐	☐	4.	Can apply/remove cell borders.
☐	☐	5.	Can use the AutoSum feature to sum a column of cells.
☐	☐	6.	Can create a basic formula
☐	☐	7.	Can adjust the print settings to fit a large spreadsheet to 1 page.
☐	☐	8.	Can apply currency, percent, and comma style to cells.
☐	☐	9.	Can select, cut, copy, and paste a range of cells.
☐	☐	10.	Can insert and delete rows and columns.
☐	☐	11.	Can insert, delete, and rename sheets.
☐	☐	12.	Can use the built-in Help features to locate instructions on how to perform an unfamiliar task.

✓	N/A	K.	Basic Presentation Skills (Microsoft PowerPoint/OpenOffice)
☐	☐	1.	Can create a new blank presentation or use a template to create a presentation.
☐	☐	2.	Can save a presentation.
☐	☐	3.	Can edit a presentation.
☐	☐	4.	Can rearrange the order of slides.
☐	☐	5.	Can add animation to a presentation.
☐	☐	6.	Can insert clip art into a presentation.
☐	☐	7.	Can insert a saved picture into a presentation.

Appendix 6-4. Information Technology Core Competencies Checklist: Core III

EMPLOYEE			START DATE		COMPLETION DATE

The following are the Information Technology Core Competencies that are suggested for all PLCMC Public Support staff who work at a location that uses Envisionware, LPT One Print Management Software, or Express Check. The employee should check each item as competency is acquired or mark N/A for competencies that are not applicable.

✓	N/A	A.	PC Reservation Staff Software Skills
☐	☐	1.	Can view and make borrower reservations.
☐	☐	2.	Can cancel a borrower's reservation.
☐	☐	3.	Can unlock a borrower's station if the borrower forgets the password used to lock the session.
☐	☐	4.	Can change a PC's status to out of service.
☐	☐	5.	Can change a PC's status to in service.
☐	☐	6.	Can view the status of PCs.
☐	☐	7.	Can extend a borrower's session time.

✓	N/A	B.	PC Reservation Borrower Software Skills
☐	☐	1.	Can assist a borrower in making a reservation.
☐	☐	2.	Can assist a borrower in making a future reservation.
☐	☐	3.	Can assist a borrower in starting a session on a PC.
☐	☐	4.	Can assist a borrower in locking and then unlocking a PC.
☐	☐	5.	Can assist a borrower in ending a session.
☐	☐	6.	Can assist a borrower in canceling a reservation.

✓	N/A	C.	LPT One Staff Software Skills
☐	☐	1.	Can release a print job for a borrower from a staff PC.
☐	☐	2.	Can create and/or change a pin number for a borrower.
☐	☐	3.	Can use the staff software to add/remove money from a borrower account.
☐	☐	4.	Can log in to the print release station as staff and view the print queue.
☐	☐	5.	Can log in to the print release station as staff and view printer status to check for errors and can clear the errors.
☐	☐	6.	Can log in to the print release station as staff and stop LPT One, save the print jobs, exit LPT One, and restart LPT One.
☐	☐	7.	Understands that deposit account money is tied to a borrower's card number not a borrower number and that LPT One does not update a borrower's library card number if a card is lost and then replaced.

(Cont'd.)

Appendix 6-4. Information Technology Core Competencies Checklist: Core III *(Continued)*

✓	N/A	C.	LPT One Staff Software Skills
☐	☐	8.	Knows the proper procedure for replacing a library card that has a print account balance.
☐	☐	9.	Knows how to look up a borrower by name to search for a print account.

✓	N/A	D.	LPT One Borrower Software Skills
☐	☐	1.	Can assist a borrower in sending a print job to the black and white and/or color printer.
☐	☐	2.	Can assist a borrower in depositing money onto a library card.
☐	☐	3.	Can assist a borrower in viewing his/her print jobs at the print release station.
☐	☐	4.	Can assist a borrower in selecting and releasing print jobs.
☐	☐	5.	Can assist a borrower in viewing deposit account balance.

✓	N/A	E.	Express Check Borrower Software Skills
☐	☐	1.	Can assist a borrower in checking out items from an Express Check station
☐	☐	2.	Can assist a borrower in paying fees by credit card using the Express Check/ACS station.

✓	N/A	F.	Express Check Staff Software Skills
☐	☐	1.	Knows how and when to turn off borrower screen.
☐	☐	2.	Can toggle between ACS and Horizon screen using ALT+TAB keystroke combination.
☐	☐	3.	Can use Horizon to clear and/or override borrower blocks

Appendix 6-5. Information Technology Core Competencies Checklist: Core IV

EMPLOYEE		START DATE		COMPLETION DATE	

The following are the Information Technology Core Competencies that cover specific technology areas. If a location does not have A/V equipment or offer technology classes, then those sections are not required. The employee should check each item as competency is acquired or mark N/A for competencies that are not applicable. Core IV competencies are suggested for all managers, supervisors, Information Specialists, and for other staff as identified by their supervisor.

✓	N/A	A.	Audiovisual Knowledge
☐	☐	1.	Knows location of all branch A/V equipment.
☐	☐	2.	Knows how to set up, operate, and troubleshoot all branch A/V equipment.
☐	☐	3.	Knows how to connect projector to a desktop PC.
☐	☐	4.	Knows how to connect projector to a laptop.
☐	☐	5.	Knows conference room and computer lab abilities (e.g., is there a telephone line, Internet connection, etc.).

✓	N/A	B.	PLCMC Intermediate Troubleshooting
☐	☐	1.	Knows the location of the server.
☐	☐	2.	Knows the location of the router.
☐	☐	3.	Can identify a network port.
☐	☐	4.	Knows the location of the PC Reservation Management Console (if using Envisionware) and knows that it must always be on.
☐	☐	5.	Knows how and under what circumstances to reset the router.

✓	N/A	C.	PLCMC Imaging
☐	☐	1.	Understands the basic concept of imaging PCs.
☐	☐	2.	Can reimage a PC with a bootable CD or bootable floppy disk with the standard image.
☐	☐	3.	Can reimage a PC with a bootable CD or bootable floppy disk with a non-standard image (e.g., a non-Envisionware image).

✓	N/A	D.	Public Technology Training Skills
☐	☐	1.	Knows how to use the PLCMC Technology Training Database as appropriate to work duties.
☐	☐	2.	Knows where training materials are located on PLCMC Central.
☐	☐	3.	Can set up the computer lab for training class.
☐	☐	4.	Can conduct a 1.5 to 2 hour hands-on technology class.

Chapter 7

Core Technology Competencies at University of Texas Southwestern Medical Library

Richard Wayne

Overview

As have almost all libraries, the University of Texas (UT) Southwestern Medical Library has encountered numerous technology challenges over the past ten plus years. UT Southwestern's primary strategy to meet this challenge was to increase the overall technical knowledge of the library staff. This chapter describes UT Southwestern's successful endeavors to help make the staff more technically proficient. Several staff technology training series, as well as the supplemental library-wide technical support team, are described in detail. The chapter also provides numerous resources to help the reader learn about evolving technologies in libraries.

Introduction

This chapter provides insight into how a large academic medical library has dealt with the issue of technology competencies. Our approach has been successful in improving staff competencies and in building a robust support structure. However, we are always looking for new techniques and tools to improve our approach.

The scope of this chapter is broad. I begin by describing the environment in which I work. Then I discuss technology training plans that were developed and delivered to the library staff. Next I describe our unit liaison program, which was designed to further propagate technical knowledge and skill into the various areas of the library. Finally, I make a few suggestions about how to keep up with technology, especially as it relates to library services.

The UT Southwestern Medical Library

Our library is part of the University of Texas Southwestern Medical Center at Dallas, also known as UT Southwestern. UT Southwestern is a component of the University of Texas system. The system consists of nine academic universities and five health institutions.

UT Southwestern has three degree-granting institutions: UT Southwestern Medical School, UT Southwestern Graduate School of Biomedical Sciences, and UT Southwestern Allied Health Sciences School. We have four Nobel Prize winners on our faculty—more than any other medical school in the world. We have three-fourths of Texas' medical members of the National Academy of Sciences on our faculty.

The library has over 258,000 volumes in all formats, including over 53,700 full-text electronic journals. Our primary clientele consists of almost 20,000 faculty, staff, students, and residents in the university and its affiliated hospitals and clinics. We are open 101 hours per week and have 54 staff members.

Our library has customarily been at or near the forefront with new technologies. We have worked with our university's Information Resources Department for many years to create the best technical environment possible given information security restraints. For example, we were an early adopter of wireless networking.

We have about 250 computing devices in the library (desktops, laptops, servers) that we try to refresh every three years or so—depending on the state budget and therefore on our budget. We manage our own library Windows domain for authentication, file sharing, and applications. We also have servers for a staff intranet, staff and public blogs, electronic dissertations, interlibrary loan (ILLiad), our integrated library system (SirsiDynix Unicorn), as well as some for other miscellaneous purposes. The library and campus wireless network was recently upgraded, and we can now use 802.1X authentication instead of virtual private networking (VPN) client software to access the wireless network.

Our library circulates laptops within the library as well as external to the library. We used to circulate PDAs but have discontinued this service—the demand did not justify further investment. We also circulate USB jump drives, multifunction card readers, and other miscellaneous equipment.

The four members of the Information Systems (IS) Unit within the library do much of the technical work. We primarily focus on tasks such as running servers and troubleshooting PCs. However, each of us has responsibilities outside the unit too. For example, I coordinate and help manage the strategic planning in the library. I am also a member of a number of interdisciplinary library teams such as the collection development team. None of our four systems people has an MLS. However, two of us have master's degrees in other areas.

Two of the staff focus on servers (including our integrated library system [ILS]) and systems analysis. They also help with the plethora of microcomputer issues. The other two staff members focus largely on microcomputer support and planning.

Development of a Multi-Session Training Series for Library Staff

The Need for Training

In 2001, our university applied for and received a large grant from the Texas Telecommunications Infrastructure Fund (TIF). The library had a number of sophisticated technical projects included in the grant. Examples include federated searching, virtual reference, electronic dissertations, migration to ILLiad, and the circulation of PDAs and laptops to library clients.

As a result of the grant and related projects, it became clear that our staff needed a higher level of technical and project management expertise. This section addresses some of our library's efforts to increase the technical competencies of the staff.

Curriculum Development

We wanted the sessions to be worthwhile for all participants. We spent a good amount of time planning a curriculum that would have something for every member of the staff.

Ideas for the training curriculum came from several sources. A primary source was the basic technical tasks required of workers in a library today. Microsoft Windows has been the predominant computing platform at our university for many years, so we based our instruction on tasks associated with Windows-based computers. We decided that, at a minimum, everyone on our staff should know how to log in to Windows, check e-mail, create documents and spreadsheets, and print. We wanted everyone on staff to be comfortable with these basic functions as a foundation for more advanced applications.

Another important source for curriculum ideas was our "Microcomputer Incident Log" (MIL). "Microcomputer" is actually a misnomer at this point, because we get requests for a wide array of technology support for which microcomputers are just one part. We encourage our staff to document every request for assistance in our MIL. This helps us to manage priorities and workflow, and it also helps us to evaluate trends, common problems, and other areas of interest. Prior to each series of classes, we analyzed the MIL to find areas of training opportunity, that is, areas of common need reported by our staff.

Changes in the computing environment initiated other training topics. For example, when we started providing network jacks and cables for clients with laptops, a training need became apparent. Our staff, especially those who work with the public, needed to learn how to assist clients with connecting to the Internet via these new conduits. We trained people and helped to create handouts on how to change browser proxy settings for Windows and Macintosh laptops.

Another training need arising from changing technology is jump drives. When clients started coming into the library with jump drives, public services staff were

189

not sure what to do with them. As a result, we incorporated the use of jump drives and other peripherals into our training program.

Once we had a draft list of training topics for our classes, we polled the staff who would be taking the classes about topics they would like included. We sent the list to the library staff for comment and incorporated their recommendations as appropriate. Then we sent the revised list out again, and so on, in an iterative manner. Everyone on the staff had the opportunity to shape the curriculum before it was finalized. Our goal was for the staff to accept the final curriculum and see it as being relevant to their needs.

Selection of Instructors

The next question became "Who would be our instructors?" At the beginning of our discussion, it seemed obvious that the staff in our IS Unit should be the instructors. They were the people with the technical expertise. This strategy has worked well. All of our technical people developed their own presentations for our training series. We also invited people from other units in the library to participate as instructors. For example, the first instructor for PDA usage was from our reference area. He had already developed a class for library clients, so expanding this to library staff was a natural and easy process.

Course Evaluations

We wanted to know how we were doing and how we could improve our classes. Appendix 7-1 shows feedback form we used. The forms were very helpful in assessing how we did and how we needed to change or improve the classes. The staff were very honest with giving us feedback. When they did not like something, they told us about it. When they really liked something, they told us about that too.

The staff took the time to fill out the surveys and provide some very useful comments. They helped us to hone the individual classes and the entire sessions so that we met their needs. Of course, the suggestion most common for improvement was to provide more chocolate and other goodies during classes.

Evolving Classes

One of the realities for libraries in the past 10 to 15 years has been change. Much, but not all, of that change has been driven by technology. As a result, our classes had to change to reflect changing technologies, needs, people, and budgets.

The first training series was offered in early 2003. It consisted of five classes of increasing technical complexity. Appendix 7-2 shows the outline for this first set of classes. You can see that we left ample time at the end of each class for questions and hopefully answers. That part of the class was very important.

Meeting One of the first training series mostly addressed our IS Unit and related issues. We thought that it was important for the rest of the library staff to understand how we work. We discussed our responsibilities and areas that were not our responsibility. We discussed the MIF system at length. We talked about how we did planning and how we set priorities. When we were done, students had a very good idea of how the IS Unit worked and how we could best help them. One topic that we discussed in this session was the Desktop Optimization Team (DOT). I will address this team in detail later in this chapter.

Meeting Two of the first training series focused on technology basics. We opened the case of several desktop PCs and let students hold and touch some of the parts. We talked about our library network, the separate student network, and the campus network in general. We discussed how the Internet was based upon Transmission Control Protocol/Internet Protocol (TCP/IP). Finally we provided a quick tour of Windows.

We started to get into some more library-specific technical issues in Meeting Three of the first training series. We demonstrated how to add and remove printers in our environment. We discussed how to use our shared network drives for storage. The topic of information security was introduced, and a number of important elements such as Windows Updates, antivirus software, and password protocols were discussed. We also talked about the increasingly important topic of connecting a laptop to the (public) library network via wires or wirelessly.

Meeting Four of the first training series explored the concepts of maintenance, troubleshooting, and where to go for help. We taught the correct disciplined approach to troubleshooting. We explained when to submit an MIF to the IS Unit and when to call the University Help Desk. We discussed the numerous options for further help. Finally, we demonstrated the basics of the personal digital assistant (PDA).

191

Meeting Five of the first training series was the last class in the series. It dealt with two issues. The first was burning data to CDs. The technology people had been experiencing extensive questions on this topic from library staff. We talked about all of the things that can go wrong and what you can do to address them. We also talked about how clients (and staff) can go about getting a VPN account and the associated software in order to access campus online services from home. Then we demonstrated how to load and configure the software on a laptop computer.

The first training series was very enthusiastically greeted and attended. Each class was offered twice so that all of our 50 plus staff could attend. The evaluations were very positive, and, most important, the outcomes were excellent. The average staff technical knowledge was appreciably higher after the classes than before the classes. We saw this demonstrated by fewer support calls on the topics that we had covered and by a greater staff persistence with technical issues.

The next three annual staff technology training series were very similar to the first series in many ways. Series II and series III are summarized in Appendix 7-3 and Appendix 7-4. After each training series, we made an ambitious attempt to improve the series based on training series attendee feedback and changing circumstances. We also reduced the number of classes in each series from five to three. Five classes were fine, but it was very difficult to schedule the entire staff for that many classes. You can see in Appendix 7-2 through Appendix 7-4 that we incorporated new topics into the curriculum as technology continued to change. For example, in series III we went into depth about the migration to Windows XP Service Pack 2 and how it changed the computing experience. We also, in series III, discussed the changing landscape of information security and how it was becoming a bigger factor in our computing lives.

In training series IV, we started to experiment with more substantial changes. In the first phase, we taught a series similar to the previous ones, but we also worked with our Information Desk (ID) Unit which provides circulation and quick reference services to our clients to create classes specifically designed for them. This special workshop series was led by the manager of that unit, and, as a result, the curriculum also had topics that were not technical. We worked with them on the technical topics and taught most of the technical classes.

A number of potential topics were proposed to the ID staff prior to the curriculum being finalized for series IV. The ID staff had the opportunity to rate topics via a SurveyMonkey survey. They rated topics on their level of expertise with that topic as well as the topic's importance for their work. As a result of the survey, we were able to select the most meaningful topics for the ID staff. Some of the topics were mandatory, and some were electives. In this manner, each student could get a customized curriculum according to his or her interests and needs.

Most of the technical topics were more specific to the ID environment than in our more general classes. For example, we taught ID staff all of the features that were available on specialized workstations. Those workstations were set up for specific purposes, such as electronic dissertations, strictly licensed databases, and advanced scanning.

We are now evaluating the fifth iteration of the staff technology training series. We are encouraged by the responses that we received from the previous four training series. However, we have some new staff, and there are certainly some new technologies. The classes will need to change substantially. We plan to work very closely with the staff to develop a new, energized training series.

We will develop the new curriculum for training series V in much the same manner that we have in the past. There are some topics—such as wireless connectivity—that need to be covered every time. There are also some new topics, as well as some topics that dropped off the list. Our campus has not yet embraced Windows Vista OS, but it's just a matter of time. It would be prudent to start preparing the staff for this product.

Extending Our Reach—Unit Liaisons

Background Information

Two specific events in the past convinced our library's management that there would be times when the IS Unit personnel would not be sufficient to deal with important or urgent issues. I have already described one such event—the TIF grant that our library won in 2001. That grant spawned many sophisticated technical projects. The projects required technical expertise as well as project management skills for staff even outside the IS Unit. In addition, two members of our IS staff were unavailable because of extended illnesses. We needed more expertise than our three remaining people (we had five total people in the unit then, now we have four total people) could offer in order to complete all of the projects in an accurate and timely manner.

The second event was more urgent. It was actually a series of events. In the late 1990s and the early 2000s, we started seeing very aggressive viruses, worms, and other malware. Some of the more famous of these were the Melissa virus, the ILOVEYOU virus, the Nimda virus, the Slammer worm, and the MyDoom worm. The malwares were continuously evolving and started using a combination of strategies to achieve their malicious goals.

The malware attacks were very disruptive. The library had to stop all non-essential activities, focus on these attacks, and ensure that each of our hundreds of computing devices was patched and immune to the attacks. As the resulting combative enterprise-level software tools developed, we tried to embrace those, but each of these attacks was still time-consuming and disruptive.

We realized that we needed additional help during these times of crisis. Good information needed to be obtained quickly, and the resulting decisions and action plans needed to be implemented very quickly by technically savvy personnel. We decided to organize a Desktop Optimization Team (DOT) that would supplement the IS Unit's capabilities.

We envisioned that every unit in the library would have a DOT representative. A large unit might even have two DOT representatives. We knew that there might be some resistance to pulling people from other units, so we agreed that some ground rules were essential. The DOT responsibility needed to be voluntary. We wanted to work with people who were particularly interested in technology and who did not mind the occasional diversion from their work. It was essential that all DOT members understood that their primary job came first and that they needed to keep their supervisor informed of potential DOT activities. Finally, we hoped that the most technically savvy staff would be interested in joining DOT, not the most technically illiterate.

DOT members did receive some minor benefits as a result of their membership. They became aware of serious technical issues when they happened. In addition, they received some extra technical training from the IS staff.

The Desktop Optimization Team in Action

The DOT was formed in 2002. It had a charter (see Appendix 7-5) and a full membership of staff representatives from every unit in the Library. After the DOT was formed, some additional technical training was provided to members on the most likely tasks that they would be performing. For example, DOT members were taught how to do Windows updates and replace basic peripherals such as keyboards and mice. All the staff in the library were encouraged to contact their DOT representative first—when feasible—when they had nonurgent technical problems or questions.

As it turns out, the DOT members were not used in emergencies as much as we had anticipated in 2001 and early 2002. Fortunately, the number of emergencies that we had anticipated (based on earlier events) did not develop. There were some problems and issues that the DOT handled, but not to the extent that we had originally predicted.

There are a number of possible reasons for this surprising outcome. One is that the training series increased the technology knowledge level of all staff and they were therefore better able to address the problems at the point of need. Another is that we started to incorporate tools into our environment to combat malware and other threats in a centralized, coordinated manner. Yet another reason might be that we tended to hire new staff with greater technical skills than the staff leaving. Finally, the number of severe malware contaminations has slowed in the recent years

However, the DOT folks have been called upon to use their special skills on a number of occasions. When the Blaster and then Sasser worms hit the Internet, the DOT members helped ensure that all computers in the library had the appropriate Microsoft updates. The DOT members have been very helpful during transitional times as well. When Internet Explorer 7.0 was released, the DOT members worked with library staff to evaluate the new version and then carry out the upgrade. When new releases of our campus e-mail software—GroupWise—were released, the DOT members helped to upgrade staff computers to the new version. When we acquired new production quality copier/printers that required a special installation, the DOT members helped to teach staff how to install the drivers.

The DOT was renamed to the Technical Liaison Team (TLT). Then in August of 2004, the TLT was renamed to the Technical Assistance Group (TAG). This new nomenclature helps to better classify and categorize the TAG. The TAG is really a group that helps the IS Unit to support library technology as opposed to being an independent team that works on cross-functional issues. The mission of TAG did not change—the name change helps to more accurately categorize what TAG has done all along.

Our technical liaison experiments have been largely successful. The liaisons have helped to provide ready expertise at the point of need or at least more closely to the point of need. They have helped to reduce stress from many potentially stressful situations.

Keeping Our Skills Up to Date

Our Jobs Keep Changing

When I started out in the information technology field, I used punch cards. Wow! When my employer in 1979 wanted to communicate with an online service for financial information, we used a 300 baud acoustical modem. Wow!

Even when I started working in this library in 1992, things were dramatically different than they are now. I managed a Novel Netware cluster that held our MEDLINE data. Mosaic—the first popular graphical Web browser—had not been invented yet. If we wanted to use the Internet, we used more primitive tools than available today, such as HyperTelnet, Lynx, FTP, and telnet. Most of the activity was via command line prompts rather than a graphical interface.

Technology has come a long way since then, and the pace of change promises to be even faster in the future. Basic assumptions continue to change. Perhaps we will not have servers in our libraries in a few years. Perhaps everything will be hosted as software as a service (SaaS) or from some similar model of network computing. There is tremendous change in the ILS market. It's possible that, in a few years, the ILS as we know it today will be something totally different.

My point is that we are involved in a field that is constantly changing. If we stay put, we fall behind. Clearly, we need to make an investment in continuous learning and continuous experiences.

How Informed Do You Need to Be?

The other way to phrase this question might be "How informed do you want to be?" If you enjoy learning about and using technology, then your task of learning about it will be much easier. If you have to force yourself to learn every bit of hi-tech information, then it will indeed be a struggle for you.

But, practically, you need to ask yourself how informed you need to be. You may even get input from your colleagues on this question. In my situation, I am responsible for the technology for a major medical library. I also have a library planning and technology consulting business. I write articles and book chapters and do presentations on library technology and library strategic planning. I need to be very informed about these and related topics. If I find that there are holes in my knowledge, I need to patch them and patch them fast.

The answer to the question of how informed you need to be will vary depending on your responsibilities. Your situation may be totally different from mine. For example, if you are the head of a library circulation department, you do not need to have a detailed awareness of all current and developing technologies in the library automation area. But perhaps your technology education can be more focused on circulation activities. For example, you need to understand the trends in ILS. You should understand the cost and benefits of self-check and Radio Frequency Identification (RFID). You probably want to be able to perform at least basic troubleshooting on your circulation computers and circulation staff computers. The body of information that you need to be familiar with is different from the body of information that a colleague in technical services needs.

Sources of Information

In this section, I would like to make some recommendations on how you might keep your technical skills up to date. This section is not oriented toward the systems librarian, because those folks probably know how to find relevant technology resources already. Instead, this section is oriented toward the library staff person who needs to have some technical skills and who needs to keep them current.

There are a great many resources "out there" to help you stay knowledgeable and adept at technology. Because the technologies are changing all of the time, the associated resources frequently change as a result. This creates a challenging situation for me to document in a book. However, there are a number of time-tested resources that are reputable and quite usable. These are the types of resources that I will be addressing in this section.

Information Technology Resources

One of my favorite resources is *PC Magazine*. I have been reading it for many years. The print version or the online version (www.pcmag.com) are both great and full of useful information. In fact, it's very rare that I read a *PC Magazine* issue and I don't find something to print or copy or scan for a current or future article or presentation that I am working on. I also regularly look at *PC World*, *Computer Shopper*, and *MacWorld*. All of these magazines have been around for a long time.

Despite the heavy rush hour traffic, there can be some advantages to living near a major city such as Dallas. We get a number of conferences, seminars, workshops, and similar events throughout the year. For example, I annually visit the International Technology Exposition and Conference (ITEC). Every year there are several sessions that help me to expand my knowledge. This past year, I attended sessions on open source tools, using Web 2.0 in business, and evolving wireless networking security standards.

Another particularly good learning opportunity is the TechNet Seminars presented by Microsoft. As new products are announced and as old products evolve, Microsoft will frequently highlight these changes in TechNet Seminars. There are TechNet Seminars aimed at a variety of audiences. The seminars are free events that are held in major cities around the country. They are a very helpful way to stay informed about products from this very important vendor. TechNet also offers a plethora of Webinars on similar topics.

In addition, there are numerous opportunities—both Web based and live—offered by a host of other companies throughout the year. The anti-malware companies seem to be particularly active in offering learning activities. Their sessions can help keep you up to speed on evolving information security threats.

ILS Users Groups

Most of the ILS vendors have a users group and perhaps a users blog or forum. Not only can you learn specific practical skills from these groups, but you can see how other libraries are utilizing their systems. Don't underestimate the potential of your vendor's users group(s) to provide education and assistance.

At UT Southwestern, we use the SirsiDynix Unicorn system and are members of that user group. There is a group that meets biannually just from the Dallas/Fort Worth area on this topic. There is another group—the South Central Unicorn Users Group (SCUUG)—that meets annually (www.scuug.us). Then there is the Unicorn Users Group International (UUGI), which also meets annually (www.uugi.org).

Library Organizations

Technology education from library organizations has the advantage of being tailored to the specific interests and needs of libraries and library staff. In the discussion of library organizations, we can start locally and move to the international arena (which is beyond the budget of most of us). The following is a sample of some library organizations in Dallas, Texas.

The Northeast Texas Library System (NETLS; www.netls.org) helps meet the needs of public libraries in this area. It is one of ten public library systems in Texas. Another local resource is HealthLine, a group of medical and hospital librarians who meet in the Dallas area approximately four times per year.

Moving to the state level, our primary organization is the Texas Library Association (TLA; www.txla.org). TLA has divisions for public, academic, school, and special libraries. It has round tables for almost every interest and need. For example, I am an active member of the Automation and Technology Round Table (ATRT). ATRT hosts multiple educational sessions during TLA's annual conference.

Now let's move to the regional and national levels. If you are a medical librarian and can't afford to go to the Medical Library Association's annual conference, then you might attend the annual conference of a regional chapter. In my area, it's the South Central Chapter (www.sccmla.org) made up of a five-state region.

The big fish of library organizations is of course the American Library Association (ALA). There are numerous divisions, units, chapters, discussion groups, and other forms of organization to suit almost every need and purpose. For technology information, the Library and Information Technology Association (LITA; www.lita.org) is a great resource. The LITA Web site archives the top technology trends compiled by library technology experts over the past several years. LITA also offers regional institutes for in-depth immersion in specialized topics.

The ALA annual conference can be an educational bonanza. There are programs on almost every imaginable library topic. You can learn from experts all over the country and the world on the slate of topics that interest you.

Many of the library organizations that I have mentioned publish an associated journal or magazine (electronic or paper). For example, LITA publishes *Information Technology and Libraries*. These resources are a wonderful source of information on technology and most other library topics.

Web Resources

In 2008, no list of key resources would be complete without a section on Internet resources. The danger in listing them is that these resources have a shorter life cycle than some of the others that I mentioned earlier. I will try to highlight a few that have stood the test of time (so far) and look like they will be around for quite a while.

1. WebJunction (www.webjunction.org): WebJunction is a portal that combines libraries and technology topics. It has been supported by the Gates Foundation and OCLC.
2. TechSoup (www.techsoup.org): TechSoup is another technology-related portal that you should know about. It bills itself as "The Technology Place for NonProfits." Its scope therefore is broader than libraries, but it has numerous useful resources for libraries and librarians.
3. Wilson Web: Our library has a subscription to the Wilson Web databases of Library Literature and Information. It is a great resource for people like me who are continuously researching topics and looking at evolving issues.
4. EDUCAUSE (www.educause.edu): EDUCAUSE is primarily aimed at improving higher education through technology. However, there are numerous useful resources available at their Website. A particularly rich area relates to information security.
5. Public Library Association Tech Notes (www.pla.org/ala/pla/plapubs/technotes/technotes.cfm): Tech Notes is a great place to find out about important library technologies. Examples are "Libraries and RSS (Really Simple Syndication)" and "Games in Libraries."

There are many other Web resources available about technology and libraries and the juncture of the two. You work in a library, so I am sure that you can find them if you want. If you can't, please e-mail me or ask your reference librarian.

Appendix 7-1. Official Library Staff Technology Training Series II Evaluation Form: Session II

The information presented in this session was:

a) Very helpful   b) Helpful   c) OK   d) Not very helpful   e) Lousy

Suggestions for future session topics:

How can we improve future sessions?

Other comments:

Appendix 7-2. Library Staff Technology Training Plan

MEETING ONE—ABOUT LIBRARY INFORMATION SYSTEMS, BASICS I

1. Unit's mission, priorities for the quarter (10 min)
2. Review our responsibilities chart (15 min)
   a. Our customers have responsibilities too
3. Our methodology—planning, planning, planning; please include us in your plans early on; budgeting (10 min)
4. Microcomputer incident form (10 min)
5. On-call schedule—interpretation (5 min)
6. Technical liaison team (5 min)
7. Some terminology (15 min)
8. Q & A (10 min)
9. Computer room tour (10 min)
10. Total time: 90 minutes

MEETING TWO—BASICS II

1. Open a PC (10 min)
2. Our LAN (10 min)
3. Student LAN (5 min)
4. Campus network (10 min)
5. Internet, Internet 2 (15 min)
6. A Windows tour (25 min)
7. Q & A (10 min)
8. Total time: 85 minutes

MEETING THREE—MEAT & POTATOES

1. Adding, removing a printer (10 min)
2. Adding a shortcut (5 min)
3. L: and P: drives (the library's shared network drives) (5 min)
4. Accessing Reference Manager, Contact Pro (5 min)
5. Microsoft Windows updates (5 min)
6. Loading software/removing software from a PC (5 min)
7. Restarting, daily procedures for staff, antivirus activities (10 min)
8. Microsoft Office (5 min)
9. Information security (10 min)
10. Connecting a laptop to the network, wired/wireless (15 min)
11. Q & A (10 min)
12. Total time: 85 minutes

MEETING FOUR—MAINTENANCE, TROUBLESHOOTING, HELP, PDAS

1. Some basic Windows tools (10 min)
2. Troubleshooting basics (10 min)
3. Microcomputer incident form redux (10 min)
4. University help desk (5 min)
5. GroupWise—who to contact (10 min)
6. IRTeam (the campus-wide IT group sponsored by campus IT) (5 min)
7. Other forms of help (10 min)
8. Using a PDA (20 min)
9. Q & A (10 min)
10. Total time: 90 minutes

MEETING FIVE—SPECIAL ISSUES: MAY BE FYI, NOT GLM

This is more an informal "For Your Information" meeting rather than a "General Library Meeting."

1. Burning data to CDs (10 min)
2. Establishing a VPN account and loading VPN software (30 min)
3. Total time: 40 minutes

Appendix 7-3. Library Staff Technology Training: Series II

MEETING ONE—SUPPORT & INFORMATION CONTEXT

1. Review I.S. responsibilities chart (15 min)
   a. Our customers have responsibilities too
2. Microcomputer incident form (10 min)
3. On-call schedule—interpretation (5 min)
4. Technical liaison team (5m)
5. Our network (10 min)
6. University help desk (5 min)
7. Information security (10 min)
8. Additional topic TBA (10 min)
   a. Includes cleaning mice demonstration
9. Q & A (10 min)
10. Computer room tour (10 min)
11. Total time: 90 minutes

MEETING TWO—BASICS

1. Open a PC (10 min)
2. Some Windows essentials (20 min)
   a. Backing up data
   b. Backing up GroupWise data
   c. Etc.
3. Restarting, daily procedures for staff, antivirus activities (5 min)
4. Some basic Windows tools (10 min)
5. Troubleshooting basics (10 min)
6. Public PC issues (25 min)
7. Q & A (10 min)
8. Total time: 90 minutes

MEETING THREE—ADVANCED TOPICS

1. Connecting a laptop to the network, wired/wireless (20 min)
2. Burning data to CDs (10 min)
3. Establishing a VPN account, loading VPN software, configuring (30 min)
4. Configuring Workflows (30 min)
5. Total time: 90 minutes

Appendix 7-4. Library Staff Technology Training: Series III

MEETING ONE—SUPPORT & INFORMATION CONTEXT

1. Review IS responsibilities chart (15 min)
   a. Our customers have responsibilities too
2. Microcomputer incident form (10 min)
3. On-call schedule—interpretation (5 min)
4. Technical liaison team (5 min)
5. Our network (10 min)
6. University help desk (5 min)
7. Information security (10 min)
8. Additional topic TBA (10 min)
   a. Includes cleaning mice demonstration
   b. XP Pro Service Pack 2 (SP2) Introduction
   c Q & A (10 min)
9. Computer room tour (10 min)
10. Total time: 90 minutes

MEETING TWO—BASICS

1. Open a PC (10 min)
2. Some Windows essentials (20 min)
   a. Backing up data
   b. Backing up GroupWise data
   c. Etc.
3. Restarting, daily procedures for staff, antivirus activities (5 min)
4. Some basic Windows tools & KB shortcuts (20 min)
5. Troubleshooting basics (10 min)
6. Public PC issues (15 min)
7. Q & A (10 min)
8. Total time = 90 minutes

MEETING THREE—ADVANCED TOPICS

1. Connecting a laptop to the network, wired/wireless (20 min)
2. Burning data to CDs (10 min)
3. Establishing a VPN account, loading VPN software, configuring (30 min)
4. Configuring Workflows (SirsiDynix Unicorn client software) (30 min)
5. Total time = 90 minutes

Appendix 7-5. Desktop Optimization Team Operating Guidelines

SCOPE OF THE DESKTOP OPTIMIZATION TEAM (DOT)

- Assist IS (Information Systems Unit) in the daily management and troubleshooting of unit technical computer problems.
- Add limited number of examples to LinkBase (library's intranet).
- Windows recommended updates.
- Driver updates.
- Troubleshooting problems on unit computers.
- Keep an updated list of computers in each unit.
- A DOT member's priority is with his or her unit, then with DOT duties.

PROCEDURES

- Maximum limit of 1 hour each issue/problem, which can take from 2 minutes to 1 hour to solve. If over 1 hour, complete a Microcomputer Incident Report and follow through as needed.
- A Microcomputer Incident Report will be recorded for every incident, and edit with DOT/(your initials).
- Whenever we e-mail IS and receive a reply about an issue, please include the unit manager.
- DOT members need to cover their own unit; managers should use their own DOT member or place a Microcomputer Incident Report if they feel their member is already overworked.
- Provide ongoing training of members, and conduct orientations for new members.

INFORMATIONAL

- Add to Linkbase a link to Incident Report saying, "To see examples of DOT problem-solving, take a look at Incident Reports solved by DOT members."
- Create a new poster to remind staff that we are here to help.
- Library-wide e-mail with the poster attached.
- DOT leader goes into manager's meeting to give mini-FYI of what DOT does.

Chapter 8

The Core Competency Program at the University of Iowa Libraries

Paul Soderdahl and Donna Hirst

Overview

At the University of Iowa Libraries the development and implementation of an information technology (IT) Core Competency Program took place over five years. There was no single individual or department who managed this entire effort, so the program evolved slowly and the focus shifted from time to time. The development of the Core Competency List is discussed, and the framework for technology training in the libraries is highlighted. Core competencies are used for training and staff evaluation.

205

Introduction

In 2003, the University of Iowa Libraries began a formal project to address the issues of core technical competencies for library staff. Section I of this chapter covers the development of a Core Competency Program at the University of Iowa Libraries. The identification of needs and the libraries' organizational context are discussed. The subsection on the University Information Technology Reclassification describes the larger university setting from which the libraries' core competencies grew.

Section II describes the elements that were in place or developed once the core competencies were put into production. An interim program was begun until a trainer was hired. An example is included of a specialized competency for a single software application that is a model for similar extensions once the general program is more fully in place. Some detail about the technical trainer is included, a position that is critical to the program. Human resources issues and concerns are presented.

The Environment at the University and the Libraries

The University of Iowa was established in 1847 and has 11 colleges—the largest is the College of Liberal Arts and Sciences, with additional colleges in Law, Business, Engineering, Medicine, Education, Pharmacy, Nursing, Dentistry, and the Graduate

College. Approximately 30,000 students are enrolled at Iowa, and 1,700 faculty and 13,000 staff are employed. The university has nationally and internationally recognized programs across the campus.

The University of Iowa Libraries is a large research library system with over 4.5 million volumes. The library system includes the Main Library, the Hardin Library for the Health Sciences, and 10 branch libraries. As of July 2007 the system employed over 100 Merit employees, over 75 Professional and Scientific employees, and one faculty member (the dean). University Merit staff include blue collar, security, technical, and clerical employees. Professional and Scientific employees are defined apart from the Merit system based on the professional, scientific, or administrative nature of their work. Librarians and other library professionals are classified as Professional and Scientific; library support staff are classified as Merit. The libraries have historically been understaffed and have had minimal technology support staff. As with all large research libraries, the University of Iowa Libraries is completely dependent on technology, and desktop applications are used by every employee in the system. This dependency has led the library system to explore a range of training programs and staff development programs to enhance the skills of library staff. The University of Iowa Libraries' Core Competency Program is an outgrowth of this exploration.

Section I: Planning the Core Competency Program

Identifying Core Competency Needs for Library Staff

As the University of Iowa Libraries entered the twenty-first century, the general IT competency of the library staff was a concern for all library units—IT departments, general library departments, and library administration. A very minimal technical orientation for new staff was in place, but everyone at the institution felt that the technical training needed to be enhanced. Staff raised concerns from a variety of perspectives:

- The libraries needed to establish a baseline of technology skills so that general staff, supervisors, and IT trainers could all work toward the same goals.
- All library employees needed to become more productive and more proficient at using the workstation and peripherals required for their day-to-day work.
- The libraries needed to shift the control for technology training from the library IT department back to the supervisor of the staff members' department.
- The libraries needed to focus IT training efforts on basic skills and leave advanced training to units or to individuals desiring advanced skills.
- Library employees wanted formal training classes to allow the staff to choose options in upgrading their technical skills.
- The libraries didn't have adequate technical staff to train general library staff to be technically competent. Training tools and focused goals would need to be developed.

The issue of core competency training was brought to the Library Information Technology Advisory Committee (LITAC) in 2003. The committee did a literature search at that time and did not find much relevant information except for a helpful article by Scott Childers (2003) titled "Computer Literacy: Necessary or Buzzword?" in *Information Technology and Libraries*.

The article by Childers included a history of computer literacy going back to the 1960s. In particular, a 1984 article by Donald Norman titled "Worsening the Knowledge Gap" provided a framework for Childers' work. Norman (1984: 222) described a hierarchy for computer literacy:

- General principles of computation
- How to use computers
- How to program computers
- The science of computation

Childers subsequently took this hierarchy and updated it to reflect requirements for libraries in the early twenty-first century. Childers' (2003: 102) hierarchy grouped competencies into three levels:

- Level 1 is the baseline proficiency level, and any skills that a staff member is lacking within this level should be approached and mastered as soon as possible.
- The second level is that of a barely computer-literate person, similar to the literacy of someone with a kindergarten reading level. This level of computer competency is the minimum level that the majority of the library staff should rate. Skills that an employee is lacking could be possibly ignored if their other job skills are high enough.
- The third, or target, level is the level of computer proficiency that all library staff should try to achieve; however, staff members who do not have these skills should not be penalized.

One section of Childers' article focused on the impact that computer literacy has on libraries. He raised the question of whether the impact of computer literacy is different for general library paraprofessionals as opposed to professionals. He concluded that the demand for computer-related skills has moved from insignificant to critical for most academic library positions, quoting Krissof and Konrad (1998: 32) that "training should be viewed as a necessity, not a luxury; as mandatory, not voluntary; and as comprehensive, not superficial."

Childers added his own information and perspectives to a chart prepared from the Basic Computer Equipment Competencies created by The Library Network (TLN) Technology Committee at tech.tln.lib.mi.us/finalbasic.htm (accessed 2007). LITAC found the Computer Proficiencies Chart in the appendix of Childers article to be particularly valuable.

207

Early Efforts Toward Core Competencies

After careful review of the Childers article, the committee decided to adapt his Basic Computer Equipment Competencies as the basis for a local implementation. The content of the Childers' competency list was largely accepted for local use, and the list from the Childers article was revised into a table format (Appendix 8-1). Additional competencies were not added, but the revision to a table facilitated its use for individual staff evaluations. The group decided that this Core Competency List would be used as the basis for staff training. Because of university hiring guidelines the list could not be used in the recruitment of new staff.

The Desktop Support Group reviewed the competencies list to see if support documentation for training was available, particularly for those baseline topics identified in the Core Competency List. These baseline topics received special attention, because all staff members were required to meet them. The university subscribes to the SkillSoft service, a collection of online professional development courses available to both Mac and PC staff users. The Libraries' Desktop Support staff searched the SkillSoft resources to determine if documentation addressing the competencies was available through this resource, again focusing on the baseline topics.

The committee agreed that it was very important that Iowa's core competency document be flexible in structure and also allow departmental customization. Customization should be easy for departments such as a public services unit or a branch library, allowing units to add competencies specific to the unit. Additionally, customization for particular special cross-departmental functional requirements, such as word processing, spreadsheets, or support for cross departmental projects, should be permitted.

After final approval by LITAC, the document was forwarded to the Director of Information Technology, who presented the document to the Libraries' Executive Council in August 2004. The council was very favorable but decided to postpone implementation so that a newly formed Technology Training Task Force could consider core competencies in the broader context of technology training.

Defining a New Framework for Staff Training, Development, and Enrichment

LITAC's discussion of core competencies began at about the same time that the libraries at large launched a major planning initiative. Recognizing that the libraries' existing strategic plan had been drafted in very different budgetary times, a planning effort was undertaken "to become more focused on a narrower group of well-chosen priorities if the Libraries intends to continue to innovate and move in new directions" (University of Iowa Libraries, Annual Report, 2003/2004). In order to implement a new strategic plan that reflected current financial realities in an ever-changing information landscape, the libraries made significant organizational changes by restructuring departments, streamlining workflows, and reevaluating services. Key to the planning effort was a focus on taking advantage of changing technologies to make the best use of an ever-decreasing number of staff. In a 2006 self-study report it was noted that the libraries experienced a $1.3 million reduction in funds for staffing from 1998 to 2006, the equivalent of approximately 25 entry-level positions (University of Iowa Libraries, Self Study Report, 2006).

In June 2004, the planning committee recommended that a task force be formed to consider how best to deliver just-in-time technology training that could be focused on individual user needs. Focusing on just-in-time training would require that training be responsive to the current needs of the individual as well as the climate and needs within the organization. A four-person task force was launched in July and quickly realized that in order to develop a new model for technology training, the notions of staff training and staff development would first need to be considered more broadly.

The libraries have had an active staff development program for many years, offering forums and workshops to all staff on a regular basis. Included in the program was a technology training series, organized by the libraries' coordinator of assessment and staff development with input from a number of technologically savvy library staff. The new task force faced the challenge of identifying which elements of the past staff development sessions were effective and should be retained and where there were gaps in meeting current technology training needs.

The task force decided to distinguish three different types of learning activities: (1) staff training, (2) staff development, and (3) enrichment. Staff training was used to describe those activities that taught skills required in order to do a job. Staff development described activities that would generally improve one's ability or quality of job performance but might not be skills that required mastery. Enrichment activities were considered slightly distinct from staff development in that they were always voluntary and not undertaken on work time. For example, enrichment activities might include brown bag sessions on hot topics only tangentially related to libraries and librarianship.

In order to clarify these distinctions, the task force crafted a Framework for Staff Training, Development, and Enrichment (see Appendix 8-5). The framework identified three different triggers for staff training: (1) something about the employee's situation has changed, (2) something about the institution or environment has changed, or (3) a remedial training need was identified. Determining who should deliver the instruction and how to deliver it would be dependent on the trigger. With the framework in hand, the task force could identify more precisely where the current technology training program was insufficient. For example, if the trigger for training was that the employee's situation has changed, then a class scheduled months in advance could not meet that individual's needs. Rather, just-in-time, point-of-need training would be most effective.

On the other hand, there are many situations where something about the institution or environment has changed, such as a new version of the library management

209

system or a change in e-mail software. In these instances, training scheduled in advance and offered in groups might be efficient. However, library staff often reported that group training was not effective, because the training classroom was an artificial environment with machines that were sometimes configured very differently from their own individual workstations. Thus, for a system-wide training need, small group sessions within the department would generally be more effective than a classroom filled with staff from other departments whose job responsibilities and workflows varied widely.

By contrast, staff development and enrichment could take place effectively in a large group setting. The task force concluded that the existing staff development program could adequately meet the needs for staff development and enrichment related to technology but was not well suited for staff training.

Putting the Supervisor in Charge

In addition to defining a new framework for training, the task force also recommended that supervisors at all levels needed to assume primary responsibility for the training required for their employees. The supervisor has knowledge of the particular responsibilities of a staff member and also knows what is likely regarding new responsibilities. Although obvious, this statement had not been made so plainly in the past. The task force acknowledged that supervisors might not be in a position to offer the training personally, but, nevertheless, an IT trainer or a staff development coordinator would rarely know the training needs of an individual in another department. In some cases it may be evident.

Placing the training responsibility on the supervisor has been critical to integrating core competencies into the performance evaluation process. The task force concluded that only the immediate supervisor is in a position to address core competency concerns in an evaluation setting, and thus the immediate supervisor needs to be the one responsible for addressing any deficiencies and arranging training as needed. The task force further recommended that administrators need to emphasize to their managers the importance of orientation and training and that the libraries need to provide opportunities for supervisors to develop and improve their training skills. The full set of recommendations made by the task force are provided in Appendix 8-6.

The task force recommended that a trainer be hired to meet the increased demand that would result from adopting a point-of-need training model. Recognizing the close link between technology training and desktop support, it was recommended that this new position also include responsibilities for general one-on-one IT support.

Standardizing University IT Classifications

Facing repeated budget cuts, the libraries would not receive new funding for the desired Desktop Support and Technical Trainer. Thus, in order to create the salary line, funds would have to be reallocated from other library staff positions. Reallocating salary funds from one functional area to another, however, was not uncommon. As part of the planning process, the libraries had adopted a pattern of reallocating positions in order to move in strategic new directions, and a priority was given to making better use of technology in order to cope with a reduced work force. Nevertheless, identifying funds for the new position was not easy. On the other hand, fitting the position into the restructured library IT division was straightforward.

In 2000, the university convened a group to overhaul the university's classification descriptions, pay grades, and career paths for IT staff in an effort to increase the ability of the university to attract and retain quality staff. Like many similarly sized state institutions, the University of Iowa has predefined job classifications for all positions, including IT professional staff. Over the decades, however, these positions had become outdated. Some job titles, such as "senior analyst" or "department information specialist," were so vague that they had lost any specific meaning. Others were tied to dated technology, such as "operations manager of mainframe computing facility." Several named specific campus units, many of which were no longer in existence, such as "CONDUIT marketing and distribution administrator." Even when relevant, these classifications were so specific that they would never have more than one incumbent, and the university felt this contributed to a lack of career path. Job classifications were used inconsistently from one department to another, and department managers often felt compelled into gaming the system in order to pay a competitive salary.

211

The IT Job Reclassification Committee was charged with developing a new system that could be applied campus-wide, provide well-defined career paths, reflect updated qualifications, and omit any references to specific technologies (e.g., names of specific programming languages). After soliciting information from peer institutions, studying IT classifications used in the private sector, and analyzing IT position descriptions currently in use at the university, the committee developed a matrix that could be applied consistently for all IT positions across the campus enterprise.

On one dimension, the committee divided IT tasks into eight job families: (1) applications development and support, (2) database administration and development, (3) data center operations, (4) IT management, (5) IT security, (6) IT support services, (7) network and communications engineer, and (8) systems administration and systems programming. A second dimension was job level, with Level I used for entry-level positions and Level V for the highest senior-level positions. This grid allowed for up to 40 job classifications—eight families with up to five levels each. In practice, however, only 27 job classifications were created. For example, no classifications were defined for IT Support Services IV or V because the most senior-level IT staff would either tend to move into a specialized functional area (such as systems administration or applications development) or into management.

Similarly, no classifications were defined for IT Management I or II. This system allowed the levels to be used consistently across all job families so that all Level IV jobs would be similar in scope and responsibility regardless of job family.

This new system provided a career path, allowing individuals to move from Level I up to Level V. It also provided for the possibility of moving into senior-level positions without necessarily moving into management. An Applications Development and Support V would be considered on par with IT Management V, roughly equivalent to a director or other senior administrator. The Chief Information Officer is the only IT position above Level V and is the equivalent of a vice president or associate provost position. As a result of the reclassification project, the number of IT classifications used on campus was reduced from 58 to 27.

For each level, a set of criteria was developed to describe the characteristics of positions at that level with respect to independent judgment, problem-solving skills, communication skills, end-user interactions, resource management responsibilities, business knowledge, sphere of influence, impact of errors, and technical competencies. The criteria that were used for each of the five levels across job families served as the foundation, and more specific criteria were defined for individual job classifications. Figure 8-1 shows how technical competencies were applied for Applications Development and Support Levels I and II.

With the criteria in hand, the committee developed a general classification description for each of the 27 new IT classifications. Each description followed a similar template: (1) basic function and responsibility (a brief paragraph describing the jobs in that family), (2) distinguishing characteristics (features that distinguish

Figure 8-1. Competencies Applied to Select Positions	
APPLICATION DEVELOPMENT LEVEL I	
Technical Competencies for all IT positions at Level I	Stays up-to-date in use of tools and skills required to perform the job, as well as major new technology trends
Technical Competencies specific to Application Development Level I	Has programming experience and/or formal logic education. Demonstrates ability to translate functional specifications into program code
APPLICATION DEVELOPMENT LEVEL II	
Technical competencies for all IT positions at Level II	Stays up-to-date in use of tools and skills required to perform the job, as well as major new technology trends. Researches and evaluates new tools/processes for area
Technical Competencies specific to Application Development Level II	Competent in one or more tools, operating systems, and languages used by the unit. May be involved with multi-platform and intersystem relationships. Demonstrates ability to write functional and technical specifications for complex integrated systems. Conceptual knowledge of databases used by the unit

jobs at that level from other jobs in the same job family), (3) characteristic duties and responsibilities, (4) supervision received, (5) minimum qualifications, and (6) knowledge, skills, and abilities. Knowledge, skills, and abilities included those competencies that may or may not be required for any given position. The section was not intended to be a checklist of competencies but rather a sampling of the types of competencies that a department might demand for a specific position. IT managers might pick and choose from the knowledge, skills, and abilities of several different classification descriptions in order to identify the competencies required for a given job.

To implement the new system, all of the approximately 500 IT jobs on campus were reviewed. Each employee was required to complete a position description questionnaire; IT managers were invited to suggest a classification; and the committee reviewed each position and placed it in one of the 27 new classifications. Dozens of interviews were held, appeals were heard, and, in July 2003, central human resources switched all IT staff to the new system. The reclassifications were generally budget neutral, with only a handful of situations where employees' current salaries were outside the range of their new classifications. Interestingly, three of these were library IT staff whose salaries needed to be raised in order to bring them up to the minimum.

Because the IT reclassifications were taking place at about the same time as the libraries' reorganization, the new library IT organizational structure was modeled after the new campus-wide job families, with separate units for applications development and support, desktop support services, and systems administration and programming. (Digital library services and Web services were later added as additional library IT departments.)

With respect to technical competencies for the University of Iowa Libraries' IT staff, the core competencies certainly apply to all staff, including IT professionals. In addition, advanced technical competencies required for each individual position are drawn from the knowledge, skills, and abilities in the classification descriptions, although they are typically not formalized except when a vacant position is advertised.

The newly created technology training position was easily placed within the IT support services family, because the job consisted of a combination of technology training and desktop support. The scope of the position placed it at Level II. The IT Support Services Level II classification is described in Appendix 8-7.

Section II: Implementing The Core Competency Program

Putting the Core Competencies into Production

After review by the Libraries' Technology Training Task Force, the library administration accepted the IT core competencies for all library staff as approved by LITAC. Iowa's Core Competency List (Appendix 8-1) includes requirements at the baseline, intermediate, and advanced levels. It organizes the requirements according to areas such as basic workstation setup, printing, Internet, computer security, Microsoft Windows operating system, e-mail, calendaring, IT policy, and a number of other categories. Some of the specific competencies are common knowledge, but many are less commonly known.

The Core Competency List was acknowledged to be a very useful IT management tool. Library administration wanted the document to serve as:

- a staff training tool,
- an orientation tool for new staff,
- a tool to build staff empowerment, and
- a tool to reduce the IT support burden.

Without an adequate IT trainer in the systems office, the core competencies were largely a symbol rather than a tool for change. The library administration acknowledged that a full, system-wide implementation could not be put into place until a technical trainer was hired. Yet the demand for IT troubleshooting and training had been strong across all library units even prior to the acceptance of the document. With the Core Competency Program the libraries could effectively address training, orientation, staff empowerment, and enhanced IT troubleshooting support.

The libraries' Head of Desktop Support Services was given responsibility to implement the core competencies until a trainer could be hired. She quickly decided that she would use the tool for all new staff and would work with experienced staff as time allowed. She developed a Core Competency Self-Checklist (Appendix 8-2) as a training aid. The self-checklist includes all of the baseline competencies, but they are formatted as a self-help tool rather than as a policy document. The checklist also embeds the answers to the questions inside the questions when possible so that the process of completing the checklist actually teaches the staff member many relevant concepts. The self-help checklist removes, or at least reduces, the need for IT staff mediation, thus saving IT department time and empowering staff.

A general technical orientation has always been necessary for new employees. When new staff members are assigned their workstation and peripherals, the IT department reviews login and security issues. A basic introduction to workstation software and policy also takes place at the orientation. The Core Competency Self-Checklist became part of this process. Frequently supervisors asked to be present at the core competency session for their new employees in order for them to learn about the baseline and to learn what was being taught to their staff.

Competencies Required for Specific Applications

The initial Core Competency List was intended to be flexible by allowing customization for particular functional requirements. This feature was tested when the libraries changed their Web page editing software from Adobe Dreamweaver to

Adobe Contribute. In addition to allowing the libraries to adopt a more standardized look and feel through the use of required templates, Contribute's user-friendly interface and lower cost permitted a much wider deployment than had been possible with Dreamweaver. The expanded usage prompted a desire to define application-specific competencies for Contribute users that were appended to the original core competencies document. Appendix 8-3 lists the Contribute competencies. Competencies for other applications have not been developed but can quickly be added when the need arises.

New Trainer and Desktop Support Staff Position

In June 2006, the university libraries began the hiring process for a Desktop Support and Technical Trainer. The position reports to the Head of Desktop Support Services and provides support to the Main Library, the Hardin Library for the Health Sciences, and 10 branch libraries. The position is described in Appendix 8-8. The trainer is expected to work with supervisors throughout the library system to develop and implement personalized technical training plans. There were many position requirements for the new trainer, but it was particularly important to the libraries to find someone who was flexible, was skilled at teaching computer concepts, and had strong interpersonal skills. Hiring someone who was comfortable with the core competency information was important.

The libraries hired a very strong candidate with lots of experience who could "hit the ground running." The trainer works with the Core Competency List and the checklist. Because of the great demand for his services, he frequently works with whole units rather than one on one, but he does do a lot of personalized training as well. During the original planning for a core competency program, analysis emphasized individual training, but demand has resulted in offering a number of group meetings. A group meeting typically includes 12 staff members. The unit meetings have been a very good forum for asking questions, because people's queries often generate additional questions from their peers.

The trainer has indicated that typically it is best if a group's supervisor does not attend the meeting, because the presence of the supervisor can suppress questions and comments. Sometimes the process, both the meetings and the questionnaire, elicit sarcastic comments. These training events can offer staff a chance to vent and describe their frustrations. Because the trainer works to make the training course a safe environment, the staff members feel comfortable in voicing concerns about their hardware, the software they are required to use, their supervisor's expertise, the physical environment (light, workstation height, etc.), and more. The trainer is not always able to solve problems voiced by participants, but sometimes problems can be resolved, and typically the participant learns that the trainer is an ally in addressing technology issues.

Orientations for new staff continue to be offered. Typically an orientation takes place mid-morning on the staff member's first work day. After the installation of the workstation, the staff member is lead through the Core Competency Self-Checklist (Appendix 8-2). Instruction is offered in any area needed. One month after the orientation, the checklist is sent to new employees in campus mail and they again review the document and ask for assistance if needed.

Experienced staff may be offered a one-on-one session when the employee or the supervisor makes the request. Often these one-on-one sessions are for employees needing remedial assistance or who have been having trouble with technology. The trainer never does special training for advanced staff. Once staff members develop beyond the baseline, they are expected to progress on their own. The trainer has limited time for training activities, and it is recognized that the trainer cannot be an expert in all the specialized software functions and packages that the libraries use. The core competency goal is to get all staff up to a baseline, and then the individual staff members can take responsibility for their own advanced training. Although staff would like the library and the trainer to offer advanced IT training, advanced users know that it is unlikely that the trainer would know more than they do about their specialized software. The trainer has considered having a supervisors' meeting to encourage supervisors to take more responsibility for training their staff in technology, but this has not yet been possible to organize.

The libraries' trainer has become well integrated into the staff. He is a strong member of the IT department's Desktop Support team. Approximately 20–25 percent of his time is spent on training, and the rest of his time is in desktop support. One of his special strengths is his ability to present technical training information in a very inviting way. The trainer has created "Weekly Tech Tips" that go to all staff each week. Appendix 8-9 includes three Weekly Tech Tips from January and February 2007. These tips are both e-mailed to all staff and posted on the Desktop Support intranet page. The tips in Appendix 8-9 focus on Internet Explorer 7 and RSS Feeds, the IE7 Menu Bar, and Phishing Scams. The tips use graphics effectively and use color to highlight sections. The tips are very informal and frequently include humor. The trainer establishes a nonthreatening environment for learning.

Through the Weekly Tech Tips the trainer began to encourage staff to submit effective or interesting tips to be promoted in the weekly publication. Competition has developed among the staff to see who could get their tips published. Generally staff sees the acceptance of a tech tip for publication to be a way that they can help each other. Appreciation of the tech tips has even extended beyond the library. One of the library staff is married to a faculty member in the College of Business, and the tips began to be routed through the Business College to rave reviews.

Core Competencies within the Human Resources Context

The libraries' human resources (HR) division was involved in the development of the core competencies policies and procedures from early in the library exploration of this support program for library staff. The early distinction between training and staff development was a significant HR concern. It was important for the Core Competency Program to include training with a hands-on component. It was important to move away from the staff development model with a large group receiving lecture-type information.

The Core Competency List is referenced in the Libraries' Personnel Evaluation Documentation. The competencies are not mentioned or included in position descriptions when advertising for new positions. They might be mentioned in interview sessions, but generally the new pool of prospective employees seem already to have most of these skills, especially the baseline skills.

A number of problems were identified with the initial computer-related staff development sessions that existed before the Core Competency Program. HR hoped to address many problems through the Libraries' Core Competency Program, including the following:

- The development sessions were not offered at a point of need.
- Sessions were not offered when there was a staff demand.
- Sessions did not include a hands-on component.
- Supervisors were not involved in the sessions.
- The sessions did not allow for one-on-one instruction.
- There was inadequate staff in Desktop Support to meet the demands.

Once the Core Competency Program was in place and a trainer was hired, various HR documents referenced these requirements. The Performance Evaluation System for professional and scientific staff members (e.g., librarians and other professionals) documented the core competencies as additional position expectations along with a guide to their use. Appendix 8-4 presents the Guide to Using the Core Competency List. Professional job responsibilities (University of Iowa Libraries, Performance Evaluation) are explicit in stating: "Competence in appropriate areas of technology (see Libraries' Core Competency List and Guide)."

Merit staff members (i.e., nonprofessional staff) are evaluated annually against the core competencies. The evaluation questionnaire is explicit in asking whether there are expectations in the Library Technology Skills: Core Competency List that need to be discussed/addressed. When Merit employees develop their annual goals, they frequently mention the core competencies. Goals might include taking a SkillSoft course or the development of other technology skills above and beyond their basic job responsibilities.

Library administration is aware that many long-term employees have a tendency to deny that change is continual in the academic library environment these days. However, change is ever present inside the library and in the larger environment as well. Flexibility and computer competency is a necessity for library employment; the Core Competency Program is a focused attempt to assist these employees in making the transitions.

217

Summary and a Look to the Future

Iowa's Core Competency Program is based on establishing a strong, deliberate baseline of competencies in staff. The baseline is very basic and provides an appropriate level of detailed information. This baseline defines a cultural foundation for the libraries across departments. The self-checklist that was developed from the Core Competency List allows staff with few computer skills to confirm that they are up to the minimum. The program raises self-confidence and expertise in staff with marginal skills. The program is well designed so that the process frees up Desktop Support staff time to handle trouble calls.

The actual training sessions, be they one-on-one or group sessions, put the trainer face to face with staff. The formal training sessions establish a focal point for subsequent informal desktop support. For new employees, the number of computer problem calls has significantly dropped since the Core Competency Program was initiated.

The Core Competency Program and its documentation need to continue to evolve. As library employees offer feedback, the trainer needs to make changes to the list and the checklist as well as to respond to suggestions about processes that occur in the training sessions themselves. As with any documentation, wording needs to be adjusted and sections need to be less ambiguous. Redundancy in the documents should be removed.

Changes in the broader technology environment will certainly influence the ongoing Core Competency Program. Changes to the operating system (e.g., Microsoft Windows Vista) and to major enterprise software (e.g., Microsoft Office 2007) have the potential to require alterations to the core competencies. The addition of new enterprise software or unit-specific software will also require that the documentation be kept current and relevant.

The intermediate and advanced levels of the Core Competency List may not be particularly relevant at Iowa. In Iowa's current program these levels don't serve any active purpose. The intermediate and advanced sections are relatively self-explanatory and do provide the supervisor with a resource for possible discussions with staff. Possible future uses of these levels may develop over time.

At the University of Iowa the first full year of the Core Competency Program is largely complete. A full cycle of personnel evaluations has taken place within this context. The libraries expect that a second year of training and evaluations based on the core competency baseline is appropriate. This coming year's work will focus on reinforcement and follow-up. It has not been decided whether, once the program is in its third year, to revise the program so that it will be positive and effective for experienced staff. It is possible that the libraries may not need to do a full core competency effort every year.

LITAC continues to have a role in the Core Competency Program, primarily in updating the official list of competencies. Four times a year the trainer updates the

Core Competency List. LITAC reviews the revised list once or twice a year as needed to provide system-wide input into the revisions.

Iowa's Core Competency Program has in large part addressed the concerns that library staff had with the earlier minimal orientation sessions for new staff. The development of the program took several years with ever-shifting leadership, but input into the program from a broad spectrum of individuals and units resulted in a program that addressed the needs of multiple constituencies. IT administrators in the university's central IT department have voiced interest in promoting the libraries' Core Competency List among other campus units. The implementation of similar programs at other institutions should be considered.

References

Childers, Scott. 2003. "Computer Literacy: Necessity or Buzzword?" *Information Technology and Libraries*, 22, no. 3 (September): 100–104.

Krissof, Alan and Lee Konrad. 1998. "Computer Training for Staff and Patron." *Computers in Libraries* 28, no. 1 (January): 28–32.

The Library Network Technology Committee. "Basic Computer Equipment Competencies." Available: tech.tln.lib.mi.us/finalbasic.htm (accessed August 3, 2007).

Norman, Donald. 1984. "Worsening the Knowledge Gap." In *Computer Culture*. New York: New York Academy of Sciences: 220–233.

University of Iowa Libraries. "Annual Report" (2003/2004). Available: www.lib.uiowa.edu/about/annualreport/03-04.pdf (accessed October 2, 2007).

University of Iowa Libraries. "Performance Evaluation System for Professional & Scientific Staff." Available: http://intranet.lib.uiowa.edu/hr/policies/P&Sperfevalsys.him (accessed October 2, 2007).

University of Iowa Libraries. "Self Study Report, 2006." Available: www.lib.uiowa.edu/admin/selfstudy/LibrariesSelfStudy2006.pdf (accessed October 2, 2007).

Appendix 8-1. Library Technology Skills: Core Competency List

	LEVEL 1: BASELINE	LEVEL 2: INTERMEDIATE	LEVEL 3: ADVANCED
Basic workstation	• Be able to identify location of equipment power buttons. • Be able to turn equipment on and off. • Understand difference between log-off, restart, and shut down. • Understand best practices for shut down or restart of equipment. • Be able to identify location of power cords so connections can be checked if there is no response from equipment. • Understand password prompts and be able to provide the appropriate password. • Know your Hawk ID and password. • Know when "iowa" or "iowa\" is needed in addition to your Hawk ID. • Understand how screen layouts for software tools should look. • Understand how various storage media work and are accessed. • Understand which files are backed up and which are not, based on storage location. • Understand that files should be cleaned up on a quarterly basis.	• Be aware that system checks are performed by the computer on start up.	• Be able to backup files to a network share or CD-ROM.
Printing	• Be able to turn the printer on. • Be able to add paper. • Be able to print specific pages (rather than the entire document). • Be able to choose a network printer.	• Be able to change toner cartridge or ribbon. • Be able to diagnose and correct printing problems for various applications. • Be able to clear a paper jam. • Be able to add a networked printer to your workstation. • Be able to check and clear the print queue. • Be able to print large PDF documents by selecting "Print as Image" command.	• Be able to print white text (if dark background). • Be able to check the printer setup for proper configuration. • Be able to install printer and drivers.

(Cont'd.)

220

Appendix 8-1. Library Technology Skills: Core Competency List *(Continued)*

	LEVEL 1: BASELINE	LEVEL 2: INTERMEDIATE	LEVEL 3: ADVANCED
Internet	• Be able to open and close browser. • Be able to use browser menu and toolbar buttons. • Be able to change browser options and preferences. • Be able to add, use, and edit browser bookmarks. • Be able to type in a URL. • Be able to understand a variety of error messages.	• Understand differences between various browsers and their versions. • Understand terms and jargon (such as telnet, chat rooms, blog, etc.). • Be able to deal with frames when printing Web pages. • Be able to use Tools and Internet Options to change the home page or delete temporary Internet files.	
Computer security	• Be able to respond to computer virus, parasite, or hacking incidents. • Understand and practice good password strategies. • Change passwords frequently, at least every 180 days. • Be able to differentiate between legitimate security threats and hoaxes. • Understand potential security and privacy threats while using e-mail, including attachments, chain letters, hoaxes, spam, and viruses. • Understand the importance of locking or logging out of a workstation when away.	• Be able to scan files or media for viruses.	• Understand how security software protects the computer. • Understand potential security problems that can arise from patron usage of library computers. • Understand potential security and privacy threats while using the Internet, including cookies, downloading malicious or unauthorized files, unsecured communications of private information, viruses, etc.
Operating System	• Be able to navigate in the folder, directory, and drive system. • Be able to create or delete folders. • Understand differences between files and folders. • Be able to open applications and documents. • Understand various save options. • Understand common menu items in applications. • Be able to create a shortcut on the desktop. • Be able to copy and paste and drag and drop within files and folders. • Be able to utilize right-click mouse options (2-button mouse).	• Be able to navigate without the mouse. • Be able to toggle or use the task bar to move between multiple open applications. • Be able to select multiple files or folders. • Understand file-naming conventions and extensions. • Be able to navigate from within an application to open, save, or delete. • Be able to share files with others.	

(Cont'd.)

221

Appendix 8-1. Library Technology Skills: Core Competency List *(Continued)*

	LEVEL 1: BASELINE	LEVEL 2: INTERMEDIATE	LEVEL 3: ADVANCED
E-mail & calendar	• Be able to use department-provided e-mail software to: —Send and receive messages and attachments —Resend bounced messages • Understand that the mailbox should be cleaned up on a quarterly basis. • Be able to use Outlook Web Access (http://email.uiowa.edu). • Be able to make calendar entries for own schedule. • Be able to check calendars of others.	• Be able to accept calendar invitations from others. • Be able to participate in e-mail listservs. • Be able to organize messages with filters and folders. • Be able to recognize questionable attachments. • Understand appropriate use of attachments. • Understand difference between a list posting address and a list owner address. • Be able to schedule meetings with others, including groups. • Be able to schedule rooms for meeting usage. • Be able to set privacy and priority levels. • Be able to subscribe and unsubscribe from lists.	• Be able to make e-mail and calendar groups. • Be able to create personal mail folders on the H: drive. • Be able to create and maintain a listserv. • Be able to designate viewing and scheduling rights.
IT Policy	• Be able to locate the libraries' IT (LIT) policies on the intranet.	• Demonstrate familiarity and understanding of acceptable use policy.	
Technology support	• Be able to relay basic, complete troubleshooting information, including error messages, to LIT. • Understand where to look for troubleshooting information. • Understand the need to reboot computer and try to replicate problem before calling for support. • Know the phone number, e-mail address, and Web site for LIT.	• Understand the procedure for requesting new hardware and software as described on the LIT Web site.	• Knowledge of file extensions and how they are used by the computer.
Voice mail	• Be able to create outgoing voice message and forward calls to voice mail (if applicable).		
Supervisor responsibilities	• Understand procedures for requesting hardware and software.		

(Cont'd.)

Appendix 8-1. Library Technology Skills: Core Competency List *(Continued)*

	LEVEL 1: BASELINE	LEVEL 2: INTERMEDIATE	LEVEL 3: ADVANCED
Application-specific skills			
Example: Contribute	• Be able to locate and open files. • Be able to make page edits.	• Be able to create pages using a template.	• Be able to create templates.
Example: SharePoint	• Be able to access a SharePoint.	• Be able to add to a SharePoint.	• Be able to create and maintain a SharePoint.
Example: MacroExpress	• Be able to use existing macros.	• Be able to create simple macros.	• Be able to create complex macros. • Be able/authorized to distribute macros to a department.
Example: MS Access	• Be able to open and use a database.	• Be able to create a simple database. • Be able to generate reports.	• Be able to create a complex (relational) database. • Be able to create queries. • Be able to create relationships between databases.
Department-specific skills	• TBD.		
Library resources	• Be familiar with the library's e-resources, including lib.uiowa.edu, InfoHawk, Google, application help files.		
Public computers	• Understand the limitations and support procedures for public computers.		

223

Appendix 8-2. Core Competency Self-Checklist

This checklist is a tool that employees and their supervisors can use to identify technology training needs. The core competencies can be viewed at http://intranet.lib.uiowa.edu/litac/core competencylist.doc.

✓	Basic Workstation Skills
☐	I am familiar with the location of the power buttons on each piece of equipment for which I am responsible.
☐	I know how to power my computer and peripherals on and off.
☐	I know how to locate power cords for the equipment I use.
☐	I know that I can hold the power button on my computer for five seconds to force it to shut down even when it's frozen.
☐	I understand the difference between log-off, restart, and shut down.
☐	I know my Hawk ID and Hawk ID password.
☐	I know which of the applications and Web services I use are tied into my Hawk ID and Hawk ID password.
☐	I know which of the applications and Web services I use require that I enter my domain "iowa\" before my Hawk ID. I know that if my Hawk ID doesn't work one way (with or without "iowa\") I can try it the other way.
☐	I am familiar with the screen layouts in the software I use.
☐	I know how removable storage media (CD, DVD+-R[W], USB) work and how to access them. When I've connected removable storage, I know how to get to the files and folders on those media.
☐	I know that files on H: and L: are backed up and that files on my hard drive are not. I understand that files on my PC should be cleaned up quarterly.

✓	Printer Skills
☐	I know how to add paper to my printer.
☐	I know how to print specific pages of a document.
☐	I know how to select the printer I want to use.
☐	I know how to set my default printer by right-clicking on a printer and choosing "Set as Default Printer."
☐	I know how to delete a print job I sent to the printer.

✓	Web Browser Skills
☐	I know how to open and close Internet Explorer (IE).
☐	I understand IE's menus and toolbars.
☐	I know how to change IE's options and preferences by choosing "Internet Options" under the "Tools" menu.

(Cont'd.)

Appendix 8-2. Core Competency Self-Checklist *(Continued)*

✓	**Web Browser Skills** *(Cont'd.)*
☐	I know how to add, use, and edit my IE favorites.
☐	I know how to get to a specific URL by typing it into the IE address bar.
☐	I am familiar with a variety of Web search engines, including Google.
☐	I understand the importance of noting exact error messages.

✓	**Computer Security Skills**
☐	I know I should turn my computer off and contact the libraries' IT (LIT) department immediately if I suspect I have a computer virus or my computer has been compromised.
☐	I am aware that The University of Iowa and other legitimate businesses will not ask me for my passwords or personal information via e-mail or phone.
☐	I know how to lock my workstation by pressing Ctrl-Alt-Del and choosing "Lock Computer.
☐	I regularly lock my workstation (or log out) any time I step away from my computer.
☐	I understand and practice strategies for keeping a strong password.
☐	I have provided my password hints at http://hawkid.uiowa.edu.
☐	I know how to change my password by pressing Ctrl-Alt-Del and choosing "Change Password."

✓	**Operating System Skills**
☐	I know the difference between a file and a folder.
☐	I know how to create and delete a folder.
☐	I know how to start a program and how to open a document.
☐	I understand the various ways to save my files.
☐	I understand the functionality of the menu options in the software I use.
☐	I know how to create a shortcut to a file or application.
☐	I know how to drag and drop and copy and paste within files and folders.
☐	I know how to utilize right-click mouse options.

✓	**Outlook Skills**
☐	I understand how to send and receive messages and attachments in Outlook.
☐	I know how to resend an undeliverable or bounced message.
☐	I know how to access and use Outlook Web Access (OWA), the Web-based version of Outlook at http://email.uiowa.edu.

(Cont'd.)

Appendix 8-2. Core Competency Self-Checklist *(Continued)*

✓	**Outlook Skills** *(Cont'd.)*
☐	I know how to create an appointment on my Outlook calendar.
☐	I know how to check the Outlook calendars of other library staff.
☐	I know how to accept a meeting invitation in Outlook.

✓	**IT Policy**
☐	I am familiar with University information technology policies at http://cio.uiowa.edu/policy.

✓	**Technology Support**
☐	I know where to report problems/issues regarding technology.
☐	I understand the importance of noting exact error messages.
☐	I understand that restarting the computer is always the first step to take when a problem occurs.
☐	I know that I should report a problem to LIT only if I can replicate it after restarting my workstation.
☐	I understand how to provide LIT with enough detail so that they have sufficient information to attempt to replicate the problem.
☐	I know how to contact LIT by phone and by e-mail.
☐	I am familiar with the LIT Web site at http://intranet.lib.uiowa.edu/lit.
☐	I know the procedure for requesting new hardware and software as described on the LIT Web site.

Rev. 2/6/07

Appendix 8-3. Adobe Contribute Software Competencies List

LEVEL 1: BASELINE	LEVEL 2: INTERMEDIATE	LEVEL 3: ADVANCED
• Understand the libraries' Web policies as stated in the Web Policies Guide. • Know where to locate Contribute documentation on the staff intranet. • Know where to look for help and troubleshooting information within Contribute. • Understand the difference between www.lib.uiowa.edu and test.lib.uiowa.edu. • Be able to locate and open files. • Be able to edit an existing page. • Be able to change text size, style, and justification. • Be able to create links to other pages and e-mail addresses. • Be able to create links to non-Web files (e.g., PDF files). • Be able to create a new page in the appropriate library template and publish it. • Know how to form a proper page title.	• Be able to add a borderless PDF icon next to PDF links. • Be able to create an anchor on a page and link to it. • Be able to insert images. • Be able to insert a table. • Know how to use the "imgborder" (image border) style. • Be able to add page keywords and descriptions.	• Be able to make a copy of an existing page. • Be able to edit images (resize, crop). • Be able to edit a table (resize, add rows and columns). • Know how to use Shared Assets (where available). • Know how to create a link to proxied URLs.

227

Appendix 8-4. Guide to Using the Core Competency List

The Libraries Information Technology Advisory Committee (LITAC) has prepared a document entitled *Library Technology Skills: Core Competency List*. This document outlines three levels of basic technology skills. **Level 1: Baseline** lists those skills in which all libraries' staff should show proficiency at the time of hire or as soon as possible thereafter. **Level 2: Intermediate** and **Level 3: Advanced** outline skills that might be required depending on individual job responsibilities. For some positions, these skills are needed in order to complete essential job junctions. For other positions, these skills are desirable, although the need to learn them is not as immediate.

New employees should be able to demonstrate Level 1 and any appropriate Level 2 and Level 3 skills, identified by the supervisor, by the end of the training period.

Although these instructions reference new employees, supervisors should also review the Core Competency List with current employees, perhaps at the time of performance appraisal.

1. **What to do when filling a vacant position:** During the search and interview process, the supervisor should keep in mind the technical skills required for the position, referring to the Core Competency List as needed, and consider including them in the stated qualifications.

2. **What to do when preparing the training plan:** Before a new employee begins, the supervisor should review the Core Competency List to determine which skills are relevant to the position. These competencies should be highlighted and prioritized.

3. **What to do the first week:** Within the first week of employment, the supervisor should review the highlighted Core Competency List with the employee and make note of which skills the employee already possesses and which will require further training. A copy of the annotated Core Competency List should be given to the employee for future reference.

4. **What to do when arranging training:** The supervisor should determine what training can be accomplished within the department. It is likely that much of the initial overview or basic training can occur there. The supervisor can then arrange with the staff of ISST (Information Systems Support Team) for any additional technical training required by the employee. When necessary, ISST staff will work with the supervisor to develop and implement a personalized technology training plan (e.g., one-on-one training sessions, SkillSoft training, etc.).

5. **What to do as follow-up:** Supervisors and employees may review the Core Competency List during performance evaluation conferences. Employees may request, or supervisors may identify, additional technical training as appropriate.

Rev. 12/8/04

Appendix 8-5. The University of Iowa Libraries' Framework for Staff Training, Development, and Enrichment

	DISTINGUISHING CHARACTERISTICS	EXAMPLES	WHO IDENTIFIES THE NEED?	WHO COORDINATES AND SCHEDULES	WHO DELIVERS THE INSTRUCTION?	HOW IS IT BEST DELIVERED?
Staff training: Employee change	• Required • New employee, employee with new tasks, job training • Something about the employee's situation triggers training need • May be handled differently for student vs. Merit/Professional and Scientific (P&S) • Immediate application in job • Typically takes place where employee works or close approximation	• Checking out a book • Cataloging a CD • Working at a public service desk • Filling out an EMJFA • Chairing a P&S search • Assuming new selection responsibilities	• Supervisor • Employee • Library administration • Library HR • ISST/Automation • University HR	• Supervisor • Library HR	• Supervisor or designee • Web-based or print documentation • SkillSoft • ISST/Automation • Library HR	• One-on-one (verbal, hands-on at desk, etc.) • Self-directed, self-paced (library intranet, online tutorial, SkillSoft, iLecture, etc.)
Staff training: System change	• Something about the institution or the environment changes • Change in procedures, change in technology or infrastructure • Improved workflow • Necessary for doing job after change is implemented	• New e-mail system • New calendar system • New version of InfoHawk • Training supervisors in new university sexual harassment policy • University workflow change • Change in library procedure	• Supervisor • Library administration • Library HR • ISST/Automation • University HR	• Supervisor • Library HR • ISST/Automation • Library staff development • InfoHawk subcommittee • Task force or working group	• Supervisor or designee • Web-based or print documentation • SkillSoft • ISST/Automation • Library HR • University HR	• Self-directed, self-paced (library intranet, online tutorial, SkillSoft, etc.) • Small group (hands-on in department, etc.) • Large group (lecture with handout, etc.)

(Cont'd.)

Appendix 8-5. The University of Iowa Libraries' Framework for Staff Training, Development, and Enrichment (Continued)

	DISTINGUISHING CHARACTERISTICS	EXAMPLES	WHO IDENTIFIES THE NEED?	WHO COORDINATES AND SCHEDULES	WHO DELIVERS THE INSTRUCTION?	HOW IS IT BEST DELIVERED?
Staff training: Remedial	• Not triggered by a change in situation • Employee evaluation may identify training need • Typically not related to primary job tasks • Typically not urgent, but still has immediate application	• Improving customer service skills • Using network directories • Changing application defaults	• Employee • Supervisor	• Library HR • ISST/Automation	• Employee • Supervisor • Supervisor or designee • Web-based or print documentation • SkillSoft • ISST/Automation • Library HR	• Self-directed, self-paced (online tutorial, SkillSoft, iLecture, etc.) • One-on-one (verbal, hands-on at desk, etc.)
Staff development: Job-related	• Typically voluntary • Will improve ability or quality of job • May or may not have immediate application • Often take notes • Requires supervisor approval • Ongoing learning, improving, updating skills • May prompt attendee to propose workflow change, which then requires training	• Customer service • Working with international students • Conducting better evaluations • Intro to Online Resources • Working with digital images • Staff recognition programs • Getting published	• Library HR • Library committee • ISST/Automation • Library staff development • Library administration	• Library staff development	• Typically university expert • May be in-house • May be outside paid instructor	• Large group (lecture with small group activities, presentation, Q&A, etc.) • Small group • Self-directed, self-paced (SkillSoft, library intranet, etc.)

Appendix 8-5. The University of Iowa Libraries' Framework for Staff Training, Development, and Enrichment (Continued)

	Distinguishing Characteristics	Examples	Who Identifies the Need?	Who Coordinates and Schedules	Who Delivers the Instruction?	How Is it Best Delivered?
Staff development: General interest	• Topics that are informational or of general library interest • Open to all staff • Typically no immediate work application • Rarely take notes • Supervisor approval only to ensure continuity of service	• What's new in InfoHawk • Update on emerging technologies • What's new in a branch library or department • Provost Hogan talk • My sabbatical as a third-world librarian • Hot topic in librarianship • Overview of university benefits	• Library administration • Library committee • Library HR • Library staff development • Branch library or department	• Library staff development	• Library staff • University staff • Guest	• Library forum • Large group (demonstration, presentation, Q&A, etc.)
Enrichment	• Voluntary • Not on work time • Informal • Open to all staff • Typically interactive, thought-provoking • Discussion format • Hot topics	• Discussion of gay marriage issues • Consumer technology gift ideas • Human rights issues • Implications of RFID (radio frequency identification)	• Any staff member • Library committee • Library HR • Library staff development • Library administration	• Library staff development	• Typically in-house, although host may arrange for others to lead or participate	• Brown bag sessions may be small group (facilitated discussion, etc.) or large group (facilitated discussion, etc.)

231

Appendix 8-6. The University of Iowa Libraries' Technology Training Recommendations for Merit and P&S Staff

GENERAL RECOMMENDATIONS

1. The Libraries should adopt the task force's Framework for Staff Training, Development, and Enrichment (Attachment A) as a model for the Libraries' staff instructional programs.

   Executive Committee (ExCo) approved this recommendation and instructed the task force to develop a plan for communicating the new model to staff (e.g., a library forum) after making final edits to the documents.

2. Supervisors at all levels should assume responsibility for the training needed by their employees. Supervisors are responsible for training in local processes and workflows.

   ExCo approved this recommendation. Directors will ensure that supervisors in their directorate are aware of these responsibilities.

3. Administrators and managers should emphasize to supervisors the importance of orientation and training of new staff and of new systems to all staff.

   ExCo approved this recommendation. Directors will emphasize this with the supervisors and department heads in their directorate.

4. The Libraries should regularly provide opportunities for supervisors to develop and improve their training skills (effective training techniques, adult learning, etc.).

   ExCo approved this recommendation. Libraries' Human Resources/Staff Development will implement.

TECHNOLOGY TRAINING RECOMMENDATIONS

5. Supervisors should make use of the Libraries' Core Competency List (maintained by Libraries Information Technology Advisory Committee) to identify technology training needs for new employees and to develop a plan to meet those needs, relying on Information Systems Support Team (ISST) staff resources as necessary. See the Guide to Using the Core Competency List for details. (The Guide and the Core Competency List are included here as Attachments B and C.)

   ExCo approved this recommendation. Libraries' Human Resources will incorporate these instructions into materials given to supervisors on orientation and training for new staff, as well as into the performance evaluation systems for staff.

6. Supervisors should contact ISST and the Automation Office to arrange for each new Merit and Professional and Scientific (P&S) staff to meet with a representative from each of the two departments within the first few weeks of employment for hands-on orientation and training in system-wide technology.

   ExCo approved this recommendation. Libraries' Human Resources will incorporate these instructions into materials given to supervisors on orientation and training for new staff.

7. Supervisors should arrange for each new P&S staff to meet with the heads of ISST and the Automation Office within the first two months of employment for a high-level overview of system-wide technology and related issues.

   ExCo approved this recommendation. Libraries' Human Resources will incorporate these instructions into materials given to supervisors on orientation and training for new staff.

(Cont'd.)

Appendix 8-6. The University of Iowa Libraries' Technology Training Recommendations for Merit and P&S Staff *(Continued)*

TECHNOLOGY TRAINING RECOMMENDATIONS *(CONT'D.)*

8. Staff from ISST and the Automation Office should assume responsibility for identifying and for providing and/or coordinating technology training that is required by all (or large numbers) of staff across multiple departments. Libraries Staff Development may provide coordination, consultation, and support.

   ExCo approved this recommendation. ISST and the Automation Office will assume these new responsibilities.

9. The Libraries should increase and improve use of the intranet as a central repository of documentation and training materials for Merit and P&S staff as a way to foster good communication and to make it easier for staff to find the materials. Toward this end, ISST and the Automation Office should oversee maintenance and availability of system-wide and cross-departmental technical documentation, and individual units should maintain their local documentation and training materials on the staff intranet.

   ExCo approved this recommendation. Department heads will ensure that local documentation is made available on the staff intranet. ISST and the Automation Office will coordinate efforts to determine and document procedures for posting on the Web.

ORGANIZATIONAL CHANGES

In order to implement these recommendations, we propose the following organizational changes:

1. The Libraries should disband the informal staff development technology training group. Responsibility for identifying technology training needs is distributed to supervisors (for local needs) and to ISST and the Automation Office (for system changes and other system-wide needs).

   ExCo approved this recommendation. The group has already been disbanded.

2. The InfoHawk Management Advisory Committee (IMAC) should disband the InfoHawk Staff Training/Documentation Subcommittee. If the need arises, an InfoHawk working group could be charged to address a specific training or documentation issue. Routine workflow documentation and training (e.g., acquisitions or cataloging) is most effectively handled locally within the department. Cross-departmental documentation and training (e.g., circulation) is most effectively handled by the InfoHawk subcommittee responsible for that function. System-related ALEPH documentation and training (e.g., installing client software) is most effectively handled by the Automation Office and/or ISST.

   ExCo endorsed this recommendation and approved forwarding it to IMAC for its discussion and action.

3. An additional employee should be hired in order for ISST to meet this increased demand for point-of-need training. This employee's primary job responsibility would be to work with supervisors to develop and implement personalized technical training plans as needed and to help identify, prepare, and deliver departmental or large group training for system changes. Recognizing the close link between technology training and desktop support, this new position would also include responsibilities for general one-on-one desktop support.

   ExCo will consider this recommendation when it reviews other staff positions as part of the Provost's reallocation plan.

Respectfully submitted by the members of the Technology Training Task Force: Sue Julich, Susan Marks, Paul Soderdahl, Carlette Washington-Hoagland

January 26, 2005

233

Appendix 8-7. Information Technology Support Services: Classification Description

Issued   October 2002   **Classification Code: PC55**
Title   Information Technology (IT) Support Services-Level II   **Grade: 08**

Basic Function and Responsibility

Positions in this job family are primarily responsible (at varying degrees) for providing assistance and consultation to technology users. Incumbents may perform help desk functions and training, provide direct user support and guidance, and assist with technology planning. Incumbents at this level typically provide advanced technical support on hardware and software applications.

Distinguishing Characteristics

This classification is the second in a series of three levels in the IT Support Services family and is distinguished from the others in the breadth and depth of skills required. Incumbents may function independently in local and/or remote locations to perform work that requires extending established procedures and interpreting moderately complex issues. Errors may result in loss of customer/user time and/or data, substantial impact on unit image, and/or minimal legal exposure from software licensing noncompliance.

Characteristic Duties and Responsibilities

- Performs advanced installation, maintenance, and support of hardware and software within a given unit
- Serves as liaison between technical staff and end users to resolve customer/user problems and concerns
- Explains computing concepts to nontechnical staff
- Provides training (one-on-one, small group, and formal presentations) in the context of delivering technical support
- Recommends procedure and workflow modifications in order to use available technology most effectively
- Provides input in determining technology needs of the unit
- Assists with user account administration and file rights management
- May provide functional and/or administrative supervision over assigned staff
- *In addition to the duties and responsibilities noted above, this classification description must include one statement from each of four categories of statements (i.e., select one statement from each category, for a total of four additional statements to be added to the duties and responsibilities section). To view the list of statements and explanations of their intended application, please go to the following web page:* www.uiowa.edu/hr/classcomp/expectations .html

Supervision Received

Direction is received from IT Support Services Level III or above or (IT or non-IT) supervisor.

Minimum Qualifications

A bachelor's degree in related field and experience (typically 1-3 years) in IT Support Services is necessary. An equivalent combination of education and related experience may also serve to meet these minimum requirements.

Knowledge, Skills, Abilities

Knowledge, skills, and abilities are cumulative from previous levels in this job family. Certain of the following items may be required based on the specific needs of the position.

- Full understanding of desktop operating systems, hardware configurations, and software
- Basic understanding of network concepts and/or administration
- Ability to work independently in local and/or remote locations
- Ability to prioritize multiple tasks
- Skill in explaining computing concepts to nontechnical staff
- Skill in providing technical training (one-on-one, small group, and formal presentations)

Appendix 8-8. Position Description: Desktop Support and Technical Trainer

Position: Desktop Support and Technical Trainer
The University of Iowa, Library Information Technology

Summary

Reporting to the Head, Desktop Support Services, this position coordinates technical training and provides desktop support for library staff located in the Main Library, Hardin Library for the Health Sciences, and 10 branch libraries.

Specific Responsibilities

- Work with supervisors to develop and implement personalized technical training plans as needed
- Help to identify, prepare, and deliver training to library staff
- Provide first- and second-tier desktop computer support and systems support for the university libraries, including all branch libraries
- Serve as backup for Information Arcade PCs and Macintosh computers
- Provide functional supervision over other LIT desktop support and training staff; provide administrative and functional supervision over LIT student staff
- Assist with the distribution, installation, and testing of hardware and software for library staff workstations
- Provide support and training to library staff in the use of applications needed for word processing, graphic design, databases, communications, spreadsheets, Web authoring, multimedia, and other areas as they arise
- Serve as information technology consultant to library staff with respect to computer use, applications, needs, networking, and support services
- Assist in evaluating the ongoing information technology needs and services provided by the university libraries
- Assist library staff with Internet applications, Web site development, educational and instructional technologies, and related technologies
- Recommend changes to procedures and staff workflow as appropriate
- Help recruit and retain a well-qualified and diverse staff

Additional Expectations of the Position

- **Civil and Respectful Interactions:** Demonstrates respect for all members of the university community in the course of performing one's duties and in response to administrators, supervisors, coworkers, and customers
- **Diversity and Inclusion:** Welcomes the richness of talent from a diverse workforce and recognizes that diversity brings stimulation, challenge, and energy that contribute to a productive and effective workplace
- **Leadership Accountability:** Represents the interests of the university and of unit leadership in the use of resources to meet service and productivity demands within unit goals and budgets; strives to promote continual process and quality improvement
- **Learning and Professional Development:** Seeks opportunities to enhance one's own professional knowledge, skills, and abilities as they relate to one's current position and/or to prepare for potential future roles and overall career development

Appendix 8-9. Selected Weekly Tech Tips, January and February 2007

2/1/07

Weekly Tech Tip-IE7 and RSS Feeds

With the upgrade from Internet Explorer (IE) 6 to IE7, we discover many exciting new ways to stay jacked into the zeitgeist. This week: RSS Feeds! (Bring the latest in Library Science, Information Technology, and celebrity gossip right to your fingertips.)

Perhaps you have noticed that in addition to Windows' many dings, beeps, balloons, and puppy dogs, different buttons occasionally begin to glow, seemingly of their own accord. In IE, see the orange button below that looks like this?

When you visit certain Web sites, this will glow to indicate that they have RSS Feeds available.

RSS stands for "Really Simple Syndication" and is an XML format used to send quickly changing digital content to subscribers. It can be read by standalone feed readers or by browser-integrated readers such as IE7. Basically, it's a way to get news blurbs quickly without going to several news sites and loading the pages with all of their ads and pop-ups (see that yellow bar above-thank you, CNN). RSS shows a distilled version of the site, which usually contains a headline, a brief, and a link to the full story. However, RSS Feeds can include images, full-length stories, blogs, or whatever.

After you subscribe, click the favorites button, then choose Feeds:

From here you can view all of the feeds you've subscribed to. Notice that it shares a space with Favorites and History, so don't forget to click back to Favorites when you want to visit other saved Web sites.

This just in! According to Linda Roth, the UofI Libraries will soon be sporting its own RSS Feed with links to newsletters and other info. Stay tuned to this e-mail and the listservs to find out when it's available.

As Fritz said, "If you're not jacked in, you're not alive." (BtVS, Season 1, I Robot . . . You, Jane)

Now, save the latest Brangelina feed for later and get back to work.

Special thanks to Paul Soderdahl for suggesting this week's topic.

(Cont'd.)

236

Appendix 8-9. Selected Weekly Tech Tips, January and February 2007
(Continued)

1/4/07

Weekly Tech Tip-IE7 Menu Bar
Greetings fellow library workers!

This is the first in a series of weekly Tech Tips I will be sending out to the lib-forum list. The subject line will show the topic for each week's e-mail, so feel free to disregard the message if you already know all about it.

This week's topic: What the heck happened to my Internet Explorer menu bar!!!?
Answer: It's still there; however, there are basically two ways to access the menu items:

- All of the menu items can be found somewhere in the new streamlined interface. For example:
  o Favorites are under the Star button on the top left.
  o "Save As" and "Send Link" are found on the right under the Page button.
  o "Internet Options" are found under the Tools button on the right.
  o Can't find something . . . ? Hit the F1 key for help!

OR

- Hit the "Alt" key on your keyboard. The menu will reappear just as before.

I encourage you to explore the new interface whenever you get a chance. Click here for a tour that highlights many of the new features of IE7. Microsoft will continue to change the appearance and function of its Office tools, so open yourself up to change and assume they are not random and senseless, but improvements based on years of market research costing millions of dollars. ;)

Finally, I encourage you to send me suggestions for future Weekly Tech Tips. Try to avoid topics that everyone should already know, such as "how to create a calendar appointment" or "how to use InfoHawk."

I'm looking for topics that are short, helpful, and fall under the heading of "Here's a cool feature that everyone ought to know about!"

1/18/07

Weekly Tech Tip-Phishing Scams
This week's topic is very near and dear to all of our hearts here in LIT. Namely, **PHISHING**. I will now avoid the obvious water sports jokes and leap directly into the education part:

Wikipedia says: "In computing, phishing is a criminal activity using social engineering techniques. Phishers attempt to fraudulently acquire sensitive information, such as passwords and credit card details, by masquerading as a trustworthy person or business in an electronic communication. Phishing is typically carried out using e-mail or an instant message, although phone contact has been used as well."

The following figure (courtesy of my UofI inbox) has several tell-tale signs of a fake e-mail:

1. "Dear Bank of America Member"—**It does not contain your name.**
2. "If this is not completed by January 16, 2007, will be forced to suspend your account indefinitely . . ."— **This threat conveys urgency and wants you to respond quickly, without thinking.**
3. **My favorite, and the one that fools the most people: Notice the pop-up balloon in the following:**

237

(Cont'd.)

Appendix 8-9. Selected Weekly Tech Tips, January and February 2007
(Continued)

Subject: [LIB-IT-HELP] Bank of America Notice

MBNA Bank and Fleet Bank are now Bank of America

Dear Bank of America Member,
We recently have discovered that multiple computers have att
the logons. We now require you to secure your account infom
If this is not completed by January 16, 2007, we will be force

To continue CLICK HERE or on th

> http://www.33rd.de/boa/
> **Click to follow link**

http://www.bankofamerica.com/secure/

Thank You

Bank of America Security Team

© 2006 Bank of America Corporation. All rights reserved.

MBNA is now part of Bank of America

If you roll over the bankofamerica.com link, you'll notice the actual link will take you to 33rd.de/boa/ (.de = some Web site based in Germany). What is this? Who knows? I didn't follow it. And neither should you.

There are hundreds of variations on this theme. If you follow this link (please don't), you will probably see a very good copy of the Bank of America Web site. When you input your username and password, you've just given it to the criminals.

If you see an e-mail like this and you're really worried about your money, type your bank URL into a browser and login to your account. DO NOT FOLLOW LINKS SUPPLIED BY QUESTIONABLE EMAIL.

Also, there is no one in Nigeria who wants to give you a cut of $21,320,000.00. Trust me.

Have you seen Snopes.com, yet? (www.snopes.com/crime/fraud/nigeria.asp) It's a great site to send to all of those annoying relatives who keep sending you chain letters about gas prices or Do Not Call lists. You're not doing that are you? I didn't think so.

Here's a final link to our good friends at Microsoft with more to say about phishing: www.microsoft.com/athome/security/email/phishing.mspx.

Remember: You are the fish. Avoid the hook.

Index

Page numbers followed by "f" indicate figures.

239

About the Editor and Contributors

Susan M. Thompson is the Coordinator for Library Systems at the California State University San Marcos (CSUSM). She has over 20 years of experience with libraries and technology. Currently, she manages the CSUSM Library Systems Department and is responsible for all aspects of library technology. During her tenure as chair of the LITA's Heads of Library Technology interest group, she developed an interest in the changing role of the systems librarian and in the need to broaden technology expectations for all library staff. She has presented at a number of national and regional forums on topics ranging from re-imagining technology's role in the library building to evaluating technology solutions to plagiarism. She has also published a number of articles, including "Riding into Uncharted Territory: The New Systems Librarian" in *Computers in Libraries* and "Remote Observation Strategies for Usability Testing" in *Information Technology and Libraries*. Sue can be reached at sthompsn@csusm.edu.

Kevin Herrera is the Head of Information Technology at the University of Mississippi Libraries where he manages and supports a wide range of hardware, software, network, and server technologies. His areas of focus include digital libraries, Web site development, and online services. He is particularly interested in new and emerging Web 2.0 technologies and ways in which they can be used to engage patrons. Kevin can be reached at kherrera@olemiss.edu.

Donna Hirst is Project Coordinator for Library Information Technology at the University of Iowa Libraries. Donna led the implementation of the libraries' Ex Libris ALEPH system and the NOTIS system that preceded it. She has authored numerous articles and given presentations throughout the United States. Her articles include "Preparing for Automation and Staff Reorganization within the Planning Process" in *Library Administration & Management* and "A Case Study of ILS Migration" in *Library Hi Tech*.

Kevin Moderow is the Chief Technology Officer for the Charlotte Mecklenburg Library. In addition to heading library technology projects, Kevin is also involved in library strategic planning and library design. He holds a Master's Degree in Urban Planning from the University of Wisconsin–Milwaukee and a Master of Library and Information Studies from the University of North Carolina–Greensboro. Kevin has nearly 25 years of experience in information technology and holds a number of leading industry certifications, including the Microsoft Certified Systems Engineer and Cisco Certified Network Associate. Currently Kevin is leading the library in a conversion from a traditional telephone system to voice over Internet protocol. Kevin lives in North Carolina with his two children.

Diane Neal is an Assistant Professor in the School of Library and Information Sciences at North Carolina Central University. She holds an MS and a PhD in Information Science from the University of North Texas. A former systems librarian, her research areas include image indexing and retrieval, information architecture, information seeking in context, and library technologies. She teaches courses in metadata, systems analysis and design, advanced database systems, human factors in systems design, and graphical representation.

Michelle Robertson is the Automated Services Librarian at Anne Arundel Community College in Arnold, Maryland. Before accepting her current position at AACC in 2001, Ms. Robertson was a cataloger and technical services librarian at Johns Hopkins University and at the University of Tennessee, Knoxville. She is active in ALA, having served on ALCTS and LITA committees. She earned her Master of Science in Library Science at the University of North Carolina, Chapel Hill in 1995. Ms. Robertson's professional interests include usability and Web design, Web 2.0 implementations, and the intersection of gaming and academic technology. Michelle can be reached at mmrobertson@aacc.edu.

Paul Soderdahl is Director of Library Information Technology at the University of Iowa Libraries. Paul has served as the head of the Libraries' Information Arcade and as coordinator for Information Systems and Technology. He has served in a number of capacities in various Ex Libris users groups, including as a steering committee member of the SFX/MetaLib Users Group and the Ex Libris Users of North America. He has authored several articles on technology in academic libraries. His publications include "Everything You Always Wanted to Know about SFX but Were Afraid to Ask" in *Serials Librarian* and "Implementing the SFX Link Server at the University of Iowa" in *Information Technology and Libraries*.

Richard Wayne is the Assistant Director for Information Systems at the University of Texas Southwestern Medical Center Library (www.utsouthwestern.edu/library). He is also the president of Strategic Information Management Services (www.strategicinformation.com), a library planning and technology firm. At UT Southwestern, Richard manages a heterogeneous environment of technology. He also helps to coordinate strategic planning for the library. At Strategic Information, Richard helps libraries to thrive in this time of change and challenge. Richard holds an MBA from the University of Texas at Arlington. One of his favorite topics is "Strong Libraries." You can read more about this topic at www.stronglibraries.com. Richard can be reached at richard.wayne@utsouthwestern.edu.